I ♥ Obama

Erin Aubry Kaplan

I

ForeEdge

ForeEdge
An imprint of University Press of New England
www.upne.com
© 2016 Erin Aubry Kaplan
All rights reserved
Manufactured in the United States of America
Designed by Mindy Basinger Hill
Typeset in Calluna

For permission to reproduce any of the material in this book, contact
Permissions, University Press of New England, One Court Street, Suite
250, Lebanon NH 03766;
or visit www.upne.com

Library of Congress Cataloging-in-Publication Data
Names: Kaplan, Erin Aubry.
Title: I heart Obama / Erin Aubry Kaplan.
Description: Lebanon, NH : ForeEdge,
An imprint of University Press of New England, 2016.
Includes bibliographical references.
Identifiers: LCCN 2015036349 | ISBN 9781611685367 (cloth)
ISBN 9781611689679 (ebook)
Subjects: LCSH: Obama, Barack—Influence. | Presidents—United States—Election—2008. |
United States—Politics and government—2009- | African American leadership. |
African Americans—Politics and government. | African Americans—Race identity.
Classification: LCC E908.3.K36 2016 | DDC 973.932092—dc23
LC record available at http://lccn.loc.gov/2015036349

5   4   3   2   1

To my beloved husband, Alan,

who taught me so much.

I ♥ you first.

Contents

Introduction

I confess, writing an introduction to a book called *I ♥ Obama* brought up in a big way the thought that never left me in the nine months I spent writing it: why write about how I feel about Barack Obama? The topic is forbidding, because it's both too big and too small. Obama is president and a politician of the highest order; what I feel about him is bound to be wrong, attached to the somewhat mutable version of himself that he presents to the world. Whatever I say, I will look like a hopelessly deluded fan, a naïf. And millions of words have already been published about Obama, about his politics, his campaign strategies, his enemies, his foreign policy, his first year in office, his momentous decisions. As the first black president of the United States and a radical departure from American history, he has had a microscopic lens trained on him from minute one. He has been examined and re-examined from every conceivable angle at every step by every kind of media platform, all before he's out of the White House. One rather unscientific view of him from one constituent hardly seems necessary.

And yet it is necessary. The same voice in my head that doubted this book also insisted that I put down my feelings because in all those millions of words published, virtually none have explored the very obvious topic of love. I do love Obama, as many other black people do. He is the first black president; we could hardly do otherwise. It's both a genuinely romantic, first-love kind of love and an agape kind of love of a brother-in-arms taking on the impossible, soul-sucking task of being president. But the twenty-first century politics and social protocols around race, especially around Obama, have prevented me, and us, from fully expressing this love. For seven years we have had to do it in silence. I was frankly tired of loving Obama in silence, tired of silence period. I was tired of wearing this particular mask. One thing that Obama has modeled and that I talk about in this book is the freedom of being yourself, even when you can't say exactly what you think. Unlike Obama, I can say what I think. The least I can do is to be honest, to cast off this false burden of neutrality black people are now expected to bear about being black in this so-called post-racial age. To do otherwise is assumed to show bias, favoritism, or even to be "racist." Even seeing that sentiment in print makes me realize how sane and perfectly logical, and how needed, this book actually is. So never mind.

As you will discover, I am not in love with all that Obama does, and has done, as president. Not by a long shot. But this book is an exploration not of his politics but of his historical, cultural, and personal meaning to ordinary black people like me. I know that his actions and his meaning are in one way inseparable; they evolve together. But the love I feel exists almost on a different plane, with a different dynamic. It's love that coexists with the policy disagreements I've had with Obama about everything from drones to the Trans-Pacific Partnership trade agreement. I disagree with him more strenuously because of the love, not in spite of it. No matter how distraught I get about his choices, I remain strangely hopeful that those choices can change. Maybe it's because I'm in Los Angeles, but part of me believes that I can talk sense to Obama any time I want to, just as actors wake up every day reasonably believing they can become a star: however dreary things get, every day holds the same amount of possibility, offers the same proximity to the fantastic. As dire as things have become, I haven't felt this kind of optimism since I was a teenager.

I am not a naïf. I don't believe that Obama has completed or resolved any history, racial or otherwise. The Tea Party has pretty much made that impossible. But he has broken a kind of emotional paralysis around electoral politics that I'd had for a long time, that I didn't quite know I had. Though I always voted faithfully—too many people died for my right to vote, I reason—I had almost no faith that the outcome of elections would change anything. Voting for black candidates in particular had become a gesture, a nod to history and to the horse race itself, little more. Obama came along and kicked up that history, turned it over, by demanding that I see him differently. He made the big questions, which I assumed were irrelevant or uninteresting to black politicians, matter again. The stakes of this new relationship, as I say in the first chapter, are extraordinarily high.

The five parts of this book are essentially five ways of looking at—and/or loving—Obama. The first chapter considers Obama as a modern-day black folk hero, fighting a racist system that we all must fight at some point in one way or another. The second chapter looks at all the ways black folk have made images of Obama—posters, t-shirts, even perfume—into a distinct historical and pop-culture iconography that we display in windows, billboards, and barber shops. Chapter 3 delves into the complicated matter of Obama as a black leader, how he fits into that vaunted tradition of Malcolm X and Martin Luther King or whether he fits into it at all (and if not there, *where?*). Chapter 4 discusses the most taboo but essential question of who Obama is at heart—as a black man, as a person, as an American who fights, like all black people, for his right to be fully American. And the last chapter looks (somewhat reluctantly, I'll admit) at the possibility that the whole phenomenon of Obama the first black U.S. president has been a massive distraction that is detrimental to our struggle on the ground. As the anti-police brutality movement—also known as Black Lives Matter—continues to gather force around the country in black communities from Ferguson to Baltimore to Los Angeles, it's a question that is implied more and more.

But none of that shifts the original phenomenon of Obama love. For me and so many of the black people I talked to for this book—accomplished but ordinary, largely nonfamous people—that love crystallized early, and it endures. Obama and his initial outrageous bid to capture the hearts and minds of not just black folks but all of us—to put us all in his thrall and lead us through the post-9/11 ideological desert to a promised land, lead us back to ourselves—still regularly seizes my imagination, and my heart. It has changed things. These days I see Obama on television or on the Internet and I catch myself thinking, I could have been him. I am very glad I am not. But my belief that I *could* have been is extraordinary. It's transformative. It's the thrill of identification, and the anxiety of identification, and something beyond that I'd never felt in my life until now, at age fifty-three. I have President Obama to thank for this transformative feeling, though I don't quite have a word for it. "Love" will have to do. For now.

Erin Aubry Kaplan

I ♥ Obama

1 Obama the Folk Hero

WHAT HE MEANS TO US

The unlikely heroism of Barack Obama began for me the first and only time I saw him, on a warm winter day in Los Angeles in 2007. He had just declared his candidacy for president and was holding a rally at Rancho Cienega Park in the Crenshaw district. Crenshaw is the last primarily black area left in the city; it is next to Dorsey High School, one of three majority black high schools left in the 700,000-student Los Angeles Unified School District, and for nearly twenty years it was the site of the African Market-place and Cultural Faire, held in late summer. In other words, anybody holding an event at Rancho Cienega was trying to get a message out to black folks. The fact that lots of white folks lived pretty close by, some just across the street at Village Green, a leafy condominium community built as a prototype of utopian urban living in the 1940s, didn't matter. Nor did it matter that whites live in considerable numbers in Ladera Heights, a few miles north of Rancho Cienega, and in much greater numbers in Culver City, a couple of miles southwest. The proximity of these places doesn't connect them at all. Crenshaw is a black nation-state, so those whites who do live here don't live outdoors, are never seen on the streets, and more than likely tell their white friends and potential visitors that they live not in Crenshaw but in adjacent places like Culver City or West Los Angeles. They will acknowledge black neighborhoods only when special events are held there such as the African Marketplace or the Martin Luther King Day parade, when the place itself is the point; on those occasions, Crenshaw lights up as local exotica, an in-house tourist destination. But for most of the year, as far as Los Angeles and Southern California and the rest of the country and the rest of the world are concerned, Crenshaw, like black hubs in big cities anywhere else in the United States, lives in shadow and uncertainty.

The special occasion of Barack Obama's rally wasn't going to change that. I was curious to see him but hardly excited, and if I hadn't been looking for fodder for a weekly op-ed column I was then writing for the *Los Angeles Times*, I probably would have stayed home. Obama was all the talk and I knew generally who he was, but I knew nothing specific except the keynote speech he'd made at the Democratic National Convention in Boston in 2004 that had made him a star. I thought Obama was good-looking and remarkably self-possessed, like many aspiring actors I've met, but I was not a fan of that speech. It made me uneasy. The call for Americans to overcome their differences and find strength in unity across party and ethnic lines hadn't moved me in at least twenty years, not since I started college in 1979 and felt almost at that very moment the 1960s officially grinding to a close. I saw a preview of it in fifth grade, when I was bused to a very white school not far west of Rancho Cienega and understood at ten years of age that integration was going to be impossible because whites simply didn't want it. Blacks would always be tolerated, never invited or freely given space.

I didn't resent this, probably because it didn't surprise me. I had grown up with a fiercely activist father, a soldier of the movement and a New Orleans native who believed in justice and equality for all, but he harbored no illusions about the depth of white American resistance to both. He was committed to changing laws and behaviors; changing hearts and minds was not a reachable goal. It depended too much on feelings, and in my father's line of work and in his own life experience, feelings were unreliable, mercurial, even dangerous, for everybody concerned. Anybody talking about feelings as they related to justice and politics had his head in the clouds or was secretly averse to the real work needed for racial progress—work that was tough, unglamorous, and distinctly unsentimental. It was also lonely. Erasing differences and coming together across color lines as a way to effect change was one of those facile '60s utopian ideas commercialized by companies like Coca-Cola that celebrated brotherhood and equality as the good *feeling* Americans get singing a song or downing a soda. Now that feeling had been resurrected as a serious message for a seriously disillusioned age that seemed to be always invoking the '60s, minus its actual events and unfinished business. The sense of possibility, of transformation being eternally on the horizon, was the only use people had for the '60s anymore. Mainstream politics had long ago stopped talking about its hard lessons and touted only hope and rainbows, talking up the idea of change rather than the mechanics of it. Obama was just the latest politician to do this.

By the time I reached the park I was more than halfway annoyed with Barack Obama and his campaign of hope. I had decided that it was hollow. The fact that he was a black man exactly my age who could make extraordinary history and put our generation on the map moved me less than the eternal question of, hope for whom? Nobody ever asked black folks what they needed. Yet everybody was always giving them something they claimed was good for them, and always at places like Rancho Cienega, throwing out encouraging words that shimmered on delivery, like strings of beads tossed from a Mardi Gras float, but that started to dull the minute the event/rally was done and everybody was walking away. The words dropped on the ground and stayed there, with good reason; no use taking anything home. I knew this firsthand. I had sat through these kinds of faux events for fifteen years now, since the citywide unrest in 1992 had made a prophet out of every black leader or figure who claimed to have a piece of the answer Going Forward, sometimes the whole answer. They called a press conference and I would come, making it as significant as I could in a write-up the following week. (The real prophets were not written about because they rarely had press conferences.) I anticipated Obama scaling down his prophetic message to fit this place, this black island in the ocean of Los Angeles that was itself by an ocean and because of that, perhaps a more hopeful place than a similar island in Des Moines or St. Louis. Los Angeles is not hallowed ground or the heartland but the end-land, the great western flourish of the American continent, a shining sea. Obama chose well, I thought: plenty of room for expanding in all directions about possibility and hope and whatnot.

His warm-up act was a choir on a stage erected in the middle of Rancho: a dozen or so bright-faced people singing and swaying to a gospel-like tune. They were black, white, Latino, and maybe an Asian or two, a human rainbow rising over the sea. They looked serene and perfectly oblivious to the fact that they were in Crenshaw, or perfectly happy that they were here and not in St. Louis. The crowd of rally-goers was considerably black, but very mixed; of course, I thought, glancing around with more than a little contempt, people hired to drive home the message of multicultural togetherness. Fellow actors. I stood and folded my arms tighter and tilted my face up to the sun. Though I'm a native, I appreciate the sun and never take it for granted, especially in winter. Sun here is ubiquitous, but it is not guaranteed, never a given in any season. It is generous but sly, temperamental.

I closed my eyes in appreciation, and when I opened them, Obama was on stage. I blinked. The sky and commanding sun had shrunk, willingly transformed into a backdrop for a figure who was striding—or pacing—in front of the choir in a white shirt and tie, holding a microphone. He was taller than I expected, more imposing, and he radiated something that I didn't expect at all. Not charisma—well, charisma, yes, but something more unwieldy than that, a restlessness that was used to sitting on itself and showing an even, polished surface that the world read as charisma. Something had pierced that surface, and now a ray of agitation that was knitting Obama's brow almost into a frown and turning his measured strides into emphatic stomps here and there that made the raised wooden stage shudder.

I know what you're thinking, he was saying to us. I know. You're tired. Tired of war, tired of Washington. Tired of too many people in prison . . .

His tenor boomed over the crowd, which cheered his every line. But that booming voice was also intimate. This was not just a voice of aspiring authority or practiced salesmanship—please vote for me—or even charisma. It was overwhelmingly the voice of Obama, one man in a white shirt and dark tie talking encouragingly to the rest of us about how crappy things had become in America and how his own ideas about the country could make it better. Not just make the country better, but make it realize the potential that it has for greatness despite a history, including a very recent history, of bullshit and broken promises and racial hypocrisy and fake populism and all the rest. So certain was he of this idea that he forgot himself—or he remembered himself—and flashed a bit of the agitation and anger that

I immediately recognized as all of ours. Oh lord, I thought, amazed, he is one of us. Most remarkably, he is one of *us,* a black man who understands the grieved nature of black anger toward crappy America and its bullshit promise, understands it even if he has not exactly lived the bullshit in the way many of us have lived and continue to live it, even if he can't describe it aloud. I forgave him that. What was more important was that despite his Harvard pedigree and lofty idea about America and his Hollywood-approved handsomeness, Obama was a common man, certainly gifted but as ordinary as so many black people with many gifts who live in agitation their whole lives, people who might be told they are somebody but who never find a stage or listening ears. For all of those folks and for everybody else, Obama was offering redemption, a voice. He was offering hope.

Another amazing thing was that unlike most black figures, including Jesse Jackson, Obama was not chasing the American ideal of togetherness—praising it but really chastising it for betraying black folks so badly. He was out in *front* of it, calmly extending the ideal in both hands as if it actually belonged it him. When he said, "You all are tired," he was saying he was sorry that his ideal had disappointed but assured us it was going to be restored; he was giving us his word about something I always thought we as black people had none to give. It had never felt possible. Obama didn't change that reality on the spot, but his confidence touched me. He was seeing something I couldn't, looking over our heads at something, largely invisible to most of us, that drove him, that had driven him all over—Chicago, St. Louis, and now here, finally, to the continent's end.

It was because of this vision of something I sensed but couldn't see, but which I knew that *he* saw, that made him a hero to me that afternoon. I saw his faith in a fully realized America, a faith that I and many other black people—certainly all the ones I knew—had put aside long ago, mostly because we felt we had no choice. Obama, on his own, was offering us back that choice. He was a hero not because he was transcendent or prophetic, but precisely because he was none of that, at least not yet. And he might never be; he might fail utterly in this undertaking, I thought. But the undertaking was what mattered. It was what moved me. I also thought that whatever he did from this point on was going to matter terribly to black folks. He was one of us, although he didn't know that yet; stalking that stage, he didn't really know what he was setting in motion, and that ignorance moved me too. Obama saw things we didn't, but we also saw things that *he* didn't, and this kind of silent dance was a dynamic between a black figure and his followers that I'd not seen or felt before, a modern romance that I knew right away was going to be the stuff of myth, not just speeches and endorsements and poll numbers. What Obama did was going to matter in a way I never thought any black person in my lifetime could matter. The stakes were too high to even measure.

When the rally was over, I didn't leave the paraphernalia of words on the ground as I ordinarily did. Instead, I was carrying something that excited me, something very physical, which also made me uneasy. I was rattled. Obama had gotten under my skin and into a psyche that belonged to another age, one in which black people followed the fortunes of people like Joe Louis and Malcolm X as if their lives depended on it, because in a way they did. I walked away knowing I would now have to follow Obama like that. I wasn't sure if I wanted to and doubted that I even had the time, but I had no choice. It was this feeling of surrender, immediate and almost titillating but mostly alarming because I had no idea where this one man would take us and how this quest would end, that made him a folk hero that day. A dangerous one, too, because this Obama, like Malcolm X, had ambition that he saw as perfectly appropriate, even patriotic, but it was going to make him an outlaw. A pariah, a loner. It didn't matter that Obama, quite unlike Malcolm, appeared utterly mainstream, that he attracted enough admiration and support from white folks to eventually put him into the highest office in the country and arguably in the world; despite that, he was going to be on his own. This isolation was another thing that he didn't see coming then, but I did. We did. Certainly Malcolm would have seen it. Martin Luther King, despite his own belief in the Beloved Community that had paved the way for Obama, would have seen it too. But Obama had cast his grand vision on an assumption never made by a black figure before: that everybody, black and otherwise, saw things exactly as he did. They, too, saw what had been lost in America and knew what needed to be reclaimed. He wasn't only a black man arguing a position on our behalf, he was a fellow

American steering the way back to an America that had once morally challenged itself on many questions, including the question of race. Obama was appointing himself primary keeper of the American story, not a critic of it, a thoroughly modern vision of black possibility that was going to get him elected, and then reviled, by white folks.

Black folks who had always seen the American story for what it was saw it all coming; we would overwhelmingly support Obama and then brace ourselves for the opposition. Our apprehension, as it turns out, has been more than justified. But that doesn't dim the miracle of Obama, which is simply that his new story, his attempt to not just belong to America but to lead it, is ours. *He* is ours. The truth of that has been alternately heady, bittersweet and tragic. The story is not over, the meaning of the particulars not sorted out. But it is already legend.

♥ From the instant he became president, Obama has been a black cultural touchstone like nothing I've seen before. His presence has changed everything, realigned our thoughts and arguments about ourselves and our progress and our country, affirming some things and disproving others. As so many people have said to me, his symbolism has been the most influential thing about him. It's also been the most controversial. As president, he is a black man waging a battle against the racist tendencies of the very system he was elected to lead, fighting daily to effect ideals of unity and common good that were never meant for black people at all. This is the spectacle that black folks have followed anxiously, more so than his policies, many of which have been shaped—not in a good way—by his failure to effect those ideals. The failures, the over-compromises, are Obama's acknowledgment of defeat; that includes his almost total silence on the subject of blackness itself, which for black folks feels like the worst defeat of all. And yet we watch Obama struggle and sympathize with him, with his thwarted ambitions and his failures, because to be what he's trying to be—black, idealistic *and* president—is nothing less than superhuman. A folk hero's errand for sure. The errand is almost complete.

True to what that electric feeling in the park presaged for me in 2007,

Obama has been a figure of unprecedented importance for black people. Throughout his turbulent presidency we have anxiously measured the breadth and meaning of every setback and every triumph, though clear-cut triumphs have been rare (and even they are cause for a certain anxiety). In the pantheon of black figures and leaders, Obama is unique, a logical extension of King and Malcolm but also detached from them because he has made most of his decisions detached from us; he has us in mind but not at the table. As president he decides things only as himself, not as an agent of other black people, which doesn't mean that we don't benefit from his decisions, but we don't know what he intends for us, if he intends anything. It is a new and strange dynamic that has left us still arguing what Obama's role as president should be as far as black people are concerned. What I have heard most often is, "He's not the president of black America, he's the president of the United States of America!" which to me is a bright red herring, a self-negating posture meant to head off a more troubling discussion about why we as black people have learned so well to have no expectations of anyone who makes any claim to represent our interests, however obliquely. Yet we support Obama because we must; his stature in the world and his still-unfolding battle with the America he claims to love demands our support. He may not actively represent us—the first black leader with that somewhat dubious distinction—but he is ours. He means more to us than anyone has meant in a long time, so even if you have soured on him since 2008, you cannot ignore him, and you especially cannot ignore what he means. As a twice-elected president, he is a towering symbol of previously unimagined black success that has reconfigured all of our conversations about race and racial progress; nobody can talk about either thing anymore without invoking his name or citing what he recently said or what's been said about him.

But his ubiquity is double-edged. In a white America that blacks must still navigate, Obama is both our armor and our Achilles' heel: on the one hand, his presence in the White House refutes stereotypes of black inferiority and fallibility; on the other, his blunders or failures of nerve confirm them. We largely forgive him the blunders, because that is our job—who else but us will give him the margin of error he needs but is never granted, the margin we seek but rarely find for ourselves? Who else will say he is human? And we forgive him because, towering figure though he is, Obama is one of the family. He is one of our bright young men who made good, the very essence of the talented-tenth vanguard that W.E.B. DuBois imagined would lead the race to new heights and eventually prove to America that equality was not a theory, nor was it some charity dispensed by white folks when it moved them, but a fact, a reality. Obama is our fortunate son who carries the weight of this proof, and we worry for him, like all parents with great expectations worry for their children. We worry not only about how he is faring in his job, but about how he is *doing*—is he eating right, keeping his head on straight, keeping it together? The front pages of newspapers and websites keep up the purely political narrative—what's happening in the White House, in the polls—while blacks keep up a parallel but shadow narrative whose core concern is how the political beast that Barack leads is also trying to eat him alive.

This is the battle royale we have been watching, with Barack our accidental folk-hero protagonist fighting an enemy far bigger and more insidious than anything faced by folk heroes such as John Henry, Joe Louis, or Malcolm X. Those men were pitted against a machine, against white men in a boxing ring, against the self-doubt of black people. But Barack is pitted against America itself. America and its entire monstrous history of racism that has been roused anew because he has dared to try and show the country something, dared to be black and chiefly idealistic rather than black and chiefly critical, imploring or righteously angry. For this sin of initiative and imagination he is still being punished, and we are still watching the battle unfold (years later he is still standing tall, but he seems to be losing by degrees, sinking into the ground by quarter inches) in a kind of collective agony and fury that will take many more years to put into words. So much is at stake: If Obama loses his idealism, loses what he began this whole enterprise with, then blacks will have lost, too, even those of us who never believed in the enterprise of One America in the first place. The question about what would happen if there was ever a black president is no longer rhetorical. It is being answered.

Yet his presidential record has little to do with his heroism. Years from now, we will tell stories and sing songs about Obama's great feat of becoming the first black president who did not ultimately change the real world in which we all suffer, who in fact succumbed to the political temptations of that world more than a little. But the feat was that he got to the top on his own volition. He did not get there as a black prop of white ideology, à la Supreme Court Justice Clarence Thomas. He succeeded as *himself.* And himself he has remained: though he lost many ideological skirmishes along the way, Obama the man/hero didn't unravel or despair on the world stage that he's occupied every day. Under terrible pressure he has kept his brilliant smile in reserve and his gravitas intact, even flashing the old agitation at times—the promise to use his veto pen in his last years of office, the quick seething at innumerable moments of hysterical opposition by the white right. Through all of it he has been approachable but unflappable and, to the puzzlement of many in the media, emotionally impervious. He bends, compromises, but does not bleed. This is what black folks appreciate and recognize as themselves, that Obama the idealist is also a survivor. He hews to a critical black tradition of forbearance in the face of great, almost inevitable disappointment, of soldiering on in spite of. This is what has endeared him to us, what ensures his place in our still-unresolved history as a hero for the ages; forbearance has already placed his image alongside the images of true freedom fighters like Harriet Tubman and Frederick Douglass, as well as folk-tale heroes such as John Henry. Like all of them, Obama risked for the sake of others. He dreamed of a different state of being. He *tried.*

♥ Before Obama, the only folk hero in my living memory was Martin Luther King. And he is barely in it; I was six when he was murdered in 1968. But his legend took root instantly. His soaring, tremulous voice became embedded in the collective black conscience and our consciousness, and his tragically unrealized ideals and aspirations became the measuring stick for racial progress after his own death punctuated the beginning of the end of the Movement. Though King has been made into a paragon of multicultural cooperation and even post-racialism over the years, I always saw and heard him as agitated, what white folks disapprovingly call "fiery."

King was first and foremost dissatisfied with the racial status quo; he later voiced dissatisfaction with other things, like war and capitalism, for which he was more or less vilified by many of the same people who agreed with his stance on civil rights. But he refused to suppress any part of himself, making him a black existential hero who prefigured Obama. Malcolm X was the same kind of precedent, an Afrocentric man whose blunt-spokenness and refusal to salve white anxieties pretty much defined "fiery" to the establishment. But Malcolm was at his core an intellectual, a methodical debater who, like King, raised his voice to make a point. The intellectual rigor, if not the raised voice, is certainly Obama, though this is where the comparison seems to end. King and Malcolm X risked all to ensure black justice, ultimately giving their lives; Obama is not aiming for black justice. It would not even seem possible. He and his ambition came on the scene in a post-post civil rights era in which black justice had become not just politically passé but actively discouraged, even among those who still believed in it. Americans in 2008 were talking seriously about post-racialism and the end of blackness as an ethnic identity and as a concept. With the end of blackness came the logical end of any movement for black equality; black leaders who challenged this even mildly were marginalized or called out of step. What had once been a mainstream idea that whites accepted, however reluctantly, had become radical. Even Jesse Jackson, King's sergeant at-arms and a two-time presidential candidate himself in the 1980s, had moved rhetorically away from racism and toward more racially inclusive issues of poverty and the growing crises of the working poor. Poverty and class stagnation became the framework for race, rather than the other way around. Gone from this picture was the idea that black people were battling the system or opposing the racism that still constrained them; in the new post post-Movement picture, a consciously black leader was irrelevant, a black folk hero out of the question entirely.

But Obama is an oddity—technically not a black leader, but a black folk hero nonetheless. As president he defies the possibility of being the first thing but resurrects the second. It's more than a little ironic, because when Obama came on the scene, he was certainly aware of the growing belief in post-racialism and knew that his appeal to white folks depended on it. He just as certainly knows that he is a hero to blacks because of his blackness, and unlike Clarence Thomas and other arch-conservatives of the post–civil rights age, he's welcomed that. It charges him. The black connection alone put a lie to the ahistorical assumptions of post-racialism: here is a post–civil rights baby who's been schooled enough by the '60s to understand that racial inequality is alive and well but is millennial enough to believe that he could create a new reality in a growing distance between the big moral questions posed by the '60s and the fractured indifference to them now. This is where Obama's big risk lay, where his heroism took shape. He was not clamoring for black justice, but he was advocating for justice being done to American ideals and American promise that included, but were certainly not limited to, racial justice. This sounds obvious, but what he was aiming for had never been attempted by a black man in the Oval Office because there had never *been* a black man there before. He is the first, a barrier-breaker like Jackie Robinson in 1947. But Jackie came to major league baseball with all the skills and experience he needed to succeed, while Obama has had to develop his skill set on the fly and in the face of great hostility and resistance from people who didn't want him or anybody like him in charge.

Yet it is his job to be in charge, not just of the executive branch of government but of the wants and aspirations of the American people. The pitfalls from the beginning of this enterprise have been so deep and numerous that for Obama to keep his feet moving has been, to most of the people I talked to, nothing short of a miracle. Great achievements would be nice, and we got them from folk heroes such as Jackie Robinson and Joe Louis; they broke barriers and proved to the world they could compete. Obama is much more susceptible to failure because being president isn't like being an athlete, or an entertainer or a doctor or any other kind of professional. It isn't accomplished by talent alone, and never without the faith of the millions who expect you to represent them. A black person has never won representation on this scale, and during the Obama era (whatever that is) we have been forced to admit, or to remember, that white folks simply don't believe that blacks who are not entertainers or athletes can validly represent them or earn their faith; certainly blacks can't articulate white people's feelings about a country that has never cared whether its black citizens have faith in it or not. Obama as president has therefore asked people for the unprecedented, if not the impossible—agreement from the majority of nonblack Americans that he can indeed speak for them.

He doesn't have to succeed for black folks to recognize the heroism in this request. I knew that from the first and only time that I saw him and signed up for what I suspected right away was a fool's errand. But walking out of the park that day in 2007, shaken as I was, I was impressed. I secretly admired the hell out of this Obama. I wished him luck.

❤ In his book *Black Culture and Black Consciousness*, Lawrence Levine posits two kinds of folk heroes in black culture: outsiders and insiders. Outsiders are bandits or outlaws, badasses along the lines of Stagger Lee and Super Fly, men who flout the rules and embrace the margins in which they live. Insiders are the opposite: social conformists, straight arrows who work hard and play by the rules of American society in order to gain its acceptance. Though they seem different, Levine says that these two archetypes are similar in that they challenge a racially exclusive system that rejects black folks on any terms. Obama is both things at once: the ultimate insider/conformist who is still an outlaw because he is black. In fact, he is treated like an outsider by white folks *because* he is an insider who has learned to work the system well enough to have become president twice. He's gotten as close to power as any black person in our history has ever gotten. Paradoxically, it's just that success that makes him illegitimate to his detractors. To them he is a silver-tongued hustler/trickster Br'er Rabbit who no more belongs in the White House than a fox belongs in a coop of chickens.

Obama is our folk hero whose exploits black people have settled into talking about daily, as in, "Did you see what they did to Barack?" (In these discussions, really an ongoing conversation, he goes by his first name, like any member of the family.) Reviewing the harrowing plot points of his presidency has been very much like dissecting Joe Louis's fights or Jack Johnson's troubles with the law; the concern is not so much about what happened as it is about whether Obama is left standing, whether he's actually outsmarted his enemies without them realizing it. (Many people I talked to took great satisfaction in the idea that Obama is quietly succeeding in the very areas in which he is assumed to be failing—health care reform, diplomacy with demonized countries like Cuba and Iran. Like the tortoise, he takes the long view.) This symbolism is the storyline that matters most, the stuff from which his legend will be made.

Much about Obama's political legacy is still forming and is already controversial, even amongst black people. But the resonance of his symbolism as a black man claiming a space denied to black people for so long is indisputable. Symbolism alone makes him a hero to blacks of all generations, from the civil rights set who never imagined they'd see such a development in their lifetime to young people who signed up to vote in 2008 in order to be part of a history that had been feeling more and more disconnected from their lives; suddenly, Obama brought it close. Voting for Obama brought black folks together like they haven't been together in forty years. In the aftermath of the Movement, we had lost our cohesion, our mojo, to the winds of change and to the great pressures of integration and individualism; Obama showed us that the collective identity had never really gone away; it had just gone underground. It had only needed a clear reason to assert itself publicly, and he gave it one. It's funny, because Obama, though a keen student of America's history of racial injustice, is at heart an integrationist who would prefer that the days of blacks even needing group cohesion and a collective identity be numbered. He appreciates blackness and identifies with it, but he would prefer that its concerns be embedded in American political discourse and in the prevailing American political agenda, whatever that happens to be. He would certainly say that they are embedded in his own. But the fact is that race is still a separate and unequal element in politics (as Obama must certainly *also* know) and pretty much all of American life, which is why Obama the idealist/integrationist is still an outlaw whose arrival on the scene had the effect of outing black people as a people. Suddenly, we had something on which everybody had to take a position. If you were black you couldn't sit this one out, nor could you take a position and then go home and not think about it; you had to participate.

It's been a good thing, a relief really. Obama-watching has shaken us out of a certain stupor that bordered on despair and revived a common purpose we haven't had in decades. The best moment by far was celebrating the moment of his first inauguration, before anything at all had happened, having the political party of our lives before settling into the less glamorous, nerve-wracking but still affirming business of him being president and us watching, constantly asking ourselves and each other, *Now what does this mean? Why is he being asked that? God, why is he responding that way? If I were him, I'd give those crazy white folks a piece of my mind. What's he got to lose that we haven't lost already?* In almost the same breath, we say—maybe uncertainly, but hopefully—*Well, he is doing the best he can. If I was under pressure like that, getting shit from Congress and big corporations and my own party, not to mention shit from black folks who righteously need so much and want me to deliver it yesterday, I'd have lost my mind or died a long time ago. Barack is staying alive to see another day, to maybe try something else.* We know better than anybody how America squeezes the goodness and hope out of people, and Barack is supposed to be Captain America now, but as black Captain America, he's getting squeezed doubly. Whether we agree with him or not, we have to appreciate his position, which we don't really know the whole of. Nobody does. This is a point I heard made over and over in his defense: only Barack really knows what he goes through. He is alone. Give him space, people told me. He may not be doing the right thing by us, but he's trying to get close. He's trying to figure something out.

Folk-hero Obama is an unintentional outlaw, but he is no bandit. Black bandits, Lawrence Levine says, are always out for themselves, rejecting the sense of community that bolstered most black people and tethered them to the hope that things might change for the better. However, the fight for self-preservation has a certain necessity and its own morality; violent as it sometimes gets, it keeps blacks from accepting the nagging belief that we don't matter at all. Bandit or not, black heroes were also antiheroes, people trying to neutralize the forces arrayed against their very humanness the best way they knew how. Bandits and outlaws were the grunt soldiers of that fight, shooting first and thinking not at all. Thinking was a luxury. "Black bandits never tried to change anything . . . they were pure force, pure vengeance, explosions of fury and futility," Levine explains. He adds that "they were not given any socially redeeming characteristics simply because in them there was no hope of social redemption." This is exactly the profile of modern-day black gang members like the Crips and the Bloods, antiheroes if there ever were any; unlike black criminal outlaws such as Super Fly, they are utterly without glamour, vilified rather than admired by the general black public, though they do enjoy a certain folk-hero status among themselves. It's useful to remember that Super Fly, the drug lord of the eponymous 1972 movie, was actually seeking social redemption, a way out of the life, if not a way into conformity. One of the more interesting images of Obama that I collected over the years is him as Super Fly—not literally Super Fly, but a clear suggestion of him. On a movie poster with the title, "Obama: Back 2 Back!" the president, in suit and tie, stands next to his wife (main woman/gun moll), Michelle, arms folded defiantly, his gaze steady and vaguely challenging; she is standing with her hands on hips, smiling but equally defiant. Together they rise like a mountain above a montage of portraits of other "badass" black heroes who came before: Ida B. Wells, Harriet Tubman, and of course Malcolm X. The message is contradictory but also complementary. Barack is a badass, a lone man living by his own rules, forging new ground; he is at the same time the very embodiment of social redemption, a believer in the true American system of democracy who espouses hope and change with a straight face.

This is the twoness—the double consciousness, if you will—of virtually every notable black leader in history, even Malcolm X, who despite his deep and abiding skepticism of the American project, did not advocate abandoning the country he considered home. Obama stands out from the pack because as president, he is attempting to take black folks' eternal outsider status not only to insider status but straight to the core of American power. He aspired not to bring pressure on the system, as black leaders typically have, but to assume the mantle of the system itself. (This fact alone is what staggers me about Barack, what initially made me so uneasy about his candidacy and where it could lead; that core of American power is rightfully ours, but it is also radioactive, full of things I'd rather not examine, let alone claim. There are things in that core that could kill him.) Advancing to that level of power is a kind of power unto itself, and Barack is the first black person to achieve it. That he achieved it more or less as an individual and not as an expression of a black movement or popular sentiment makes it that much more impressive, only because it was so unlikely—John Henry swinging his hammer and actually beating the mighty machines in a contest. While Obama's single-minded journey to the center of American power technically makes him the ultimate conformist, it also makes him the baddest black motherfucker on the planet—a bandit in a category all his own. In his book, Levine writes that "many of the qualities which white Americans invested in their bandit heroes were reserved in Negro lore for another kind of hero who by transcending society's restrictions and stereotypes could directly confront it on its own terms and emerge victorious." We're not sure if Obama will emerge victorious at the end of his time in office—probably not, at least not literally—but his transcending of stereotypes and restrictions imposed on black men and the confrontations he's endured because of that transcendence are victories in their own right. And he fights on, because as president he really has no choice. He is both bandit and martyr, outlaw and do-gooder for whom no act of challenge or compromise goes unpunished.

♥ Obama's enemies see him as much worse than a bandit. They see him as a kind of cultural terrorist blowing up the usual order of things, a man who must therefore be stopped at all costs; black folks, of course, regard Obama as a benevolent insider, or as Levine puts it, someone who has followed all the rules, operated within society's moral code and been rewarded for it. Obama has beat the system by conforming to it, by being an exemplar when society still insists that black men cannot really be exemplars—for their own kind, perhaps, but not for anyone else. If Obama doesn't directly aid black people, he doesn't prey upon them as bandits often did in black folklore, sometimes killing them and feeling no remorse about it. Bandits were hardened, amoral at best, admired by blacks for their exploits and their refusal to lie down for white folks but not known for their compassion. Obama's image is that of a good guy, a stand-up man. He radiates caring and thoughtfulness, even sensitivity. He loves his wife and children and, despite the efforts of some tabloids to render him otherwise, is a straight arrow with no skeletons in any closet. He is a symbol of resistance to a hostile system, but a reluctant symbol; he strives to appeal to the public as himself, a man who is inclusive and unconfrontational by nature.

But the fact is that he did seek out this fight. He is not a boxer whose great skill thrust him into the limelight, as happened with Joe Louis; Obama put himself there. He wanted the attention, the opportunity to be in charge. He set it all in motion, set up the deal and then closed it in dramatic fashion. Unlike so many black folks, he got exactly what he wanted, and he didn't get it by hanging back or by having a weak stomach. There is certainly badass-ness in that, and more than a little ruthlessness. Despite concerns that Obama is not carrying the torch of black justice into his presidency, as history needs him to do, black people can't help but admire his singular vision, applaud the force of his own individual determination to get where he wanted to go. That is power we tend to doubt exists, even in talented-tenthers like Obama. Even if he ends up being the only black person to ever power himself to the White House, he has shown us it is possible. Not likely or necessarily something other black folk would even want to do in the future, not after what we've seen in his eight years. Obama's rocky odyssey thus far may actually reseal the doors of white privilege and make it harder, not easier, for another black person to be elected president; this is one of those barriers that may not fall just because a black person has broken it. But the precedent will stand. That is victory enough. By simply standing in opposition, by taking out Osama bin Laden (slaying the giant), by going through the hell of his entire presidency without breaking down or showing defeat, Obama triumphs. And unlike John Henry, who was a grunt, Obama is leader of the free world. That automatically qualifies him as baaaad on a level we have never seen and never imagined a folk hero could attain. Republicans keep trying to kill him, metaphorically, and he won't die—unlike John Henry, who after he beat back the machines, expired on the spot, gave his life for the cause. Obama is heroic for living. Nor is he arrested or pursued or run out of town, like Jack Johnson (or Shine, or Super Fly). He can't really be touched. He is a folk hero in a category of one, the archetype of an altogether new type.

The question is, what kind of songs will we sing for him? When he is gone from office, and then just gone, what kind of stories will we tell?

Lawrence Levine says that whatever their temperamental differences, black folk heroes have largely shared the same symbolism and fulfilled the same purpose in black culture because the American racial order simply hasn't changed that much over time. He makes that point in contrasting "fiery" Jack Johnson and Joe Louis:

> Johnson lived a public life, defying the larger society at almost every turn. Louis lived a relatively private, controlled life, speaking continually of how much he owed his mother, his friends, his country, coming across as the epitome of decency and respectability. Yet this paragon must take his place in the pantheon of folk heroes alongside other "hard" men because, however quietly and with whatever degree of humility he did it, Joe Louis, like Jack Johnson before him (and Obama after him), stood as a black man in the midst of a white society and in various ways beat representatives of the dominant group to their knees. In this sense, no degree of respectability could prevent Louis from becoming a breaker of stereotypes and a destroyer of norms. He literally did allow his fists to talk for him, and they spoke so eloquently that no other contemporary member of the group was celebrated more fully and identified with more intensely by the black folk.

Obama's "fists" are his eloquent words, his intellect, his dignified—presidential—bearing. In this, he beats the white boys at their own game. However naive and shopworn it sounds at times, the one-America mantra coming from a black president is a pointed challenge that says to the powers that have been: Did you all mean this all-men-are-equal business or not? Are you prepared to make good on the promise that you all are always waving flags about? It's the same challenge King made, that sharp question wrapped in his own eloquent rhetoric about brotherhood and entreaties to white Americans to live up to the true spirit of the Constitution. For a black man to invoke the flag as Obama does cannot help but be a criticism of how the flag is usually invoked, especially by the likes of the ultra-patriotic, nativist Tea Party. For a black person to be nativist he would have to be blindly conservative or delusional, and Obama is neither.

The journalist William Rhoden wrote about how he finally understood the power of Joe Louis the night Obama was elected in 2008, what he calls his "Brown Bomber" moment. It was that night that he got the collective black euphoria that his generation had never experienced, and it awakened in him a sense of possibility and genuine hope that he seemed surprised was there. But unlike the Bomber's victory, Obama's election victory wasn't self-contained. It was a victory of access, not of outcome. Joe Louis either won his fight or he didn't; if he won, as he did when he beat Max Schmeling, the euphoria was full and unqualified. There was no doubt about the nature of the victory or what it meant. But even at the height of black euphoria in 2008, there was doubt about what the victory of 2008 would mean and widespread caution about wanting it to mean too much. Rhoden says that we blacks will wake up tomorrow and still be poor and at the bottom of the barrel in so many ways. Of course, that was true in Joe Louis's time; his triumphs in the ring did not change social conditions outside of it. But they were not expected to. Obama's political ascent is *expected* to do just that because that is considered his job. Joe Louis was merely Joe Louis, but Barack Obama is leader of the free world.

This is another paradox. Barack is, as friends of mine repeatedly insist, "just a man." But a man in a position that requires symbolism and deference to certain American mythologies about its leadership can never just be a man. Add to that the symbolism that Barack already carries as a black man and how that symbolism collides with racialized notions of American superiority and exceptionalism, and the nature of this victory gets very murky. For years the fight between Obama and the presidency has ground on; at points it has gotten hard for me to watch. But it won't end until this president's time is up, until he can perhaps reclaim himself as "just a man." Until then the Tea Partyers repeatedly recoil at Obama's offer to share the American dream in compromise, because in their eyes what he is offering is his dream, not theirs. He is in many ways a stain on their dream, an impediment to their progress and their narrative of the ideal America. That is why Republicans pledged in 2009 that their primary order of business would be to unseat Obama. They truly can't go forward if someone like him is standing in the way, reminding them daily of the hypocrisy and racism etched deeply into a belief system they'd much rather conserve than take apart or question even mildly. A black man prompting a white man to search his soul is fine in a certain context—when the black man is a slave or social inferior, wise old Black Joe inadvertently teaching boss man the true meaning of life, in the movies or other works of fiction such as the *Adventures of Huckleberry Finn*. But a black man expecting to be treated not just as a social equal but as a political superior—*the* superior—is cognitive dissonance at a decibel level that conservatives simply don't want to hear; the sound is too painful, disorienting. The natural response is for them to shut out the noise, make it go away by any means necessary.

The dissonance isn't just the noise Obama makes, it's the noise he makes *as* Obama the president/hero/symbol. He may never raise his voice, but his resonance is deafening, because what he champions for himself he is also championing for other black folks. He probably doesn't intend that, but it happens. Levine says that, in the same way, John Henry's epic bare-handed contest against the machine was never individual; instead, he is "a representative figure whose life and struggle are symbolic of the struggle of the worker against machine, individual against society, the lowly against the powerful, black against white." Obama's struggle to find his footing in the very unfamiliar role of president—to figure out how to tame the machine set against him, as it were—is our ongoing struggle to find our own footing as fully engaged Americans, whatever our day jobs. It's the struggle of both black outlaws and insiders, though the insiders are more unsettling to the social order because they want in. They are infiltrators who might be applauded but who cannot be allowed to succeed. Obama persisted and charmed and eventually slipped through the looking glass into wonderland, and the strange characters on the other side of the mirror who were used to being seen only by each other were immediately determined to drive him back, make him lose his way. Black folks support Barack's right to stay in wonderland, to navigate treacherous terrain that we all navigate to some degree. But his particular terrain is a minefield, fraught with dangers that those of us living outside the inner sanctum of Washington can't begin to imagine. How he navigates it is the hero's journey in which all black folks have a stake. Even those openly disgruntled about the path Barack has taken so far are keenly interested in the path he has left to travel. It still matters.

Levine says that figures like Joe Louis "were so important because they were never perceived as isolated men but rather as an integral part of the entire network of black culture." That goes for Obama as well. However much the media says he is singular, above the fray of our sorrowful slave past because of his white American heartland mother and African father, he is an integral part of black culture. Black people may see him as isolated politically, but he has never been estranged from us, has never denied his place in our universe, which has always shadowed the larger American universe (or perhaps *it* shadows *us*). He knows full well that in the blazing limelight of the American universe, he still represents us. In the boxing limelight, Joe Louis proved over and over that we were the strongest people in the world. Barack is proving something more radical: that we are the most sophisticated and intellectually competent people in the world. Of course, traits like sophistication and intellect in blacks are always seen as anomalies or exceptions to the rule; acknowledging the prevalence of physical gifts in black men is one thing, acknowledging a prevalence of intellect is another. There are always ways around this. To his nemeses, and probably even to many of his supporters, Obama is one of a relative handful of talented coloreds who exist at any given time and in any given generation, but talented coloreds don't disprove the negative. That negative is still impossible to disprove, even with Obama in office. The collective belief in the black negative trumps the collective power of black individual achievements every time. It's because of this that I take a peculiar but nonetheless deep satisfaction in Barack being the *nigger* who has become president, the nigger with the smooth good looks and agile mind who occupies the White House against the wishes and the fundamental values of so many of his fellow Americans. If that's not the best revenge, I don't know what is.

Black people have been acutely aware of the nigger comparison from the very beginning of Obama. "You *know* they think he's a nigger," we say to each other, matter-of-factly and almost without emotion, because of course that's what they think. It's unavoidable. The old Malcolm X rhetorical question, what do you call a black person with a Ph.D.? will almost certainly become, what do you call a black person who's president of the United States? The answer remains the same: a nigger. This isn't funny and never has been, more like a rib-poke reality check that might produce an embittered laugh that says, Yeah, you right. But if white people *really* think Obama's a nigger, they must be steaming mad, and that's worth something. Obama beats them down just by standing up. The recalcitrance of certain white folks is a badge of honor, one we've all worn at one time or another. Obama would prefer not to wear it, not as president; he needs people to acquiesce, not to resist. I don't know if Joe Louis or John Henry ever really thought about what white people wanted when they were doing their work, but Obama must think about it. The fact that he has largely failed to convert that fury into love but still tries, though not quite as intensely as he did in the beginning, is part of his lore, his cross to bear. He didn't beat the machine, but he keeps charging at it. This is one of the things that already makes him heroic: the failure to change the hearts or minds of people who have been against black people for hundreds of years is virtually no failure at all.

♥　Tell the truth, a friend warned me more than once when I told her about this book. Now and then she repeated the warning: make *sure* that you tell the truth. I knew what she meant was not just to be accurate with facts, but to consider everything Obama is up against before passing judgment on him, either as president or as a man (for her, and for her many black folks, those two things are inseparable). To my friend, the truth about Obama is something very specific, something good and affirming and necessarily antithetical to the ugly narrative of less-than and incompetence that had already begun to envelop Obama like a fog during his first months in office. My friend was visibly agitated by that narrative, which is why she kept monitoring the "truth" of the Obama story that I was telling. She brought it up at a backyard barbecue in the summer of 2013, at a birthday party for a mutual friend who lived in a very spacious, well-appointed house in a historic part of town. When I asked her about her thoughts on the latest geopolitical developments and Obama's reactions to them—Syria, Libya, post–Arab spring—she waved the questions away before the words were out of my mouth. For her, Obama's significance had been settled long ago. Syria, Libya, the economy, Guantanamo, even historically black issues like discrimination and police brutality are, for her, all separate from the daz-zling fact that Obama is president and in a position to deal with issues at all. Not that she doesn't care about those issues; she does. But she wants very much to savor the advent of President Obama, to marvel about his meaning to black folks for longer than the moment we were all allotted in 2008 before reality began setting in. She already knows what it is about Obama she wants to remember, and why. "As long as he's standing and wav-ing from that Air Force One plane, I don't give a fuck about anything else," she told me cheerily. "He's *there*. That's what matters. That's his legacy." She has harsh words for those black folks who are indifferent or who seek to discredit Obama in the eyes of other black folks, to dull the shine—the limelight—of the man waving from Air Force One.

She's still concerned that I won't talk to people who "understand Obama," who know how to assess him; she fears that the people I talk to won't see the big picture because they haven't been taught how. Most of all, she fears for his legacy because she thinks black people's judgment about their own history and sense of place in the bigger American story is so skewed and so meager, we won't give Obama his due. And we can't do that to Obama, my friend insists. We have done that many times already, forgotten or remained largely ignorant about the true significance of figures such as Ida B. Wells and William Monroe Trotter and even Martin Luther King, whose mean-ing we've simplified and sanitized over the decades along with the rest of America. We can't do that, not this time. Obama is hardly in any danger of being forgotten, but he is in imminent danger of being underestimated, my friend says, of being labeled in the end a black man who became president and meant no more or less to black people than he did to other groups. My friend bristles at the thought. We can't let that happen, she says again. Not this time. We have to tell the truth.

When the poet/activist/historian Amiri Baraka died in 2014, the news-papers struggled for days over what he'd meant—to the academy, to the literati, to the consciousness of white folks who, once they called him "fiery," felt there was nothing else he needed to be called. In most of the articles and obituaries, Baraka seemed to have no finer points, and his most seminal and subtle works were not quoted at all. Black people eulogized him differently. In one conversation I heard on the radio, a black professor dismissed the minimizing and doubt about the ultimate meaning of Baraka as proof that blacks and whites are not on the same page about the meaning of most things. "We don't have the same heroes," he said. It made me wonder if it was really possible for Obama, *because* he is a hero for so many of us, to be a hero for everyone else. Does our embrace preclude other embraces, make the whole American ideal of interethnic cooperation and seeing eye to eye the farce we've always known it was? Even as Obama praises that ideal, he exposes it as false. It's nothing he says, it's who he is. Like a Greek tragedy, the spectacular rise of Obama that we all created together in 2008—the heroic social equalizer—was also preordained to fall. Thanks to our racial history and its own inherent tragedy, that fate was already written.

A line in the last chapter of *Black Culture and Black Consciousness*, "A Pantheon of Heroes," could apply to the moment now, and to Barack. Figures like Jack Johnson, it concludes, "were important folk figures because they signified the growing Negro insistence, borne of black culture and white oppression, that they be accepted in American society not merely as Americans but as black Americans, not merely as individuals but as a people." Despite his "raceless" image, Obama knows and we know that he has to be accepted simultaneously as both a black and an individual. This is what's never happened before, though it surely must happen before he's accepted as president. But that dual acceptance of being both black and American—what DuBois saw as the holy grail that might finally slay the ghosts of slavery—is not forthcoming. Which is why Obama is our folk hero, and no one else's. No one else can claim this problem.

♥   "America has not changed," says Brenda Jackson, a Los Angeles county worker in her '60s. She is frowning. Brenda is tall, wears her hair short, cut close to the scalp, and small earrings; her mouth is set in determination. Talking about Obama, Brenda is indignant, at points defiant. She relaxes—if you can call it that—only now and then into an air of pride, a fierce kind of love, before recalling some anti-Obama moment and resuming her indignation. Those moments include early press conferences in which some reporters failed to call Obama "Mr. President," South Carolina Representative Joe Wilson's shouted accusation "You lie!" interrupting a speech about health care reform that Obama delivered to Congress in the first year of his presidency, the entire Republican leadership's cultivated air of contempt that, to Brenda, is not merely political but personal. Her indignation about all of this isn't theatrical but normal, the default position of many black people schooled by the '60s who never believed America changed heart about its racial strata. Embattled Obama—the congressional stonewalling, the barely coded epithets from well-known conservative gadflies from Ted Nugent to pop-ups like Clive Bundy—is simply more evidence of that. Brenda is nothing less than disgusted. "I just feel that in the era of a colored person being leader of the free world, we have not come as far as we should," she says. "Obama does not reflect our progress but our limitations, the reality that we have much further to go." Those limitations are part of the failure that makes Obama heroic, or antiheroic: in his attempts to assure Americans that we have gotten past our worst character defects, he exposes them. Brenda appreciates the failure that amounts to a kind of martyrdom—King was a martyr, as was Malcolm. Barack follows in this tradition, even though he'd rather not. She also appreciates the struggle Obama is waging not just for his own presidential legacy, but for so many black folks who have not been granted the legitimacy or authority they also deserve, no matter how well they present.

The writer and '60s icon Ishmael Reed is unapologetically Afrocentric, a man with plenty of criticism for both blacks and whites for continually failing the cause of racial justice for at least the last thirty years. Obama seems to occupy a special, rather fluid place in this critique. Reed says at points that Obama is hardly perfect, far from a solution to the political enervation that has ailed black folks since the '60s; at other points he goes further and complains that Obama is part of the problem of stagnated black progress, his dazzling symbolism really just another brick in the wall of delusion. But at every point he allows that Obama as president is dealing with a level of white supremacy and acrimony that is almost off the charts, and simply dealing with that on a daily basis as Obama has done makes him a warrior, a folk hero extraordinaire. "With all the Negrophobia out there, you have to give Obama credit for running," Reed says with typical bluntness. "He could have stayed at Harvard, but he didn't. He could've been killed." To illustrate his point, Reed shows me a digital scrapbook that he calls the "Rogue's Gallery"—virulently anti-Obama clippings and videos he has been collecting from the news media and the Internet, I suppose for posterity. Among his collection is an announcement of Obama shooting targets for sale; an image from the National Rifle Association depicting him with a green face and intensely red mouth, an unsettling combination of the villainous Joker, a vampire, and a minstrel performer; reports about Arizona talk-show host Barbara Espinosa in 2012 declaring Obama the "first monkey president." Reed actually seems to enjoy himself as he browses through the collection, which he's treating almost like a family album, pointing out the denigration that confirms what he's been saying about racism all these years; he's like an anthropologist who's discovered new and powerful clues that validate his theory of a life form that people have said doesn't exist. Thanks to Obama, we know very well that it does.

Reed's animation and Brenda's indignation—strong feelings, to say the least—illuminate Lawrence Levine's point that prominent black figures like Barack Obama never exist in isolation from other black people. At this point in our history, with racism still so potent, it simply isn't possible. Reeds says the media subtly fuels the problem by always denying or downplaying race while at the same time allowing race and racism to shape the coverage, or non-coverage, of black issues. The media has been the focal point of much of Reed's racial analysis of the last twenty years and also the subject of his provocatively titled 2009 book, *Barack Obama and the Jim Crow Media: The Return of the Nigger Breakers*. Reed considers the title not provocative so much as truthful; reporters in the mainstream media, he explains in the book, are separatists, "a kind of white government in exile, ready to pounce on the black young president's missteps." (The errant media sometimes also includes non-mainstream, progressive outlets such as Pacifica Radio, which despite being progressive is white-dominated and therefore imbued with its own particular sense of racial superiority.) Reed sees Obama's chief problem as being black. Being in charge of drone warfare or building the national security state is problematic for sure, but he says problems of policy are secondary to the president's battle for his own agency. For Reed and so many other black folks, Obama inhabits two separate worlds that don't touch, one existential and one practical. The first world is the one in which all black people have a stake, where all of us bask (or not) in the proximate glory of this most accomplished brother. The second is Obama's leadership in Washington, which is tedious and workaday, the political sausage-making that historically has almost never worked to our benefit. Why taint the first thing with the second? Black folks assumed Obama's job would be hellish, and it has been. If his policies are bad for us, that is no cause for surprise or despair. Better to celebrate what has happened—a black man has gained the presidency, twice—than to fret about what has not happened or what is going wrong. Things always go wrong. Black history is so full of what hasn't happened, it's hard to get exercised about all that hasn't happened still in Obama's time, which is why policymaking simply isn't part of the folklore. If Obama had come in and integrated the military or something of that sweep, such policymaking would be part of the folklore, but those things have already been done. Obama's heroism, his own breaking of a color barrier, was therefore going to be of a different nature than the heroism of Martin Luther King or Joe Louis or Jackie Robinson or Jesse Jackson—less action-driven, more existential. It wasn't going be so much about doing (hitting home runs, marching, committing acts of civil disobedience) than about *being*. In trying to fill a large, mythical, inherently exclusive space with conviction, Obama was going to have to not *be* as small as history has tried to make black people; he was going to have to permanently enlarge all of us. Which means that despite the fact that all the major desegregating was years in the past when he came to the White House, Obama may have had the most daunting job of any black who has been first in our long and illustrious history of firsts.

♥ Not that Obama doesn't have a little bit of Joe Louis in him, maybe more than a little. One of his great attractions is the possibility that our lanky, sometimes pathologically circumspect president can become pugilistic when things get serious. I have seen the flash in his eyes and the hard set of his mouth when he is angered and wants to push back or say more, but the Mask—the face that all black folk wear in mixed company—and presidential decorum forbid it. But he has been pugilistic at least once, and in politics, no less—not at home or in a bar, but in the middle of work. That says a lot. In *Young Mr. Obama*, Edward McClellan, a Chicago reporter who closely covered the career of the pre-presidential Barack Obama in Illinois, describes a pivotal moment in 2002 between Obama and a fellow black senator in the state legislature, Ricky Herndon. Herndon had long needled State Senator Obama for not being black enough, for being down enough, for being allied with too many white folks and trying to carpetbag into the black community. One day in the state capitol in Springfield, Obama snapped. Try and embarrass me again on the floor, he told Herndon, and I'll kick your ass. Next thing anyone knew the two were squaring off in the Senate chamber; they shoved and cursed until another concerned black senator, Obama's mentor Emil Jones, came and broke it up. But after that, according to McClellan, Herndon stopped messing with Obama because he had demonstrated that he was indeed willing to lose his cool and fight—in other words, proven that he was indeed a black man. A folk-hero moment if ever there was one, albeit one that most of us living outside of Chicago and the state of Illinois knew nothing about.

During his time in office, many black people have questioned Obama's willingness to fight; I don't know about his willingness, but he does have the ability. That he would threaten to kick a colleague's ass and then make good on the threat gives me great comfort when I think about all the shit-talking Republicans who could truly use a whupping from the man they always like to insinuate isn't big enough or masculine enough to be president. Maybe by the time this book is published it will have finally happened, deep into the second term as Obama slowly sheds the burden of proof of competency and fair-mindedness. Of course, he began to shed it in 2013 in his State of the Union address, when he declared that he would start using the power of executive order to effect things it had become clear he could not effect through Congress. Immediately he was criticized by the right for being heavy-handed, for overstepping his boundaries and trying to be king when he is only president. But to those critics Obama simply being in office was overstepping boundaries; any authority he exercised was always going to be too much. Going on the offensive in the endless battle for legitimacy was a briefly heartening moment, one that took me back to 2007 at Rancho Cienega when, against history and my better judgment, I believed.

(But I have moved on from that: now, with a year left in the journey, I am entirely willing to believe. I have no reservations at all. It makes no sense to have reservations. In 2007, Barack was dazzling but a stranger to me; over the last six years, I've gotten to know him and have seen how much alike we are and how alike we were. He and I were raised with the radical idea that as the very first post-Movement New Negroes, we could reason with the world in a way no previous generation ever could, maybe conquer the world in the process. Obama reasoned with the world enough to get himself into the White House. Faithlessness would be foolish now.)

"The question isn't what is Obama doing for us, it's what is Obama *not* doing for us," says Z, who recently retired from a life in Los Angeles politics. She doesn't want me to use her name because black politics is a small world that frequently spans cities, a world in which what you say has an impact, whether you're officially still in the game or not. At sixty-two, Z is upbeat, charming in a very youthful way, and plainspoken in a way that's rare in politics at any level. She tells people if they're on point or full of shit, and she'll tell them so in public. She unabashedly loves Obama—not romantically or conceptually, as I do. She loves his historic presidential enterprise and the way it has unexpectedly infused the black American narrative with something no one quite knows how to describe yet. Z doesn't talk very much about his policies—his practical side. "He has to be judged by the system he's in, and it's a racist system," she explains. A fast talker, she is being a little more deliberate than usual with this discussion of Obama because she wants me to get it; she sounds like she's explaining a recipe. "He's like the brother who's been frisked and profiled six times a week and is still standing with dignity. This system is against him"—against *us*, she means—"and he's doing the best he can. He uses the bully pulpit of his presidency, makes statements with judicial appointments and things like that. He *is* for us. He's one guy. If he gets up every day and fights, that's enough."

Ishmael Reed agrees with that. He says that the white supremacy that

Obama fights is so diffused yet so pervasive, if Obama is killed (a frequently voiced concern of black folk, even now), it will be the media that will be responsible—not because it is overtly racist, but because it fails to address the poisonous atmosphere that makes such a thing possible, even logical. Reed muses, not altogether sarcastically, that Obama would probably be blamed for his own death because of his allegedly Marxist leanings, for "the total non-crime of being a socialist," Marxist and socialist being mostly Tea Party code language for black. Concern about violence and the more ominous dynamics of racism seems to outweigh other concerns Reed has about Obama's own political neglect of blacks—both are bad, but the former is simply more dangerous than the latter. To him, the president's lack of a substantive black agenda (which virtually all forty-four presidents have lacked, with a few notable exceptions) pales in comparison to the machinations of the "white government in exile" that has been aiding and abetting Obama's marginalization, if not his demise. That is a much more serious problem than what I'll call the Bill Cosby problem—the president's tendency to criticize black people for their alleged dysfunction—that is, letting their kids watch too much television or blaming racism for their problems instead of taking personal initiative. Obama has brought these things up in several public speeches, most famously in a 2008 Father's Day speech at a church in Chicago, later before the Congressional Black Caucus and to graduates of Howard University. Reed and many other Obama observers—critics and supporters alike—have decried these sentiments every time Obama utters them, or even implies them. But for Reed at least, that's an issue that exists on another plane; like Z, he believes that Obama's main job is to remain an upright black man in a hostile white environment and deflect the bullshit, a job he is doing pretty well so far. That is essential, because if doesn't do that, he isn't in a position to do anything for anybody. The fact that we can even complain about his Father's Day chastising means Obama is winning that battle to stay upright; directing bullshit at us from the bully pulpit so hard won is, in an odd way, a good sign. That is why some of us applaud when he delivers these sermons on black responsibility—not because we entirely agree with the sentiment, but because we feel damn lucky and not a little proud to have a black president up there saying *anything*.

Most of us also understand that this sort of criticism, cringe-inducing though it often is, is not the same barely coded racial damnation delivered by the likes of Ronald Reagan and George Bush, Sr., and even Bill Clinton. Obama's admonishments to us about watching too much television are not made of the black fear and loathing stoked by Willie Horton on furlough from prison or indolent welfare queens and young bucks buying T-bone steaks. Obama's diatribes are more intimate, and differently intended. Our battle-scarred folk hero is telling us what *we* should do to get in the game, maybe even to win big at the game, as he did. I am not saying that there aren't any politics in this stance, that Obama is not obliging his white supporters by scolding black folks (and, significantly, nobody else) for their shortcomings, which is politically so easy to do. I do think there is some of that. But I also believe Obama is sending a coded message of his own that *he* is in some ways powerless to undo a deeply racialized belief system in America that holds that black people are always to blame for their predicament. There are no extenuating circumstances. As president, he himself has been victimized by this belief; the anti-Obama cultists blame him for virtually everything that goes wrong. So what he is saying from the pulpit is that as black folks we have to be realistic about the situation and practical, cleaning up whatever we can on our side of the street. This is hardly a novel view, by the way; nobody, from far-leftists to liberals to arch conservatives like Clarence Thomas, think that black people should do otherwise. Nobody believes that individual behavior isn't some part of group liberation. It is this liberation that Obama is addressing in his speeches, but I believe that, unlike Reagan, he is advising black people, not damning them. He is at these moments talking to us more than he is talking to a fearful and put-upon white electorate, even though both groups are listening. It's another example of tightrope walking that makes Obama's way forward on this journey so precarious and his heroism even more so, but we applaud (or keep our critiques muted or our mouths closed altogether) because we understand the precariousness and want him to keep his balance and prevail, even if he takes a bit of our hide in the process. The sacrifice would be more than worth it. Admittedly, we have been hurt a lot worse.

Ishmael Reed was one of several black voices warning ahead of time against any sustained euphoria of an Obama triumph in 2008. In *Barack Obama and the Jim Crow Media*, he wrote that "if many African Americans agree with [conservative] John McWhorter that racist attacks on African Americans, including predatory mortgages, racial profiling, racism in the criminal justice system, etc. will end the day after the election of a black president, they're in for a big letdown. Again."

How telling is the last word—"again." It speaks to all the unredeemed hope we've had for black elected officials who have ultimately failed to make big changes, all the patience on our part that has yielded relatively little justice. But "again" also speaks to the persistent hope that eventually that hope will be warranted, and the sacrifices made good; as long as racial justice is undone, we keep making the offer. That President Obama could actually redeem our suffering, even just some of it, is an idea of almost religious power that moves even skeptics like Reed. That's because Reed is at heart an idealist, a true believer in the '60s (he was an early proponent of multiculturalism, though not the soft-focus sort we know today) who can't help responding to the energy of the Obama phenomenon, however tenuous or short-lived. After fuming that Obama's Jeremiah Wright pre-election "race" speech in 2008 pandered to an ancient white resentment of blacks benefiting from social programs, he is almost relieved to make this post-election confession: "Nevertheless, as the cameras roamed over the millions who turned out to watch Obama take his oath and deliver his speech, one couldn't help being infused with excitement and pride. I thought of the 600 years of resistance and agitation that led to this moment, and when he was introduced as president-elect with trumpets blaring like in the 'Gladiator' movies, and walked down the steps toward his seat, I was really moved. This was . . . a triumph for the persistence of the African American movement."

I am moved by Reed's being moved, by his willing embrace of the drama and enormity of the moment. He acknowledges the power of Obama mania, which he didn't expect but which pleasantly surprised him, especially the widespread activism and optimism of young people that had not been a part of any presidential zeitgeist since Kennedy. Reed is especially impressed by the ethnic and cultural depth and breadth of Obama's following—the rainbow coalition redux, but a real force this time that Reed dubs "the big wave, all fired up and ready to go." He again admits the error of his own cynicism when he says, "I should have known something was different when I heard a black man call into C-SPAN's (normally staid) *Washington Journal*. He said, 'When I hear Obama speak, I just feel like doing something!'"

When I ask him how he feels about Obama now, five years later, Reed looks a little blank; the question doesn't seem to quite register. He was exuberant then, but that was then. I realize after some discussion that what lives for Reed is the moment and the profound meaning of the first campaign, the magic of the inauguration; what matters for him is the story, not necessarily the protagonist. He understands the heroism of protagonist Obama, defends his honor vigorously—or picks it apart—but he doesn't really personalize him. He seems to consciously resist that because the inevitable letdown of a black president whom he warns us about in his book will be that much worse. I also realize that black people are not in the habit of publicly assessing each other on the basis of intrinsic qualities such as good character or insightfulness or thriftiness; what matters first, especially to those in Reed's generation, is what you do. The external defines the internal, which sounds dehumanizing in one way—racial stereotypes operate on that very principle. But within black culture it's a valid way to describe the collective consciousness that is so vital to everybody's survival, even happiness. The question of liking someone therefore can't be separated from what that someone is doing for himself, and especially whether what he's doing is benefiting the race. "I like Obama," Reed finally says. "I think he's a good guy." That's as much praise as he can muster.

♥   In the introduction to his 2010 book, *The Making of African America*, historian Ira Berlin declares that with the election of a black man to the presidency, "African American life was totally transformed." It's an unsurprising but still curious statement. Berlin doesn't say how that life was transformed—apparently he thinks that's self-evident. But what does he mean? Presumably, he means that Obama fits into Berlin's stated view of black history in America not as a linear story but as a series of transformations. First there was the Middle Passage of slavery, then the forced transformation of Africans to Americans (a transformation still under way), then emancipation, then the hundred-year ordeal of Jim Crow segregation, and finally the second emancipation of the 1960s, the civil rights movement. Is Obama in and of himself a force of transformation? That feels too big, even though his symbolism is bigger than just about any symbolism that's come before. I do agree with Berlin that blacks have a collective consciousness, that they tend to see themselves as individuals who experience life as a group. From all that I've read and seen about Obama—especially in his own memoir, *Dreams from My Father*—it's clear that he sees himself this way too. (*Dreams* in fact affirms the primacy of his black consciousness rather than repudiates or deconstructs it, as many critics in the thrall of post-racialism liked to suggest.) Obama, the son of a man from Kenya, nicely fits with *The Making of African America*'s theme of how black immigrants have remade black American life over the last fifty years or so, which Berlin sees as a critical substory of how immigrants generally have shaped and transformed American life. Black immigrants do and do not fit the slavery-to-freedom narrative of black America; there has always been some concern among native-born black Americans that the immigrant narrative will always obscure what has already been obscured by a country that prefers almost any narrative to the one about the people victimized by its homegrown tradition of slavery.

We don't need to worry about Obama obscuring anything. He is the son of an immigrant, yes, but he is American, and one of the most delicious ironies to emerge in the last few years is that it is his white mother from Kansas, not his black father from Kenya, who ties him genetically to the inescapable realities of black American history and his place in it. (Genealogists somewhat accidentally discovered in 2012 that Stanley Anne Dunham, Obama's mother, is descended from John Punch, a black man and former indentured servant whose court case in Maryland in 1640 declared him the nation's first legally sanctioned slave.) In *Dreams from My Father*, Obama shows that he understands this place fully, long before he encounters Africa; it is in Africa where he seems a stranger, a tourist, part of a blood family, of course, but ultimately an observer. But he's never been a stranger to the black American family, has always been a participant even as he was finding his place at the table. While Obama straddles two identities—something we all do, but an image remade by multiculturalists who like to hold Obama apart from us ordinary black folk—he doesn't resolve anything or preach a new black immigrant narrative that overwrites or ennobles the domestic one. The slavery-to-freedom narrative is not over, and Obama knows it. He is part of the narrative. He is still on that freedom journey, like all of us.

Psychologically, though, Berlin is right: Obama has transformed things. Our conversations about ourselves have shifted permanently in his direction; he has reoriented them like a compass. And in the process he has become everything in that long-running conversation—the high point, the status quo, the shining example, the manipulated black face of empire, the ultimate black man, the put-upon black man, the fighter, the striver, the race man, the new deal. He is an individual who is at once a composite, a Rorschach image, the very definition of a folk hero, or of a myth.

Obama's own folk hero was Harold Washington, the first black mayor of Chicago, who fired the yes-we-can imagination of black communities in a city famous for a long and ugly history of racial strife. Washington modeled the big-tent appeal to whites and others that Obama would later adopt, but he was first and foremost a black man who was an unqualified hero in the hood, celebrated for his savvy across racial lines that led to his historic election in 1983. He was both part of the black family and bigger than life; black people around town called him warmly by his first name but also revered him as a symbol of progress that was bigger than any they'd had before. His election over his white opponent, Bernard Epton, was the Brown Bomber all over again. In *Dreams*, Obama gets a reverent earful from an old-timer named Smitty as they both sit in a Chicago barbershop getting haircuts. "The night Harold won, let me tell you, people just ran out in the streets," Smitty tells Obama. "It was like the day Joe Louis knocked out Max Schmeling.... People weren't just proud of Harold. They were proud of themselves."

The same thing was true about the fateful Obama victory in 2008, when black people filled streets and parks and living rooms, all of us incredibly proud of what had happened and the fact that we had helped to make it happen; our passion had made a difference this time. The difference between

1943 and 2008 is that even as blacks were celebrating our greatest political victory ever, we were also being discouraged—warned away—from claiming Obama as ours. He was not *our* hero, the media narrative went; he was everybody's hero. The president of the United States, not the president of black folks. That's true, of course, but that big-tent talk is also an unsubtle attempt to cut Obama off from his biggest constituency, to once again render black folks as atomized, isolated, invisible, and inconsequential. It was (and still is) an attempt to cut us off from ourselves and reinforce the ideal of post-racialism, which is not for black people's benefit and never has been.

But the warning away has had the opposite effect. That nonblack narrative, and Obama's own big-tent rhetoric, has only increased the sense of black collective consciousness. The timing couldn't be better: In the twenty-first century, that consciousness was at a low ebb. Ironically, the man who was supposed to retire blackness for good has instead resuscitated it, called it back to center stage, which might be his most heroic act of all—especially for being so unintended. Because of Obama and his odyssey, "we've got to wear our black *seriously* now," said Robert Hill, a University of California, Los Angeles (UCLA), history professor and lifetime scholar of Marcus Garvey. Garvey preceded Obama as a black folk hero with international appeal; his legend was made not by his success but by the fact that he was ultimately taken down by American law enforcement, which saw him and his grand vision of black superiority as a threat. Obama has advanced no such visions, but his presidency models a kind of black self-assurance and innate authority that is equally threatening for being so unprecedented. What he does—how he sees himself—violates a social order that has literally made America what it is. Nor can Obama be repressed or dispensed with, as Garvey and Malcolm X were, because he *is* the leader of all, not a leader of black dissent. He is on a plane with Lincoln and FDR and Kennedy, men who faced mighty opposition and even assassination, but their playing field and purview was all of America. It is Obama's too. But the landscape he's looking at is vastly different, chiefly because the landscape is looking differently at him. Obama is not the national folk hero Lincoln and FDR were because he still represents some part of black dissent—he is its product, the shiny outcome of its culmination in the '60s—and therefore he can never be national in that way. Nonblack people may support or admire him or empathize with him. They can contribute money to his cause. But as a folk hero, he belongs only to us. He may not be our "black shining prince"— what actor Ossie Davis famously dubbed Malcolm X after his death—but he shines. He has not died for us, but he has taken some slings and arrows on our behalf. He is ours.

Contrary to the Obama myth, Hawaii was not entirely the exotic outpost away from the mainland that nurtured a worldly, racially transcendent Barack. Obama confirms more than once in *Dreams from My Father* that Hawaii is actually where his black education began in earnest. As a teenager he was friends with a black man named Frank, a good friend of Barack's white grandfather, Sydney, or more accurately, Sydney was good friends with him. Frank was one of the first elders to school Barack on the historical realities of blackness, which he did away from Sydney, of course. One of the things Frank told him as he was preparing to go off to college was that a degree, or two or three degrees, wouldn't essentially change those realities. Frank saw integration as the mother of all illusions, especially for Barack's generation, because it implied equality, official arrival at the feast. But the fact is that the terms of integration are always dictated by white folks. (This was why Sydney could take refuge at Frank's house, be comfortable enough to fall asleep there, but Frank could never do the same at Sydney's place.) They'll give you a degree, Frank tells Barack soberly, but if you ever want to start "running things," you're guaranteed to hit a brick wall.

As a teenager, Barack gets schooled in basketball from a "handful of black men" who teach him not only the basics of the game but respect, which Barack learns is derived from "what you did, not who your daddy was." Hawaii is where he realizes that he is going to need guidance from someone other than his grandfather, whom he loves dearly, but like the vast majority of white Americans, his grandfather has a limited understanding of what it means to be black. Barack senses this early. He recalls in the book that "by the time I had reached junior high, I had learned to beg off from Grandpa's invitations (invitations to a black bar that he liked to frequent with a very young Barack in tow), knowing that whatever I was after, whatever it was that I needed, would have to come from some other source." That source wasn't just Frank or fellow ballplayers, but black pop culture, notably music and dance. This was the stuff that Barack absorbed and that solidified his own iconography among the black masses years later: "I couldn't sing like Marvin," he writes with typically wry understatement, but he could certainly learn moves from *Soul Train*; he couldn't be Shaft or Super Fly—those movie folk heroes of the '70s who, like John Henry, were regarded almost as real people—but he could curse like Richard Pryor. He loves his grandparents and his mother's family, but being black is, for him, *being.* He knows who he is, but he needs to know more.

Growing up, Barack hangs with black boys, notably a badass named Ray; it is Ray who shows him the impressive force and occasional fatalism of black anger. The young Barack seems fascinated by the phenomenon of black anger, probably because it isn't his own natural temperament and also because he realizes that it's central to how black people navigate, and perhaps conquer, a primarily hostile white world. For his friend Ray, anger needs no object; it is a constant that can be switched on and off at will. Sometimes he deploys it to make a point. By contrast, Barack moves in and out of white and black spheres easily, and unlike Ray, he goes home to a family that is white.

That dichotomy is what makes Obama unique to the broader American public. But to me it only makes him another one of us—a black man negotiating a double consciousness that happens to be directly reflected in the doubleness of his own family. Though unlike the rest of us (including many of us who are not biracial but who share with him roughly the same genetic mix), Obama really believes that the black and white worlds will eventually cohere. It's that optimism that makes him unique, the thing that made me simultaneously doubt and admire him when I first saw him and was left modestly (but significantly) changed. It was not *my* optimism, though it could be. It could be all of ours, which was the message that presidential candidate Obama bore that day and that he still bears, though much more wearily than before. The hero's journey is taking a toll.

Now I understand why. I see that the 2008 message of "One America" is more serious a challenge than I initially thought, deeper than the Pollyanna notion that I discarded some thirty years ago after my own run-ins with integration. Barack's optimism is a reminder of how blacks always carry the burden of American optimism precisely because they have been so badly treated and so dimly viewed; the One America message is therefore not just a challenge to America but a specific request for black folks to do what they have become so adept at doing—that is, keeping up their spirits when things look terrible (which is most of the time). Six years on, I think Obama was saying, I know things are terrible for us, but why not believe in this improbable idea with me and show the rest of the country how it's done? Get on the Love Train, and all that. Act like who we are, America's moral vanguard. The change we need and believe in matters, or it's supposed to matter. Our optimism is not so much a burden as a kind of obligation—why did we suffer so long, if not for the right to tell the country what it needs to do to save its own soul? I guess we got tired of telling the country and of not being listened to. Obama is reviving that tradition and telling the country what it needs—nicely, per his style—but as president he's also just the guy in a position to listen. That's the strange thing: he's both the messenger and the power structure for whom the message is intended, vanguard and old guard, challenger and status quo. That makes him doubly heroic, potentially, or doubly not. What he is lies somewhere in the middle, which, as we all know by now, is where he feels most at home.

♥ Oliver Stone, the filmmaker and student of American history who produced the documentary series *A Brief History of the United States*, told Bill Maher on his show *Real Time* in 2013 that he thought Obama had missed his moment. Stone sounded regretful, more than a little distraught to say it, but the bottom line for him was that Obama, a black man who had staked his election and his legacy on change, should have been the one to help restore the meaning of democracy, which had been eroding since the '60s; *he* should have been the one to light the way back, rekindle the flame that had nearly been extinguished by the corporate takeover of government and all the rest. I understood the expectation and even appreciated it—I had frankly been hoping for that rekindling myself—but at the same time, the criticism struck me as willfully naive, offered without any of the historical or cultural context that Stone is famous for. I thought, how in the world can Obama light the way back when he stands against so many cherished American ideals, among them freedom and democracy, simply in being black? How much help does Stone think the president is getting on his ideas from a Congress that is so opposed to all things Obama that it has shifted its whole governing ideology to accommodate that opposition? The modest bits of democracy Obama has tried to advance, such as health care reform and better federal meat inspection, have been fiercely resisted, attacked, snuffed out, twisted, or at best, tepidly supported. He is not allowed to own any democratic ideals, to say nothing of implementing them. I like Oliver Stone, but on this point about Obama he sounds like so many white progressives who sincerely think, and have always thought, that it is the job of black people, as the moral vanguard of American history, to enact the revolution that we all desperately need.

To be fair, I know that Stone would certainly have leveled a similar critique at any Democratic president who came into office facing a towering pile of mostly Republican-made shit that required nothing less than swift and decisive action to clean up. But the opposition to action that Obama has faced has been as unprecedented as his election to the White House. Previous Democratic presidents have favored hostile and seemingly immovable Republican Congresses, notably Harry Truman in 1947. But the difference with these Tea Party–driven Republicans is that their hatred of the president is less political than personal; they hate him even when they're given what they want. As Erik Taroff noted in his 2011 article in the *Atlantic*, speaking of the Republicans' total refusal to consider any tax cuts in an age of staggering income inequality that was only becoming more staggering, "This position can no longer be considered economics, and it can't even be considered politics. It's more like religious dogma. And it isn't only absurd, it's *obscene*."

I do agree with Stone that as a black man, Obama should carry a certain consciousness into office about the plight of people of color and about the oppressed in general. But as for advancing democracy, nobody I know is naive enough to think that is Obama's job. Black people don't usually believe their representatives can advance *their* issues, let alone democracy's.

The irony that Stone also fails, or refuses, to see is that Obama is, like him, an idealist about democracy; like Stone, he is a student of history who has made it clear that he perfectly understands the transgressions of empire, including hundreds of years of slavery and wars of aggression repeatedly sold as wars of liberation. Perhaps somewhat less like Stone, Obama also believes that capitalism and free market-ism are cornerstones of American well-being that actually facilitate making things equal for all—part of his "we are a great country" rhetoric that both alarms me and thrills me to the core. Obama believes this despite the fact that he's hammered away at the problem of "income equality" for the last couple of years, as the economy recovers speedily from the crash of '08 for those with money and continues to sputter along for everybody else. Though he doesn't say it, Obama is keenly aware of the more fundamental, intractable inequalities of race that underlie those of income. But since he is forbidden from voicing that awareness, that fundamental truth is ignored, even by the progressive likes of Oliver Stone—because really, only a black person can say it convincingly—and so goes the exhausting cycle of unspoken truth, inaction, and reaction that has been the story of race relations in Obama's America, and decades before that.

Contrast Oliver Stone's disappointment with Obama to the reaction of Angela Davis, another '60s-era progressive who became timeless because many of her ideas—prison abolition, for one—turned out to be so ahead of their time. When I interviewed Davis at a fundraising dinner in 2011 at which she was being honored, she saw Obama's election not as another brick in the wall of oppression—which is frankly what I expected her to say—but as a crowning moment for the Movement. Obama was a black man who understood and empathized with the black radical tradition, if he wasn't exactly a practitioner of it himself; electing someone like this, Davis said, was a radical act. The problem was that after the first election, we the people didn't capitalize on our own courage. "That was exactly the moment we should have seized on to enact change," Davis said. "That was our moment to demand everything," health care, income equality, climate justice, all of it. What evaporated after that first election was not Obama's will for change but his base of supporters who had rallied like hell, and then gone home. It was the people's fault, Davis said—in that even, almost musical voice that fairly crackles with optimism, even about the most dire subjects—the *people* were responsible for the failure of its leaders, especially in this case.

Yet the reason people went home was that they really thought that Obama possessed some kind of change magic *because* he is black, when the truth is the opposite. Color is always a problem. Being black, or even half-black, has always been a millstone, a negative to disprove, however successful you are or aren't. Obama's magic may only be that he disproved that negative so convincingly (at least for an election season) that he became president. Actually, I think Obama supporters considered both things—that Obama was truly magic and that he was simply a great exception to the rule of the black negative—and believed both things. But they decided that the first thing would overwhelm the second. He had accomplished the hardest part by getting there, right? Getting there had to mark the beginning of revolution, yes? It was all perfectly logical. No further action by the electorate was required; it would all be easy for black people from now on, and Obama would be the first to enjoy that new ease. He had earned it. Black supporters, however, never believed the first thing, and so we never went home. We stayed vigilant. The Republican siege of Obama that set in immediately didn't surprise us at all. The forces of white supremacy that asserted themselves more and more boldly as Obama's time in office wore on were always visible to us and no one else, apparently least of all the mainstream media, which is, as Ishmael Reed insists, part of the problem: it's not what they see, it's what they don't see. Oliver Stone is one of millions who does see the racial animus against Obama—it's hard to miss—but has decided that Obama's ineffectiveness is mainly about his character and resolve; what he is not able to do is not the fault of history or the fault of people. For a filmmaker who regularly and unsparingly picks apart American mythos, it's a surprisingly facile take.

♥ Obama knows American history. And he knows what it means, though he's careful not to show his feelings about it. Yet this is what black people want so desperately for him to do: vindicate us by finally putting American history and its goddamned mythos in its place. This is what his bully pulpit can accomplish for us. But he won't do it—remember, he is that insider black folk hero who allies himself with the system rather than against it.

Yet because he does understand history so well, Obama understands that he is an outsider, too. In *Dreams from My Father*, he presents a lawyerly but impassioned, brutally frank breakdown of the ultimate meaning of blackness in a white world. Reflecting on the views and behavior of his black friends, young Obama concludes that the white man wields control of blacks not just economically but psychologically. Decisions about their lives are ultimately his to make: "We were always playing on the white man's court." They not only own the court, he says, they own the ambitions of anybody wanting to play on it. In fact, "the only thing you could choose as your own was withdrawal into a smaller and smaller coil of rage, until being black meant only the knowledge of your own powerlessness, your own defeat. And the final irony: should you refuse this defeat and lash out at your captors, they would have a name for that, too. Militant. Violent. Nigger."

An irony Obama never could have predicted was that, as president, he would find himself struggling against becoming yet another thwarted, angry black man who self-immolates because he sees no way not to be angry. Obama is not naturally disposed to anger, as so many people have noted, but it doesn't matter. The more he doesn't ignite, the more intensely burns the world around him. He feels the heat of an anger not his own, and it is *that* anger that he is trying to keep from destroying him. That's been his battle, though you probably wouldn't see it if you aren't black, even if you'd been closely watching all along. Obama understood from his days in Hawaii that to be black is to engage in a war of psychological operations with the white world. His war as president with the Tea Party, the gun lobby, the Christian right, and so forth is the mother of all such wars. He is absorbing the full range of racial toxins that most of us have only absorbed a bit of or are always on guard against. So Obama the idealist quickly became the martyr, a word he very likely hates. He is a man of god (so he says) who would prefer not to believe that he suffers for all our sins, not just the sins of black people but those of all Americans. He prefers to focus on America's good, not its sins. The fiercely race-polarized America that he helped redefine is hardly the one he imagined delivering to all of us, starting with himself.

♥   Thirty-one-year-old Brandon Brooks remembers exactly the transformative moment when he "met" Obama. (Already it's become something on par with remembering where you were or what you were doing the first time you saw Jackie Robinson play or Paul Robeson perform.) I had that moment. But it was even bigger for Brandon, who had experienced nothing like that moment before and never expected to; his generation, unlike mine, has no living memory of the Movement and always regarded political heroes and leaders in general as more hagiography than possibility, a figment cleverly or wistfully described in a line of hip-hop. Obama changed that, made the figment real. Talking about the president, Brooks is animated, almost giddy, astonished and re-astonished anew that Obama was elected to the White House and is still there. Brandon is an editor for the *Los Angeles Sentinel*, the black paper in town that's housed in an office on Crenshaw Boulevard, not far from Rancho Cienega. On one wall of the *Sentinel's* spacious conference room is an oil portrait of Malcolm X, and next to it is a blown-up photo of a radiantly smiling Obama with Danny Bakewell, the *Sentinel's* longtime publisher and Brandon's uncle. For more than a year leading up to the first election and afterward, a banner hung outside on the front of the building, high above the entrance, declaring to the traffic below: "CRENSHAW IS OBAMA COUNTRY!"

Like lots of people, Brandon first saw Obama in 2004 when he gave his now-famous address to the Democratic convention in Boston. "I was working at a bookstore at Cal State Long Beach, watching television, and it hit me—'who's that black man?' Within five minutes I thought, 'He could be president,'" he says. "'I thought, this guy is strong, believable, authentic. . . . For a young black guy of my era, he stood out from Jesse and Al and those guys. I thought, 'Who is this guy who's got the floor? Why *can't* he be president?'" The thought took root, anchoring a public expression of black pride that had previously been limited to books and history and historiography. Obama was history, and not: he was just starting out. He was *becoming.*

Brandon felt part of that process, swept along by events, moving toward something, whereas before he had been more or less running in place. That Obama was black like him and *seemed* like him was inspiring beyond description, almost surreal. "He was commanding the Democratic floor, speaking strong, and I felt the black-thang connection, that moment of identification—it was a thrill, electric," Brandon recalls. *"And* he was charismatic."

In college, Brandon studied history and rhetoric with a man who wrote speeches for Reagan. King and Malcolm X had an aura, Brandon says, a clear sense of the prophet about them. Charismatic as he is, Obama is not in that category. But he is in a category that nothing and no one else permeates. "I don't put him on that pedestal, do the Mt. Rushmore thing," says Brandon. "Those guys, King and Malcolm, put their lives on the line. Barack is not that—he's an elected official, a great marketer." He thinks for a moment and then says: "Here's where I put him: a calculating individual who will have a legacy even if I don't prop him up. He doesn't *need* me."

Still, Brandon can't resist crowing about Obama's sheer audacity in claiming the rarefied space of the presidency as his own, of methodically taking what he wanted rather than waiting for it to be given or handed down. This boldness is worth at least ten braggadocio hip-hop lyrics, and it's what the hip-hop set, with its often muddled politics that nonetheless lean toward black justice, likes about Obama. He has done something worth rapping about. "He's a living legend," says Brandon. "It's like, 'Wow, I'm the president!' Go on ahead, I am the motherfuckin' president!" Grinning, he straightens his tie and strikes a supremely cocky pose in an imagined moment of the president in private delighting in his own achievements, maybe in front of a mirror. Cockiness aside, Brandon admires Obama for aspiring to an altruism that has always animated black struggle. "During his first term he took health care. He said, 'Look guys, health care affects everybody.' He had to do it. This was him in the Gandhi category. It's also what puts him in the Martin category—as president, he'll go on record as having paved the way. It's where he showed his vision, his humanity. It's him saying, 'All of us are in this.'" If you don't remember anything else about Obama, Brandon says, you'll remember that. Not the particulars of the Affordable Care Act, but certainly the impetus of change behind it.

That impetus is fine, but Brandon acknowledges that black people would like to remember something about Obama that is more visceral, more personal. Something more along the lines of the stance that he took, with some reluctance, after the controversial not-guilty verdict in the criminal trial of George Zimmerman, the white gunman who fatally shot black teenager Trayvon Martin in 2012. In the aftermath of that verdict, Obama said that, but for his age and the fact that he wasn't in Florida on that particular day, *he* could have been Trayvon. I found the admission sobering, at the same time heady in its simplicity and vulnerability—here was our careful man Obama standing before the cameras and baring himself to a world that thought he was made of stone, colorless, unmarked stone at that.

Politically, the response changed nothing, but it affirmed the integrity, the truth, of black experience from a height from which it had never before been affirmed. To hear Obama including himself in the tragedy of Trayvon made me ecstatic. Brandon knows why, because it was "a moment that was a confession of the obvious, of what blacks have wanted him to say all along: 'Yes, that is me. Yes, we *are* each other.'" The relief I felt at that confession was tremendous, though I know many blacks wanted Obama to go further than that on their behalf, much further—after all, to admit being part of a community when everybody in that community already knows you're a part of it is only a start, if not an actual insult. If you're going to confess to being black, why not go all the way and talk about the crises associated with the condition? It's a perfectly reasonable question to which we already know the answer—to talk about black crises is to indict white folks. "They want him to raise his fist and say, 'Fuck Whitey,'" says Brandon, laughing almost ruefully. "But Obama is in uncharted territory and knows that every day. Nobody has worn these shoes." Brandon speculates that in his worst, most isolated moments, Obama "calls on Martin or Malcolm. He doesn't lose touch with the black American struggle, and part of that struggle is winning the battle against the negative perceptions of blacks. He can't just go blowing his own horn." Or blowing the horn for us.

Pam Ward, a graphic designer and writer who worked on Obama's first campaign, says that however hard he fights that battle against racial perception, Obama remains in a bind that neither blacks nor whites want to describe, for different reasons. "Ultimately, Obama needs to change the hearts and minds of white people in order to help *us,* and he can't do that," she says. "You can have a thousand laws on the books, but changing racism is what needs to happen. Look what happened to his push for gun laws"—not after the Trayvon travesty, but after the Sandy Hook shooting in Connecticut, in which twenty-six people, mostly children, were killed by a mentally disturbed gunman who opened fire at the elementary school campus just before Christmas 2012. The shooter and the victims and the community were overwhelmingly white and middle-class; the country was horrified and, in the shooting's aftermath, largely supportive of stricter gun laws. Obama stumped for those laws with uncharacteristic passion. But with him as national spokesman for the cause, Republicans—notably the pro-gun wing of the white right—dug in. That was hardly unprecedented, but the recalcitrance of gun advocates this time had not the barest hint of apology; they were almost gleeful about the opportunity to deny the president a modest policy victory and, more important, an opportunity to deny him an emotional connection with a white public that had connected deeply with Obama once, and might have again.

It struck me that the real battle the GOP was fighting was not for gun rights, or any rights, but for the hearts and minds of white people who may not hate Obama but who don't love him either and are more prone to doubt than belief—people who don't see themselves as racist but who hesitate to join hands with Obama even on issues they support. That battleground is where the fight for change is really won or lost. This is why black people knew early on that Obama would probably fail to do what he set out to do, and it's also why we knew that his failure would not make us love him any less. His failures have little to do with us. In the end, Pam Ward says, "leading by example is all he can do. Be a good father, a good husband, a decent person. That's the mark of a man. He's part of the historical struggle to just be who he is, day in and day out. Like all of us."

Eric Priestley is also a writer, a student of the Watts Writers Workshop, founded by the screenwriter Budd Schulberg after the conflagration of the 1965 riots in Los Angeles, which kicked off a whole season of riots in big cities across the country. Eric is a remarkable poet who merges literariness, street sensibility, and lyrical observations about family and history—his people, like mine, are from Louisiana. He is what I call a professional observer. Since the '60s, he has observed somewhat anxiously the steady decline of black consciousness into a stagnation of which black people have seemed utterly unaware. Obama's bursting onto this stagnant scene has heartened him greatly. But it has worried him more. It has worried him that Obama has not been received better, by whites and also by blacks, especially young blacks, who he says fail to appreciate all that Obama stands for and all that it took for him to get to where he stands now.

Symbolism is crucial for Eric, as it is for all poets. But it is especially crucial for one who has tried for a lifetime to reconcile the disappointing realities of racial progress with high expectations fueled by a fierce belief in the transformative power of literary aesthetics and education. Eric lives on very little money, as he has for much of his life, or at least for as long as I've known him, twenty-two years; he takes the bus and train everywhere, still a relative rarity among Angelenos. When he talks, he bristles with ideas and indignation, much as I imagine he did as a young artist in the '60s, when the world seemed like his to make over. These days, it is his to reject. "I never thought I'd live to see the day when we had a black president, yet it seems like all that excitement has evaporated in the streets," he says to me over lunch at Farmers Market in mid-Wilshire.

Eric spends a lot of time at the Writers Guild library across the street from here, reading classic screenplays to study screenwriting techniques that he might apply to his movie projects, of which he has many at any given time. The possibilities once described by his mentor, Schulberg, have stayed with him. But his Hollywood aspirations never clouded the reality of Watts, where he grew up, and the black state of things in general. Obama doesn't change that state simply by being president, of course, although Eric thinks his presence on the international stage should at least improve the moribund consciousness of young black people who have never known heroes, folk or otherwise. But he is not hopeful. "Kids call each other 'nigger,' Latinos and Asians and whites do it too," he says almost angrily. "Bigotry carries over to the workplace, especially if you're black and male. Penal institutions are the biggest businesses we got going, and yet and *still*—Obama can't break the bigotry because of the Republican agenda. There are all these murders happening, like Sandy Hook, but the NRA has more money than God. How do you implement change if you're Obama, or even if you're Superman?" He shakes his head in disgust. "Laws tighten up as soon as a black man gets elected. The raw hatred out there is fueled by bigotry. If you're spoon-fed this shit for thirty years or more, how do you lay it down?"

For all this, Eric says that the times should still be more enlightened than they are; Obama the folk hero fighting for the betterment of all of us, black and otherwise, should be able to align things more than he has. But things are gravely out of whack for black people, economically and also spiritually. "I'm a black writer, but more white folks read books," Eric says. "Ask black youth about anything and they don't know anything, they don't know nothing, not a damn thing. Obama's too soft on them"—meaning that he doesn't call them out for their cultural miseducation. Some people would argue that in his Father's Day remarks, Obama has. Regardless, Eric says that "they don't understand the sacrifices made so that they can even go to the public bathroom. White people look at that behavior and say, 'Well, they're ignorant, they don't know anything.' That *bothers* me to be put in that paradigm."

He's being a bit too damning, but I get Eric's angst. The thrill of Obama claiming us all, as he did in his remark about Trayvon Martin—a young person—has its complications. Obama being Trayvon is poignant, resonant; Trayvon being Obama is, outside the realm of the symbolic, a little tough to fathom. Eric says he can't fathom it at all. "[The young people] have no respect where they come from, so how can you know where you're going in the future?" he says of Generation Z. "Obama has no impact on this kind of attitude—in fact, he exacerbates it. These youth want to say, this brother made it, but they're so full of rage, that fact escapes them—they're that paradigm that Ralph Ellison describes in *Invisible Man*. And they don't even *know* they're invisible.

"These kids don't believe in themselves, therefore they don't believe in Obama's possibility—how can they?" he continues. His anger is a bit softened by something—sorrow. "They've *disappeared* into their rage. If you don't fight [the rage] and you don't wake up, you're lost."

Pam Ward agrees that it is this kind of black internalized rage, more than the externalized rage of the Tea Party and the whole white right, that undermines Obama most. "White folks can hate on us all day long, but black folk who will put you down, that will do the worst damage," she says. "Self-hate is the worst."

This is not Obama, says Ward. Whatever racial issues he has politically, he appears to be easy in his own skin. "Obama is proud of his race—he never disassociated from black," says Ward with more than a trace of pride. "He embraces black women, he got his mom-in-law in the White House—all that speaks to the kind of man he is. He isn't a token black president like Clarence Thomas has been the token black justice on the Supreme Court. He hasn't done everything, but he has done what he can for *everybody*. I'm sure he wants to do more." Ward says that Obama simply wanting to do more is in sharp and encouraging contrast to his predecessor, George W. Bush. "The crushing things that went on with Bush—Hurricane Katrina, black people pissing on themselves in the Superdome for nine days, no water or help, a president who didn't acknowledge anything was wrong—that was a travesty," Ward says, sounding more than a little angry at the memory. "We're still living out that legacy."

As for Obama's legacy, the best thing he can do is to literally keep himself together: "With all the backbiting coming from other people, on any given day, all he can really be is himself." In an era of retrogressive racism and widespread fragmentation among black folks, to be black and be yourself—especially while being president—is more than an accomplishment. It is more than heartening symbolism. It is the very essence of heroism.

2 Obama Represents

There's a house around the corner from me that since 2008 has had Barack Obama in its front window. The first time I saw him, glancing up as I walked my dogs, I thought for a brief, astonishing second that it was *him*—was he related to the family that lived there?—before realizing that it was cardboard. It's an image of him that's become stock: serious but relaxed, sincere gaze bordering on intense, incipient smile, dark suit and tie. It's a generic political pose that Obama, a black president who has dared to make the normal presidential claim that he stands for all of America, has made utterly specific. Throughout his presidency, this Obama replica has looked out over my black working- to middle-class neighborhood like a patron saint of aspiration and inclusion, a stark figure against the white of the window shade, which is never open, probably because the family that lives there doesn't want to move the figure and risk disturbing the real Obama's mojo—or ours. The main message of this display seems to be that the president's success, the fundamental legitimacy of his claim that he can indeed stand for all of America, depends on the black faithful keeping him visible, posting him on street corners and in windows just as people hang American flags from their houses year-round. The world has to know that we believe, and that we believe in someone in common, something that hasn't happened since Jesse Jackson ran for president in the '80s. That campaign was a trial balloon, another very good black cause that reverberated deeply in the political monde, but it was destined to fail. Jesse ran twice and lost. Obama ran twice and *won*.

That's an astounding reversal of fortune in twenty years' time, and it couldn't have come at a better moment. In the midst of the exquisite disillusion that defined the black condition in the late twentieth century and continued into the twenty-first, the Obama victories were freakishly spectacular good news, and black people had no intention of letting ourselves and the rest of the world forget it. This hasn't meant sitting around being nostalgic. Remembering Obama has become a serious job, a full-time endeavor. The longer Obama is president, the more he is demonized, deracinated, insulted, and minimized by the white right and its affiliates, the harder and more necessary our job gets. The Obama paraphernalia, kitsch though it may be, captures the important details of the good memory—the straight-ahead smile, sincere gaze, and determined air all invoke the pre-inauguration glow of Obama primed for his first day on a job that most of us assumed could never be captured by a black person in our lifetime. That workday suit-and-tie image that I see on my daily walks (all he needs is a briefcase) suggest his expectation of great things after the first election, which we hoped against hope was only the first of many great things—this kind of optimism will feed our collective mojo for a long time, long after Obama has left the scene. Embattled Obama is for another day, another discussion; the proud, upright, unbent Obama is what we go back to again and again in these hard times (which actually never stopped being hard). In the future, that image is what we'll seek out repeatedly, like favorite photos in a family album that describe in simple but powerful visuals a moment that can't be repeated enough. It sustains us.

I meet Obama not just at the house around the corner but everywhere in the hood. Crenshaw Boulevard was proclaimed Obama country in '08 by the *Los Angeles Sentinel*, and unlike much of the news the paper prints every week, that wasn't really hyperbole. Obama has become a street-corner commodity, his likeness printed on T-shirts sold alongside the Lakers shirts and Bob Marley shirts and carpets and incense and bean pies; initially a novelty item, Obama-wear and other keepsakes (I once bought a vial of Obama perfume oil at a street festival out of sheer curiosity) have become part of modern black memorabilia, as distinct yet as unremarkable as the images of Malcolm X and Jimi Hendrix. For a long time there was a large billboard at Crenshaw and 43rd Place featuring a picture of Obama in mid-oration, one hand outstretched to the masses—an echo of King at the podium in Washington in 1963, delivering his "I Have a Dream" speech. Billboard Obama presided over black Crenshaw just as he presides over my own neighborhood in that window; his image and his presence in black spaces are as ubiquitous as the Virgen de Guadalupe, the Virgin Mary icon associated with the indigenous people of Mexico, who adorns everything from liquor stores to car windshields in Latino neighborhoods here. It isn't the place, it's the belief in the Virgen that matters, the iconography itself that makes her powerful. The same is true of Obama.

A man who lives a few blocks north of me still sports an Obama campaign sticker from 2012 on the bumper of his SUV. One day he invited me into his house to show off a collection of Obama paraphernalia that at that point already filled an entire room. I spotted the same life-size Obama cutout in my neighbor's window in another, larger window of an office on Crenshaw that sells car insurance. Why not? Obama selling insurance (or anything) with that ingenuous, encouraging smile makes as much sense as him selling the notion of full democracy around the world and cooperation across color lines. Whatever his limitations as president, he has the true salesman's gift of empathy and authenticity, of looking like he cares about whatever it is he's standing next to or has his hand on. Like it or not, Obama has also joined the pantheon of freedom fighters and civil rights folk heroes whose images grace every black space from salons to barber shops to churches and living rooms and family rooms and offices; upon his election, Obama was drafted into the mix like a latter-day Che Guevara, not in revolutionary garb but a suit and tie (or shirtsleeves, at his most daring). Still, like Che, Obama's face exudes a calm that covers fire, reflecting the tension between optimism and realism that marks the iconic portraits of Frederick Douglass and Martin and Malcolm. He *looks* like he belongs.

Obama didn't qualify for this vaunted pantheon in the usual way. He was not a black leader thrust to the fore by the demands of history or the intensifying grievances of black people, the first in this fighter's club to not fit the profile. Yet his actions qualify him to be there, less as a traditional black freedom fighter than as a Wild West hero: though a symbol of black community, he is also a lone force, a guy who followed his own vision. It was a vision made possible by all the heroes who came before and whose arguments for racial equality and self-worth were also implicit arguments for the kind of independent-mindedness that Obama has exercised to great effect. So his image belongs to us, with us. We know that and have always known it, despite what white folks say, even the most well-meaning among them who are fond of saying that Obama belongs to *everyone,* thinking that's the greatest compliment they could pay us. In reality that is the greatest compliment they could pay themselves. The fact is, they don't put him in their windows or beauty shops or billboards; we do. That part of him that precedes political approval or debate, that essence, is ours.

The root of the whole modern Obama iconography is something almost never mentioned: his looks. There is the sheer physical persuasion of Obama, the pop-star magnetism that Sarah Palin and other Republicans immediately derided as shallow, which looked to the rest of us like envy, white envy at that. Black people I talked to agreed that white folks are more or less forbidden from stating the obvious, that Obama is good-looking and charismatic and therefore more threatening to the establishment than a black man elected president would inherently be, because those qualities give him power. We know perfectly well that his walk, energy, alertness, athletic bearing, and relaxed but interested air (alternatively known as "cool") all compelled people to his side and accounted for a huge part of the difference that Obama brought to the political scene, a difference that the media obsessively noted but didn't, or couldn't, really describe. Black people described it to each other all the time, particularly women, either matter-of-factly or with great relish, sometimes both ways in the same conversation. The writer Stanley Crouch, who has followed with interest the role of gender in Obama's success, said to me, with typical candor, "Obama is tall, has a low voice, he's what women in general consider an attractive guy. I've heard exceptional things about him from women who've expressed how they'd like to have sex with him." He added, as a kind of caution, that "his sexuality is a strike against him because the Republicans don't appeal to women, by and large." It's maddening enough to the GOP that someone like Bill Clinton would remain popular with women; the idea that Obama does the same—Obama, who shouldn't have gotten to the White House at all—is infuriating.

Though it may be a political liability in some ways, that sexuality is an undeniable force. It is something to be reckoned with. I asked my friend William Flynn, a seventy-three-year-old retiree, about the nature of that force, and instead of answering, he sprang from his chair, stood as upright as possible, and proceeded to do a shoulders-back, chest-out, slow-drag walk. He was of course doing the black-man cool walk, arrogant, physically assured, at once self-conscious and completely natural. William was exaggerating to make a point, but not by much. Watching him approvingly was another friend and fellow retiree, Yvonne Divans Hutchinson. She's a master teacher of English and writing who's made a career of mentoring black boys in middle and high school. She laughs appreciatively as William approximates the Obama walk, exclaiming with a kind of wicked satisfaction, "Oh, honey, yes indeed, indeedy *yes!*" I laugh with her.

The three of us are sitting upstairs at a black bookstore, in a room cluttered with odds and ends of the business; yet another one of those six-foot life-size cardboard figures of Obama rises above the clutter. Yvonne studies it with a fire but also a certain reverence in her eyes. For her, Obama is not just a heartthrob—though that's a clear part of his appeal—he's a heartthrob who's also a stand-up man, the living embodiment of middle-class solidity that many black women seek in every issue of *Essence* magazine. Obama is the dream black man who, for starters, is devoted to wife and family; he's ambitious, gainfully employed, highly educated, professional, hardworking, politically astute, and racially conscious but not embittered or beaten down by experience, meaning he's optimistic—what more could anyone ask? This true prince of the black romantic imagination is as hard to come by as a black president, maybe harder. Obama is not perfect—Yvonne is too seasoned and too sensible to think that—but he has the goods. That is its own perfection. No surprise then that he's graced the covers of *Essence*, *Ebony*, *Upscale*, and other publications that still espouse a black ideal and represent it every month on the cover as a matter of principle, and of progress. Obama has for them been The Man.

These days the cover people seem to fall short of that; hip-hop mogul Jay Z has a good head for pop music and makes a lot of money, but how much he models a black ideal is questionable. Obama closes the question. He bears the standard now, a standard that he himself might not ultimately live up to, even as president (especially as president, I suppose), but he is heroic in setting it. We need that. For so long, before Obama, blacks had no fixed standard for politicians. We supported our favorites, voted consistently for black representation within the Democratic Party, from city councils up to Congress. It was part of the fruit of the Movement, this representation. But we went on autopilot. We drifted from one moment and one crisis and one personality to the next, from cover to cover, more focused on survival and quick gratification than on anything resembling long-range accountability for elected officials. Obama has at least shaken us out of that torpor. He has made us think about what black elected officials are supposed to be doing, what we should expect them to do, and why.

These sound like merely practical considerations, but there's a lot more to it than that. The Obama phenomenon is sexy. Before Obama, black folks of course had no need to measure a black president; we seem to need a measurement now, a development that is sexy for being so elusive, so improbable. It didn't strike me that way until we were well into the first term and I heard Obama being called an Eisenhower Republican. That's meant as a criticism, but when I heard that, I was thrilled because it reminded me that we now actually have a black president who must be compared to all forty-three nonblack presidents who have gone before him. We have someone in the lineup now who demands to be considered and compared to what you now have to call his peers. He demands it. In the past, we could never make that comparison, never compare Shirley Chisholm or Jesse Jackson to anyone because they had no white counterparts, really. As presidential candidates they were understood as outgrowths of black empowerment movements, and as such weren't competing with other white candidates; they were running as challengers of the system, not agents of it. They were clearly outsiders.

But Obama is understood in a much more mainstream way, which is why he's invited so much hostility: he cuts too close to normal. Many people would prefer not to feel that they have to compare him to Eisenhower or Kennedy or Reagan, but they have no choice now. History requires it. Obama is a two-term black president whose time in office has been described as an era; that his presence in the Oval Office during this time has sustained such chaos—a mash-up of derision and adulation, doubt and even despair—is unsettling, but at the same time, it's sexy. Obama made stuff that was once strictly procedural hold-your-breath unpredictable: in 2013, constant budget battles led to tense showdowns over raising the federal debt ceiling, eventually to a two-week government shutdown. Ridiculous, yes, but the face-off between Republicans and Obama—not the Democratic Party, because it was really all about the president, *this* president—was intense, and, strangely enough, sexy. When House Speaker John Boehner declared, "We will not surrender," Obama was made into a war general, an aggressor executing his advantage, a very powerful (i.e., sexy) figure. To say nothing of the fact that a white man declaring to a black man in authority, "I will not surrender" is a delicious role reversal, a historical fantasy, except that it's happened now, more than once.

So much that has happened and continues to happen during Obama's tenure cannot be compared with anything that happened during previous presidencies; Obama is breaking new ground just by being where he is. He appears unflappable through all the politics, which are so contorted and potentially tragic—with so many moving parts. The constant tension between his unflappability and the opposition's fury is sexy, too; it feels as though at any moment, the whole enterprise could veer out of control. All of us in this country are waiting for a black man to lead us out of the morass, yet his opponents are determined to maintain the morass because they would frankly rather die—fall on their own swords out of spite and imagined superiority—than follow him. What a ride.

The bottom line is that Obama the man reflects and absorbs so many conditions out there—black uncertainty, white aggression, black tentativeness about leading instead of simply reacting, black inexperience in representing white folks, not just politically but psychologically and culturally, as presidents are charged to do. This is all new; it is just not done. Obama or any black man leading as president is as unthinkable now as race mixing was in another age, though in a fundamental way that age never left us. The Great Emancipator himself, Lincoln, worried about the quandary of freed slaves living among whites; he just couldn't imagine how it could be done.

Black people were too different, too despoiled, and white people who had despoiled them were too convinced of their own singularity. That is still the case. Obama, who claims Lincoln as one of his heroes, surely knows this.

Crouch says that Obama has become the center of a modern-day Lost Cause, what with Tea Party types almost constantly rallying to save the union from Obama. The threats against the union inherent in race drive the antipathy, but so does sex; the combination has always been indivisible. Crouch believes that Obama shook things up immediately when he came in "as this half-white guy who chooses Michelle," breaking with an expectation of biracial black people to partner with someone white, or at least someone not black. That choice might have mollified those whites who see in Obama a half-breed whose very existence is more, not less, of a threat to the sanctified racial order and genetic separation than a "regular" black person such as Jesse Jackson or Condoleezza Rice; unlike them, his biracial-ness makes him a double agent, an infiltrator who must always prove his good intentions toward white folk, and a white wife would have been a good place to start. Ulli Ryder, a professor and visiting scholar at Brown University who specializes in racial identities and is also biracial, says that while some people were hoping Obama might boost the visibility of mixed-race people as a distinct people, that hasn't happened—largely because of America's history of observing hard and fast racial lines, but also because of Obama's own choices. "Because of his wife and daughters and his whole context, he's more black than half-black," she says. Still, his half-blackness resonates in a specific way. "He's the slave master's son," says Ryder. "Historically, they had certain privileges, but he has the keys to the kingdom. That wasn't supposed to happen."

Nor was Michelle supposed to happen. She is another finger in the eye of mainstream American expectations, a die that was cast early when she got a reputation as a big mouth (what other kind of mouth does a regular black woman have?) by remarking brightly during the '08 campaign, "For the first time in my life, I'm proud of my country." That sentiment was certainly nothing that other black people didn't also feel, myself included. Patriotism has been problematic for every black generation, with good reason, and the Obama candidacy was giving those of us in his post-Movement Joshua generation a real reason to feel part of the democratic experiment we allegedly inherited from the '60s. But for the anti-Obama crowd swiftly forming at the time, Michelle's comment only stoked a vision of old-fashioned radical blackness infiltrating the White House, maybe even taking it over. It didn't matter that Michelle is herself a talented-tenth striver who is eminently middle-class, that she is in most ways "light years away from that firebrand thing," as Crouch put it. A few months after that remark, the New Yorker magazine did an equally controversial cover depicting Michelle as an Angela Davis–style militant with a gun strapped to her back and ammo slung across her chest; she is grinning slyly and fist-bumping her husband Barack, who is dressed in a white Muslim garb, complete with a turban. They are standing in the Oval Office, where an American flag is burning in the fireplace, above which hangs a leering portrait of Osama bin Laden.

The New Yorker said the cover was entirely satirical, a jab at all the anti-Obama hysteria that draws on anti-black, anti-Muslim, and general anti-Other hysteria that's always in America's political atmosphere. The problem is that the image couldn't really satirize an outsized suspicion that lots of people saw as perfectly reasonable (including, no doubt, more than a few New Yorker readers). The New Yorker cover, while it may have refuted that suspicion for some, only reinforced it for many others. The Obama campaign knew that, which is why it criticized the cover instead of applauding the magazine for its wickedly observant humor.

But that dustup in which the dust never really settled didn't keep Michelle from having a certain symbolic power and influence as First Lady. Crouch thinks she's actually helped close a fundamental cultural gap between black and white women by acting as a kind of bridge-building, universally appealing Oprah who stresses a cross-racial sisterhood of struggle. This may be true—Michelle has always been more consistently popular in the polls than her husband. But what's also true is that as a black woman she is an icon in her own right, for many of the same reasons Barack is an icon as a black man: she is the do-it-all, conscientious wife and mother who is highly educated but highly nurturing, erudite but down-to-earth, racially conscious but (contrary to those early critiques) also graceful under enormous pressure. She has probably been on more magazine covers than

Barack, in part because there are so many more women's magazines; her appearance in hoary, notably white publications such as *Vogue* speaks to Crouch's theory that she indeed crosses over with white women, certainly more easily than her husband does with white men. But the enduring love black folk have for Michelle isn't so much about her crossover appeal as it is about the particular strength and forbearance of a black woman navigating a white world that can be more accommodating of black women than of black men, but that is still hostile—a quality also known as being fierce. In the "Back 2 Back!" poster commemorating Barack's twin presidential victories, it is Michelle who looks more heroic, and comfortable that way: dressed in her own workday suit but with head up, hands on hips, a wide, triumphant smile radiating into the middle distance. She looks at home. Barack is on a hero's journey with a still uncertain destination. Michelle looks like she's already arrived.

❤   One bit of Obama iconography that stopped my breath is a painting of him as Superman by comic-book artist Alex Ross. There have been more than a few Obama-as-Superman images out there, but this one isn't meant as a broadside or as kitsch. This one is the moment of Clark Kent *becoming* Superman, pulling apart his gray suit jacket and button-down shirt to reveal a blazing *S*, in this case a blazing *O*. The suit-jacket breakaway is a staple of the Superman mythos, that culminating moment of transformation from secret to public, observation to action, doubt to daring. Comic books were never my thing, but that particular moment of revelation always thrilled me, which is why *Superman* was my favorite movie in the late '70s when I was a somewhat timorous high school senior preparing to take the world by storm, or so the movie and that moment helped me imagine. I must have seen it ten times.

In Ross's painting, Obama replaces Clark Kent/Superman; the result is not a cartoon or a spoof but a compelling metaphor of a lone black man's heroic venture into the unknown that is so heightened and so purely sexy in its promise, it's alarming; I've had to close my eyes to it. In keeping with the comic-book aesthetic, this Obama Superman is more muscle-bound than the real-life counterpart. But the preternatural determination and sense of purpose that is uniquely Superman is also Obama's, especially in the slightly weary but expressive eyes that look up, up and away from his own inspired but terrible commitment. There's an anxiety just beneath the optimism that speaks to the reality on the ground—the rough social terrain that the real Obama must navigate in order to be anything close to super, in order to reach the point where his true self underneath the natty gray suit will be accepted without cover.

Actually, the Obama of press conferences and weekly addresses is in some ways very Clark Kent—good-looking but geeky, smart, diligent but somewhat wonkish and deliberative. This is Obama but not all of him—or we fervently hope it's not all of him. There's nothing wrong with being geeky, but from the beginning, black people have fantasized about him metaphorically taking off the glasses and finally dispensing with the mask; then and only then can he unequivocally state his case, make a stand for us and take care of business. (The most restive among us see him going into a phone booth and coming out Super Black Man—Huey Newton?) It's more than tempting to believe Superman lurks in Obama because we have all seen flashes of anger in him, the moments of consciously holding back. There is another man in there, even if Obama doesn't know it or won't let him out. White progressives—Oliver Stone, probably—certainly had something of the same fantasy when they voted for him the first time, and even the second, though they saw him unmasking not himself so much as the hypocrisy of America, exposing the gap between ideals and reality. Who better to do that than a black man? Their effusiveness faded as Obama continued on as mild-mannered Clark Kent or, worse, emerged as a villain who had initially posed as a hero. But black people kept the faith in his transformation, or redemption, because that faith never depended solely Obama's actions, or what he did to redress American hypocrisy. Our faith is personal and goes much deeper than that.

The Superman metaphor appeal also because it recasts repression as a personal and ennobling choice: Superman wears a disguise until he must do what he's called in life to do, which is much different from being another black man forced to wear the mask among white folks because he has no choice. One kind of repression is strategic, concealing power until the proper moment of unleashing that power to work for good in the world (and the moment will arrive, again and again); the other kind is impotence. The ordinary black version is a mask that wears *you*, not the other way around. We pray that Obama is the former. Much as we empathize with how he wears the mask like us, we don't want that to limit him as it limits us. We don't want him to be us, not in that way. No, we want him to very publicly liberate himself from that identity-stifling mask, which he can choose to do—he is president, after all. He can model the breakaway, the moment of personal transformation, that all black folk need to see. He can do this despite the virulent racial antipathy and the various forces arrayed against him. This is where being president truly matters: his political status gives him the option of personal revelation and a national audience to witness it. He alone can break the emotional invisibility that we have all been living for much too long.

You will believe a man can fly. This was the ad for *Superman*, the movie, in 1979, the year in which the sun permanently set on the '60s and "Morning in America," its mindless Republican antithesis, dawned. Hence Superman's arrival to return us to the primary-colored notions of truth, justice, and the American way. Thirty years later, politics came full circle as Obama's "Hope/Change/Believe" campaign delivered a similar promise of change, the lifting of a long darkness. The similarity to the *Superman* ad went beyond its message: For a while, Obama really *was* the man who could fly, vaulting over our racist history in a single bound, against the odds and against reason, to win an election and reaffirm core American values of fairness and democracy that had been almost forgotten. It really was a movie. And then it was over, and we emerged from the magic atmosphere of a dark movie theater into the harsh light of the afternoon. Superman isn't Clark Kent anymore; he doesn't exist at all. We are left with a black man with undeniable attraction, but with no superpowers.

Still, that a black man with virtually no name recognition could hold the fevered attention of so many long enough to get into the White House— that proves that he's got power nobody else has. At the very least, he enlisted white folks' willingness to choose a black man out of desperation—they were falling off the burning building of the Bush years and really did need a Superman-like intervention to save them from certain death. That Barack Obama could be that man, overcoming the skepticism that went along with hope, is still historic; electing him required an act of national imagination of a scale that I don't think any of us have witnessed before. The leap from the burning building to Obama, though pragmatic, was still one of faith. It turns out Americans had something under our collective gray suit of indifference that we didn't even know we had. It took a Superman that we all believed in at the same moment to show us our own flash of blue.

♥ One institution that early on sensed the transformational effects of Obama is the California African American Museum. It's located at the northern edge of South Central Los Angeles near downtown, a couple of blocks away from the University of Southern California (USC). In 2007, the museum mounted an exhibit of Obama iconography that was already dotting the landscape and shifting the political zeitgeist at the time. Curator and historian Christopher Jimenez y West said he knew something big was on the horizon the year before, when the museum hosted a book signing for *Dreams from My Father*, which Obama was touring. West said the crowd was so massive, the museum staff was forced to bring Obama into the building through the loading dock, something that had only happened with one other visiting author—Muhammad Ali. For West, forty-one years old, it was a revelation, a glimpse of raw idolizing that he, like Brandon Brooks, the *Los Angeles Sentinel* editor, had studied in history but never seen up close.

"I thought, 'Oooh, this is what it was like with Malcolm X. This is what physical charisma looks like,'" West recalls "Clearly, this was the guy who was *going to*." More impressive was the fact that Obama was getting all this adoration not as a hero/athlete of established legend—Ali or Joe Louis—but as an untested entity with possibility; he was being vaunted by black people not for what he was but for what he might be and where he might go. That alone had a physical power that gave Obama's natural charisma a whole other quality that in some ways defied description. West is still trying to find the words. "Obama was this new hybridity of masculinity," he says.

"He's still about changing the dimension, the tone of black masculinity. He's evoking it not because he wants to. I don't know what it is about the brother, something—maybe the cigarette smoking? I don't know." (Obama subsequently quit the habit.)

The familiar idea that Obama straddles racial lines is part of the appeal too, West says. But for black people that straddling means something specific, and powerful. At least during the honeymoon period of '08, Obama elevated the impossible conundrum of reconciling the double consciousness into an art. He made it look easy, not to mention sexy. "He's a child of the African diaspora, clearly, but he could negotiate white privilege," muses West. "You can always see him pull out of the river of the black diaspora, which is troubling for us. But we were also impressed. We're like, 'Damn!'"

As far as Obama might venture out of that diaspora, he's regularly assured us that we are always within his sights, blackness grounding him spiritually if not politically. That spirit is what counts first, sometimes most. West says that's what makes moments like Obama's impromptu (but credible) crooning of the Al Green ballad "Let's Stay Together" before a black crowd at the Apollo Theater in 2012 so iconic, and so heart-stopping to black supporters who are used to being spoken to indirectly, if at all, by politicians, even black politicians, who tend to talk *at* them, not to them. Being publicly serenaded with a message like that was, to put it mildly, mind-blowing. West says that Bill Clinton, the so-called first black president, could never negotiate such a moment. "When you go into a bedroom singing voice, you're making a statement, communicating something, especially him," says West. "It's very calculated, but it's not performative." In other words, it's authentic. West says the Al Green moment was also Obama subtly defying critics who charged that he was only superficially connected to black culture and therefore to the broader meaning of post-Movement pop tunes like "Let's Stay Together."

West is a fan, but he's not starry-eyed. After giving Obama his due, according him his place in the tribe, West says he's troubled by the president's glossing over—or passing over—of the myriad crises of black Americans that demand but never seem to get sufficient attention from whoever's in the White House. Those crises are ongoing, an exhausting continuum that includes overincarceration, underemployment, and undereducation. All have their roots in the racial inequality and black devaluation that began with slavery. Perhaps because West can't help but understand this big picture, his concern about Obama's reticence to address black crises is not separate from an admiration of Obama himself, something I observe in many other black people. He argues first for giving Obama a greater margin of error ("What, a brother can't be complicated? Can't make *mistakes?*"), criticizes the scholar and activist Cornel West for his criticism of Obama displaying a bust of Martin Luther King in his office ("I mean, come *on!* That's too personal!"), then details his own growing disappointment with Obama's failure so far to express politically the vital black connection he expresses so readily in other ways. If he can sing to us so directly, flash a winning smile in our direction, surely he can use the bully pulpit to voice our pain, legitimize it in a way it has not been legitimized. Surely he can do *that* much. Voicing the pain and the crises may not translate into the kind of policy changes black people need, but without Obama clearly stating the problem those changes feel that much harder to effect. In a discomfiting way, the president becomes part of the obstruction. Preserving our great and necessary admiration for him puts us in an odd but all-too-familiar limbo between hope and disappointment.

"Criticizing Obama for having a bust of King is too personal, but it's also personal that he hasn't figured out that he could do something through executive order to address us," says West (who, by the way, is no relation to Cornel). "It actually hurts him. If he wasn't Obama, we'd be back to the good old days of George Bush. He's not living up to the moral authority of the river; he's just pulling from it. For me as a black man, I'm thinking I was bamboozled"—Malcolm X's derisive term for America's repeated betrayal of black hopes for equality. It makes me wonder uneasily what Malcolm, our black prince, would have said about Obama.

"I don't know," says West. "His agenda has narrowed and narrowed; now it's so narrow and militaristic. He keeps saying [to black people], 'I'm one of you, give me a break,' but you don't get to do that. The river is what makes you. Respect it."

I agree with West. But I think it's harder to respect the river when an ocean of disrespect from the white opposition early on rendered Obama an icon of an entirely different nature—a symbol of evil, a kind of anti-icon. Ulli Ryder at Brown University says that Obama's negative symbolism is at least as powerful as his symbolism for good. The negative symbolism for black folks, however, is not about Evil Obama; it's about how his shortcomings reflect our own, and the racial shortcomings of the country at large. "He's at once a symbol of progress *and* regression, of how far we haven't come," Ryder says. By "we," she means both black folk and America at large. "It's more than [just that] they don't like him. It's dislike, and it's particular. It's racial. Bush was disliked too, but he was never called out for being white. Obama critics hate him so much, they're willing to do anything to oppose him, even if it hurts other Americans."

None of this particularly surprises her. "I'm biracial—black and white—and this kind of stuff happened to me all the time," she says. "Why not to him?"

Samarrah Blackman is a Ph.D. student in education at UCLA who, like West, has her criticisms of Obama. But like many black people, she doesn't lead with them. Nor does she consider his addressing those criticisms a litmus test for her support. In her view, Obama has already made his greatest contribution to black progress by persevering and becoming president. Whatever he does in office can't possibly match the impact that perseverance has had, and will have, on black people from now on. "Somebody had to be the first one," Samarrah says. "A black president has got to mean *something.* That's powerful in and of itself. It's beneficial, regardless of what happens in office. Regardless of what he ends up doing with his life, he'll matter."

And mattering is no small thing, as most black people understand; mattering is the metaphysical opposite of being invisible. As we have watched the Tea Party try to ensure that Obama's ultimate meaning is minimized or erased from the American history that he so rudely interrupted, we are increasingly reluctant to do anything that might help an effort that most of us consider immoral. We prefer to concentrate on keeping Obama in our front window, not idealized—not just cardboard—but in no way demonized. Keeping a balance that we know President Obama deserves, both the man and the idea of justice that he claims to represent, feels more important than airing individual grievances. We don't discard those grievances but keep them close, as we have always done. Though I have to admit, the fact that we still have to hang on to those grievances in the time of a black president who is putatively sympathetic to us, who unselfconsciously counts himself among us and sings our songs, is more than a little galling: when, O Lord, can those grievances have the kind of hearing they have not had in forty years? If not now, when? If not Obama, who is himself a grievance for so many white Americans, then who?

For black people, the question of Obama's political inattention to us hangs around him like a mist or, in our most doubtful and disappointed moments, like a fog. He is good, he is heroic, he is history. But his silence on black people will keep him from being great. It might, as Christopher Jimenez y West warns, hurt him. But West knows that the emotional and psychological hunger for Obama that drives black people to him—he saw it in person—is almost certainly more powerful than any critique we can muster. The hunger is deep and wide and cuts across class lines and gender lines and generational lines; it's probably bigger the higher up the educational and economic ladder you go, because middle-class blacks see themselves reflected more clearly in Obama than do the less affluent blacks (that is, most of us) who support him but are further from him in so many ways.

This fact hit me in 2013, during an awards dinner held by a black lawyers' organization in downtown Los Angeles. It was a "hall of fame" event at one of the more well-appointed hotels that have become part of the city's gentrified and increasingly rarefied downtown, which is no longer stigmatized by Skid Row and other expressions of desperate, notably black poverty that tend to fester at the core of all big cities. After the cocktail hour and opening remarks and dinner, the awards presentation kicked off with the audience rising to its feet for a rendition of "Lift Ev'ry Voice and Sing," the black national anthem that's standard at events like this.

We sing robustly as a familiar montage of images play on video monitors mounted on either side of the enormous room—Rosa Parks, Malcolm pounding the podium, Fannie Lou Hamer, civil rights protesters being dragged away on Southern streets. The images play, and the crowd is moved to sing louder. As the song winds down to its last verse, slowing to a solemn pace, gathering its breath for the finale, I am suddenly conscious that I am searching for Obama in this montage, seeking him out in this big narrative of our lives. Where is he? I am a bit alarmed. They wouldn't leave him out, would they? What if somebody decided, or we decided, that he doesn't belong in that company of heroes? Where would that leave *us?* I realize as I search for him how much we truly need him, how quickly I've come to depend on him. For all the talk about how he means too much or doesn't mean enough or he's just another Negro who will disappoint or who sincerely wants to do well for us but can't—for all of that—we need him here.

The music is swelling to a last crescendo ("True to our God/True to our native land"), and there he is! Obama bursts forth at last to carry the evening home, flanked by American flags, smiling and waving from the red, white, and blue as if it's the most natural thing in the world.

The room erupts in cheers, and relief. He has saved the evening and rescued us from the sense of despair, of futility, that always threatens; he has beaten it back. Obama has completed our story in dramatic fashion tonight, given the culminating lyric "true to our native land" a meaning it has never had before, given it something besides the bitter irony of black folks always being true to our native land, truer than many, but never being rewarded for it. Obama is our reward, but not from white folks. His lineage is there in the video—Malcolm, Martin, Fannie, unnamed men and women down on their knees getting bloodied. He is all of them. He damn well belongs, but he also belongs to this country, something James Baldwin argued with great eloquence and sometimes anger but never with evidence like this. Obama is, again, breathtaking. The lawyers and their guests in the room feel the unexpected electricity of the moment, and they all continue to applaud at the sight of the president capping this sacred montage as our latest triumph, Obama taking us home. It is the first time that I can recall a roomful of black people really clapping for themselves, giving themselves a hand sincerely instead of doing it at the urging of an emcee or a preacher who reflexively urges us to give ourselves a hand as a kind of unabashed affirmation that we don't tend to get in the real world. I always cringe at the boosterism, even though I understand it: if we don't readily applaud ourselves, nobody will. But Obama makes a rote and sometimes desperate-looking gesture honest (give yourselves a hand, his smile says), and for that alone, I love him.

I am standing and clapping madly, even though half the people in the audience have sat down. My father, sitting next to me, feels the relief in the room and is moved by it. He looks cheered and shouts impulsively over the noise: "I don't like everything he's done, we've got a lot problems, but I'm still with him." He sounds almost proud of Obama and a little surprised by the feeling. My father is a veteran of the '6os; having reservations about younger upstarts like Obama comes naturally to him. But that doesn't nullify his love or idealism. To the contrary, my father has always had hope. It's what toughens him and renders him almost impervious to the pain of failure or disappointment. Hope is serious business. He has written off those who always praise hope but have never really practiced it, people who fall short of ideals and then, instead of keeping at it, fall away. Obama has disappointed my father but has not officially fallen short, not yet. My father and a whole lot of other people are banking on the possibility that he will still fulfill the long-delayed promise of racial justice that he once worked toward in the streets of Chicago and that his presidency has always suggested. It could happen—after all, *Obama* happened. He happened despite the entrenchment of that immovable beast called the status quo, which said for so long that there could be no black president.

A journalist friend of mine is fond of saying that the status quo is the status quo, until it changes. That's a secular way of saying that the unlikely appearance of Obama was divinely ordered, watched over by higher powers who made it possible. Obama as a religious (but not holy) phenomenon is something implied a lot among churchgoing folks I know. At my monthly block club meetings, the opening prayer circle (which I'm never comfortable with but have learned to accept) always includes intonations to keep our president healthy, prosperous, and out of harm's way. One of my best friends, Bernice, is a lifelong churchgoer who told me that she and her friends pray for Obama all the time, just as they pray for peace and deliverance. They pray for his safety, as my neighbors in the block club do, but they're also praying for something bigger.

After the 2012 re-election, Bernice said matter-of-factly that Obama is in the White House twice because God wants him there. What else explained the fact that he won relatively easily after all the speculation and expert predictions of a race too close to call and ungodly amounts of money spent by the white right to achieve their goal of making Obama a one-term president with no legacy to speak of? I admit, the second victory surprised me, almost as much as the first. Not Bernice. She says Obama's fate is not about political horse races and never has been; it's about faith and keeping to a larger purpose. In other words, Obama is here for a reason that's already been determined and that nobody can alter one way or the other. "It's like my house," Bernice says. "If God wants me to stay here, I will, and if he doesn't, I won't. It's that simple. No use worrying about it." (That makes Obama sound more than a little like Christ, who to me is a big source of all the iterations of Superman: mild-mannered cult hero on an endless journey to redeem a weary, corrupted world.)

Of course, Bernice doesn't equate President Obama with Jesus—that would be blasphemy—although she acknowledges that there is more than something a little sacrificial about him. But unlike Jesus, he didn't choose to be sacrificed; martyrdom is something he was hoping to avoid entirely. The criticism that Obama dims his vision out of political necessity irritates Bernice, because in her mind he's doing exactly what he was put here to do, part of a positive energy field she calls the "universal force" that must be left alone to work its magic. The problem, as Bernice sees it, is that people are deliberately screwing with that magic. "You know it's all about *racism*," she says, an edge in her voice. "It's like the disbelievers who crucified Jesus—racism is nothing but a lack of faith." But, she adds, the faith that does exist and that has bolstered Obama is unstoppable. She describes the many photos she's seen of Obama with an adoring public around the world—people with eyes fixed rapturously on his face, mouths open in amazement, photos taken during but also well after the honeymoon period of his first campaign. They could be praying.

Prayers for Obama sometimes inform a public statement, like the one Bernice's A.M.E. church made about the government shutdown in October 2013 after Obama rejected a Republican budget that included a partial repeal of his hard-fought Affordable Care Act. Standing in solidarity with Obama on the act is, to Bernice, a moral issue that required a distinctly moral response, and a response to the immorality of racism that the church saw at work in yet another deliberate stonewalling of President Obama's will. The statement is dignified but underneath the dignity, furious: "The Affordable Health Care Act is the signature achievement of this president, and the effort of the Tea Party Republicans not to fund it is nothing more than a cynical attempt to undo this historic achievement, and also to deny health care to more than 50 million Americans, a large number of whom are African American," it reads. "We congratulate Obama and urge him to *stand tall and strong* against this effort to blackmail him and hold the country hostage." This is Superman holding his ground against Lex Luthor and worse villains who, like Heath Ledger's terrifying Joker in the Batman movie *The Dark Knight Returns*, can't be bargained with because his determination to annihilate the caped crusader overwhelms every other impulse—he actually enjoyed setting the world on fire and watching it burn. Obama needs all the universal force he can muster.

Obama came through the shutdown, as it turns out, though not before it brought me to the edge of a certain despair. For the first time, it hit me that it wasn't just the world, it was Obama himself the Republicans were trying to set fire to, either to burn at the stake as a heretic or to lynch the old-fashioned way. The whole standoff was theatrical, yes, even sexy to a point—Captain America versus the goons. And then it was at a point too far. The racial hatred was too mighty for the president's own party to oppose, which made me despair even more (though timidity about racial hatred has been characteristic of the Democrats for a long time). Within my despair, I felt bad for the president, who couldn't do shit now except stand his ground and keep looking dignified and above it all, just like Jackie Robinson and all the other barrier breakers; take it all in, ride it out. That was fine strategy for 1947, but in 2013 it was insulting. Jackie Robinson battled baseball, but now the playing field was as big and as formidable as it gets: now it was Obama versus the American people who he was trying to integrate into *his* team, his way of thinking. It simply couldn't be done, I thought. And Obama will take the heat of failure because of course he had no right to be doing this in the first place; he is not an American person but a black interloper who had the nerve to champion a law that passed: a thoroughly imperfect, moderately reforming law that nonetheless passed, like a lot of laws. The damn nerve of him. Better to ruin the world than to have Obama and his arrogance living in it, like a cancerous tumor that has to be blasted with the twin poisons of radiation and chemo; the body might die in the process, but the effort to save it is justified, even noble. Obama leaves his detractors no choice. That racism had come to such a point of feverish self-destruction, and in plain view of the whole country—no longer was it the South doing what it does within its own borders—was sickening. It had all become spectacle again, like lynching a hundred years ago. People were disturbed, they didn't agree, but they were more or less content to watch. They could do nothing about it.

I talk to Brenda Jackson right around the time of the impending shutdown. She is beyond agitated. She stabs a forefinger in the air and says, with finality, "Listen. They're pissed because he's a *fine* black man with a *fine* family who's smart, smarter than they are. He's got a mind of his own." She is talking about herself as well, fuming about Obama and venting about her own workplace, where she's managing all right, but those bosses, the things she can say and not say, the crap she takes from both white and black who are leery of her being black or being gay, most likely both. In Brenda's mind, it's all the same indignity: a few more of those million knifepoints. But Obama being cut is the worst of all, he's the fucking president, after all. Here he is the president of all, president of even the white-collar and blue-collar crackers and rednecks who can't see him as anything much higher than a nigger. Worked up as Brenda is, I can see the resignation in the middle of her rage, the equivalent of my despair. She is about as non-churchgoing as I am, but she understands that Obama has to wear the crown of thorns, like so many black firsts before him. His people will cheer him, but the more powerful, faithless Romans will scream from the sidelines or shrug with indifference as Obama walks calmly toward possible destruction with the cross of health care on his back.

Brenda says suddenly, conspiratorially, "I believe, you know. I believe because I have faith." She has read *Dreams from My Father* and feels like she knows Obama personally. She is thoroughly convinced (more than she was already convinced) that Obama is one of us. He is worth the fight and the heartache. I am surprised, pleasantly, to hear her say that. Brenda is tough but not very optimistic about things turning out well for black folks, to say nothing for the country at large, another legacy from the Movement. She doubts. Surely her belief now means something, will move something.

Some days later, I see my neighbor Laurie, whose backyard adjoins mine. We fall into a conversation about Obama, as happens so often with people I know. Laurie has worked in the defense industry for nearly thirty years and has weathered several furloughs and potential layoffs since Obama's been in office and the economy has teetered, especially in our neighborhood. Obama comes up because I mention the impending shutdown, and she says in response to a question I don't ask in so many words, "It's because he's black." She's standing in front of her well-appointed house with her arms folded, and she sounds like Brenda. I am surprised again, but hesitant, because though I like Laurie and have talked to her for years, I know almost nothing about her politics. I think I didn't want to know, exactly; she is so pleasant, so *middle-class* in a solid, unselfconscious way (in a black way, I suppose) that I didn't want politics to disturb whatever connection we had going. In these lonely times, I preferred the connection to any principle that might require me to break it. For those and other reasons, Laurie and I talked about dogs and sweet potato pies and her daughters' careers (or lack thereof), and new grandchildren; we never talked about Obama and what he was, what he's meant. But now she is telling me, not argumentatively but matter-of-factly: he's hated because he's black.

Then she tells me her own story, because it feels required now. Her mother came to Los Angeles from Chicago—her second migration; she had gone to Chicago from Mississippi, with a carful of kids and virtually no money. But Chicago was done, Laurie says, by which she means it had become a dead end for black people of a certain stratum. But on the pre-sumably more tolerant West Coast in the early '70s, people wouldn't rent to her mother, and the family ended up in the projects in Harbor City, a strip of city territory in the roughest part of South Bay. That was at least integrated, with blacks and Samoans and Mexicans. Eventually, they moved to Inglewood, when it was still considerably white, though that population was waning fast in the flight touched off by the Watts riots in '65. Laurie knew the first people who had ever lived in my house—the white architect who had designed the whole tract in 1953; he lived here until the mid '80s. Whites were more or less gone by then, but this was his place—he envisioned it, after all—and he was loath to leave it just because.

The story loops back to Obama and the shutdown and the intractability of racism. The hatred of black folks is as venomous as hate gets in this country, Laurie says a little grimly, her arms folded tighter. Her mother knew it, relatives who lived in the deep South and had to flee home in the middle of the night to avoid lynching knew it, the former white residents of our city who fled almost en masse knew it, and the two of us having this conversation right now and recalling this whole chain of events certainly know it. Laurie knows, which I am glad to know. She decries the treatment of Obama, but she isn't shocked by it; it's frankly hard to be shocked. We shake our heads and mm-hmm and commiserate. What neither of us says because it is so obvious and unsettling, is this: if he is treated like this and he is president, what hope is there for us? That's why Confident Obama sitting in the window of our neighbor's house just around the corner reassures us that, however badly we're treated and however far we don't get, we are entitled to hope. That is ours to display flagrantly, even vulgarly, to wave like a red flag under the nose of a bull. Or to just wave.

♥ Professor Peniel Joseph, talking about his 2013 biography of activist Stokely Carmichael, said that Carmichael chose a different path at a crucial moment in the Movement. After achieving instant notoriety as the proponent of "Black Power," he changed his name to Kwame Ture and elected to go with revolution. Peniel said Carmichael didn't go the route of Jesse Jackson or Julian Bond—"go off and become mayor of a city somewhere," as he put it—that is, do the bourgeois thing and actually try to integrate. That which black people had theoretically been working toward since the end of slavery he suddenly saw as futile, liberation pointing in the wrong direction. Carmichael saw the United States as a failed system for black people and didn't want to be absorbed by it. He would probably have seen President Obama as total capitulation, the worst kind of absorption into the system—an enormous symbol of the failure of revolution. But the middle class sees Obama as a symbol of the greatest achievement *because* he is so totally absorbed. He's infiltrated as far as one can infiltrate. Obama is rare in that he brings those two disparate things together. Actually, black folks can feel both things at the same time: that Obama is a great success because he is so much the insider and is a great failure for the same reason. To make things even more complicated, I suspect that at the bottom of the most middle-class heart lies a bit of the revolutionary, and though we all know better, we project our inner revolutionary onto Obama. He is, after all, one of us and might be capable of it, of going where we can't or don't have access. Just maybe, he could redeem us all for our own sins of inaction.

"I Am Not a Perfect Man" is the framed image of Obama on the wall in Dulan's Soul Food on Crenshaw, and it's one of the more interesting examples of Obama iconography. Obama's face is at the center of a kind of vortex, surrounded by smaller images of notable people from the '60s and decades before that. They are his conscience, his sense memory, exploding from the center of the picture like rays shooting from the sun that Obama has become. Obama's brow is furrowed, and he is shouting or yelling, probably in rhetorical fervor but possibly in anger or discontent. "I Am Not a Perfect Man" is a quote from a speech he made in 2012 before the second election, a disclaimer in which he cautioned that he was not a perfect man or a perfect president. But, he said, his vision would endure, his determination to make change and forge a better America. (It recalls Martin Luther King's somewhat grim speculation that his vision would prevail even though "I may not get there with you.")

The figures surrounding Obama in this picture are his rightful past, the ghosts who went before and who make his presence in the White House possible now. But the figures also include critics of the present, people holding signs that protest, "Bail Out People, Not Banks" and the more sardonic "War Is Good for Business." Obama is literally in the midst of the chaos, the unresolved history, shouting into the wind. He is proclaiming his innocence or owning his fallibility or both. But you don't see any of this from a distance, which is what makes this particular iconizing interesting—it's so ambiguous. Up close you see that a replicated photo of Obama is actually pixel-like dots made up of small print—his very face and eyes are an assemblage of words, and feelings. "I Am Not A Perfect Man" puts Obama at the center of the political universe as a personal triumph and as a prisoner of the desires of everyone around him. The image also reminds me of Ralph Ellison's *Invisible Man*, in which the unnamed protagonist studies a statue of pioneering black leader Booker T. Washington. Washington is standing and holding a veil before the eyes of a kneeling slave, prompting the Invisible Man to wonder, is he lifting the veil or holding it more firmly in place?

I wonder, is Obama that slave? As the first black president battling so much opposition, is he rising to his feet newly free, or is he being forced to crouch down from a standing position? Is his liberator—the American people—also his captor, willing him to rise up but forcing him down at the same time? In this photo that's not a photo, Obama is shouting to spread his gospel of cooperation—that's why this image hangs in Dulan's, which caters to the Sunday post-church crowd. But Obama could also just be shouting, perhaps screaming in exasperation. He seems to be saying, Can't you all see? Can't you?

I visited my doctor recently and saw in her exam room the very iconic blue-and-red Shepard Fairey illustration of Obama that is labeled "HOPE." I'm glad it's in her office—it's hung there a while now, going back to '08. But it also makes me uneasy because it brings me closer to what she believes. I am curious but also fearful of knowing what my doctor believes, which is similar to how I felt about my neighbor Laurie. But the nature and contours of this fear are different. I've been seeing my doctor for almost twenty years and we have a very good relationship, as good as I can get with a white person who asks me personal questions on a regular basis. She asks them without being unduly nosy or overly clinical. She is interested, compassionate, but she doesn't push. She is cool in a good way, the black way, I think because she sees a lot of black patients even though this is the West Side. I know because I see photos of other patients or friends on the wall who are black, and the magazines in her exam room are sometimes *Ebony* or *Essence*. I'm glad for that, for her awareness, but her awareness also makes me self-conscious, because with the pictures over the years, and now the Obama print on the wall, my doctor is announcing something to me that she probably wants me to acknowledge aloud. I don't know that I can, or if I should. I never had to think much about it until now. I suppose I've never known how to take her unusual level of racial comfort. In the past, I just took it.

That was always enough for me, but now it isn't. I actually do want to acknowledge our mutual interest in Obama. But I also want to ask her: why *are* you comfortable with us? It sounds accusatory, paranoid, not curious, and maybe it is. It is part of the racial unsettledness that this single Obama image has stirred up, the unsettledness that Obama himself has stirred up. The only time my doctor actually said something about him was during the first campaign, when the picture went up in her exam room and she murmured happily, a little conspiratorially over her chart, "Isn't this exciting? He's so different!"

I agreed. But something about the comment stirred resentment, entirely unexpected. A low voice in my head muttered, what do you mean, different? Different from me? Can't we find another word for him? If he was different to her, was I also different—that is, exceptional? Or was I an average black person, different from Obama, who was uniquely different? I very much liked my doctor and preferred to believe in her innocence and the innocence of her comment. I had believed in that innocence, or the possibility of it, for nearly twenty years without incident. It was a good run. And now Obama was disturbing the whole arrangement by insinuating himself and his straightforward but complicated call for togetherness into the exam room. I know my doctor assumed that I believed in the togetherness, that we shared in the "Believe." But she didn't know that for sure. Even in our most intimate talks about the bouts of depression I had suffered since I'd been in her care, I had not detailed to her *all* the things that often made me feel constricted, repressed, badly fooled, and isolated. I had not talked to her about the anxiety rooted not just in growing up in an imperfect family, but in being black. I never told her any of that second thing or even hinted at it, which meant I couldn't talk about Obama now and believing and about things in the country being so potentially different. I couldn't fully return the confidence. I smiled and nodded—because I did agree, to a point. Things were different. And I did believe. I left it there.

Pam Ward, the graphic artist, says Obama is the first branded president. By branded she means not just the name association, slogans, or sound bites that have defined presidential politics since its inception, from "Tippecanoe and Tyler, Too" to "You're Still the One," Fleetwood Mac's boomer-minded rock anthem, which Bill Clinton adopted for his second run in 1996. Ward means the high-tech, up-to-the-minute wraparound marketing of the Internet age that is meant to transform an individual (or a company, or something else) into a symbol of a very particular kind of hope, change, excitement, fashion, etc. Branding is not simply about selling a product; it's about projecting the inviolable uniqueness of that product. It's also about setting trends, which means that a lot of branding is created with young people in mind. Though technically a baby boomer himself, Obama has always appealed to young people of all colors. He used the Internet and social media—very effectively—to make his case to them and to build an electorate in a nontraditional way. The sound bites and slogans of "Hope/Change/Believe" and "Yes We Can" were expanded into YouTube videos and testimonials.

But none of the branding would mean as much if Obama weren't unique—if he weren't black. As such, he symbolizes a particular kind of hope that goes back to Frederick Douglass and continued up to Jesse Jackson, who of course made hope the center of his own campaigns. Fusing that long tradition of black hope with a modern sensibility of doing things his own way, outside of tradition—in marketing it's called "re-imagining"—is what really makes Obama a brand. Throw in the fact that his own cultural tastes and reference points tend less toward Fleetwood Mac and more toward Al Green, Jay Z, Beyoncé, and basketball, and it's little wonder that his image fascinates: besides being an old-style, keep-hope-alive folk hero, he's also a model of self-definition that black folks, and white folks, have never seen. His good looks don't hurt; this all works because, as I've said, Obama looks the part. Opponents like to try and physically marginalize him as a character actor, cast him as the tall, hapless, skinny guy with big ears who waffles too much and never gets the girl. But we know Obama is a leading man—Superman, actually, though he may never get a chance to really fly. He may wind up, like too many black folks, stuck in the process of becoming. But as long as he's on the national scene, his presence, starting with but not limited to his physical presence, will provoke a strong response. He is at the very least a good story. (He may not advance a coherent narrative for black people or for the country, but his own story playing out in the White House is like an action movie.)

Whatever its political views, the media loves Obama because he and the controversy that attends his every attempted move make for a good show. Bush was certainly controversial, but he didn't make for good television or good drama because he frankly didn't look the part. More important, he exhibited almost no signs of a political, moral, or internal struggle. The story was already written. He was part of a political dynasty with an ideology that preceded his arrival at the White House and dictated his moves once he got there. Obama came to the White House as a man truly alone, with no dynasty or family heritage or favorable Supreme Court decision to put him there. In that way, he is the rugged individual of American myth, the John Wayne or Clint Eastwood of the political Wild West, minus the guns. The romance and intrigue of Obama's saga are undeniable.

He is entertaining, and I mean that not in a pejorative way. I mean that Obama commands attention. People are watching his moves almost obsessively, daily, just as they watch a weekly, sometimes daily, reality show. I have to say that I've been so thoroughly absorbed by Obama, I have paid even less attention than usual to what's on television. But I don't need to. Obama has become a kind of one-man black entertainment source whose exploits inside the Beltway match everything television has to offer—farce, drama, reality, and the democratic, DIY digital iterations of television, like YouTube. He is our first performance president, an actor improvising on the stage of his own groundbreaking experience. For his whole time in office, nothing has been routine about his routines; every press conference or statement is an act or scene, fodder for a video or tweet going viral. For a man nobody seems to know deeply, he gets a hell of a lot of scrutiny, making him like so many other black people who may be admired or loathed, but not known.

To not be known by your own admirers is strange, especially in politics. Politics depends on intimacy. People who loved Bobby Kennedy or Ronald Reagan or even Bush II felt they knew those men, but those who love Obama—including black people—would not say the same thing. They cannot say the same thing. Loving Obama feels forbidden to most of us, dangerous for reasons that differ from one person to another, so instead we watch intently, daring him to betray a love we could never confess to him in the first place. But it does get said; at Obama rallies people have screamed, "I love you!" with the spontaneous energy of fans at high-stakes sporting events. It's like a burst of applause, but it's also a blurting out of the forbidden—I love you—in the guise of political and moral encouragement. And I have seen Obama stop, flash that brilliant smile in near relief, and in a moment of reclamation and remembrance, reply evenly, "I love you, too." The crowd screams again and swoons like it's never, ever supposed to. He loves us! Nothing matters anymore. The world of his failure, and ours, falls away.

Pam Ward says that while campaigning for Obama in the San Fernando Valley, she realized that his power turned on emotion. Emotion was built from the beginning into the message, and the image. Part of his branding is not having to think too hard; you know that Obama and hope and believe (and love, another word for hope and believe) all go together like happiness and Coke. And like Coke, that happiness is available to everyone. The Obama message was pitched not simply to the affluent demographic of the Valley, but to those people not on Facebook or Twitter, those outside the digital gathering places that have become mainstream. Obama was, in a word, accessible. "It was amazing how tight his ship was, but very easy to get involved," Ward says of the campaign. "Whoever wrote the book on how to run that campaign was a social media genius. He wasn't just speaking to the social media set, he was also speaking to the unempowered people, the ones not in the loop, including them in the 'One America' thing . . . the shifting color bar of the 'change' coalition, that was them." This was open-door Obama: he was inviting to the dance the girl, and the guy, who never gets picked. He was romancing us, the crucial prelude to love. The invitation is extended again when he stops and says with that easy, almost thoughtless intimacy, "I love you too." Maybe he never helps us at all, but he first loves us, and that counts, probably too much. Love blinds like that.

One of my favorite Obama moments was his impromptu exchange in a Chicago voting booth in 2014 with a nervous young black woman whose boyfriend had good-naturedly warned the president not to make any overtures. The president didn't miss a beat. With his eyes fixed on the ballot, Obama carried on a low-toned conversation with the woman that was straightforward but also intimate ("Now why'd he have to embarrass a brother like that? What's his name?"). He was being flirtatious, which clearly delighted the young woman, and the boyfriend too, despite his protestations. In that chance encounter they all shared the same energy, the same language, the same private love, in public; there was no president and the citizenry, just three black folks talking. It was heady.

Love doesn't convince everybody. Obama detractors actually find his accessibility repugnant, a threat or an attempt at sabotage. To them, Obama extending a hand is a trick, another black-man hustle; by its very nature it cannot be sincere or even neutral. Katie Taylor, a thirty-year-old actor and waitress raised in Pittsburgh, notes that in the Trayvon Martin tragedy, nobody wondered why shooter George Zimmerman had said to the black teenager, whom he had never seen before, "Why are you here?" instead of "How can I help you?" Katie says that Trayvon and other black men up to and including Obama represent something white people don't identify with at all. They can't imagine having that sit-down beer with Obama, nor do they want to; his extended hand, the invitation, is always a taunt, an intrusion into a circle they would prefer remain unbroken. "These guys have their own circle, which I really hear after they've had some drinks," says Katie. "What he's doing simply isn't done by a black man. He is moving people forward, black people, gay people—he's been criticized for not starting out that way, but *come on.*" Katie is almost professionally pleasant, but she very quickly sounds irritated, sharp. She is pretty. She has a black father and a white mother, like Obama; with her copper skin and brilliant smile, she could be his sister. She is approachable—accessible—easygoing, though that might be the mask she wears for certain customers she admits can be trying; more than a few have quite unpleasantly surprised her with their frank disapproval of a black president: "They said to me, 'He'll ruin your generation!'" The disapproval has only affirmed her love of him, strengthened a familial loyalty that for most black folks tends to double down in adversity. Adversity for Obama was assumed, though not to this degree or for this duration. Katie said it was actually her white mother who worried the most about racial backlash. It makes sense, and it made me wonder if Obama's own mother was more race-conscious and less laissez-faire about the meaning of color than we've all been led to believe, even by Obama himself—particularly by Obama himself.

In any event, Katie resents the notion that Obama should be cut no slack on his idealizing, that the payoff for "hope and believe" must be clear and instantaneous. She believes in his symbolism and takes the practical view of Obama as the folk hero on a journey toward an unknown destination, with all of us as fellow travelers. "He is just a man," she says, making me think again of Jesus. "He's spent his life trying to better the world. How many people have made that their life's goal? Not to make money, not to get fame. He wants all of us to stand together. I believe that *he* believes in his mission." She also believes that Obama, unlike other presidents and elected officials in general, sincerely *wants* the people in on that mission; he likes the historical spotlight, maybe even savors it, but wants company in his endeavor. This is in stark contrast to the style of the president before him. "Every time Bush spoke, it was like I was at a party that I wasn't invited to," says Katie. "I really feel like Obama is talking to me. Sometimes he's saying, 'I don't know that I have the right answer, but I'm trying.' He got me to care."

Katie says she feels fortunate; her parents never got their Obama, her father especially. She describes him as an alumnus of the Movement who "figured there was only so much Obama could do, didn't want to get his hopes up. He said, 'I know how heartbreaking it is when it doesn't happen.'" Whether "it" has happened depends on how you define the word and the breadth of expectations you still hold for a more just and perfect union, though it's fair to say that Obama, despite two historic electoral victories, has not converted Americans to a new or progressive way of thinking. He has not, in other words, completed the revolution begun in the '60s. That deters Katie from her love of him not at all. As Obama does himself, she takes the long view. "He's had to fight like hell from the very beginning because of his color, and he's wiser, if not happier," she says. "Don't throw up your hands and say 'Fuck it' because the truth isn't going anywhere. He hasn't dealt with everything yet. We got to this bad place for a reason."

♥ When the television series *The Misadventures of Awkward Black Girl* debuted on the web in 2011, a new black millennial character was born. In J, writer/actor Issa Rae created a complex, post-postmodern black pro-tagonist trying (and usually failing) to navigate life's daily absurdities and indignities, an earnest but appealing comic antihero in the mold of Jerry Seinfeld or Ellen DeGeneres. The difference is that J is black, and her daily trials are chiefly described by race: being the only tall, black, dark-skinned girl at a mostly white house party, going on a first date with a white guy who conspicuously takes her to a soul food joint when she would have pre-ferred Thai. The show has been a hit and is being developed as a full-blown series for HBO. Issa Rae, twenty-eight, says success has been gratifying on many levels, starting with how it seems to be overcoming the conventional Hollywood disinterest in the inner lives of black people, especially middle-class black people. Satirical but empathetic, *Awkward Black Girl* is really a thinking man's reality show in black, presented as comedy. In its relatively brief time on the web, it built a following and garnered critical praise that culminated in a major award in 2012 for best web TV series.

That's when a certain ugly truth that *Awkward Black Girl* routinely tries to deconstruct with humor hit the fan. Issa Rae was inundated with racially tinged hate mail, much of it from industry folk who called her talentless and unattractive, claiming her success was a fluke or the result of racial favoritism. The backlash was so intense, Issa Rae says, she finally responded to it with an open letter. The experience was quite an education. "I got seventy-five iterations of the word *nigger* in the comments," she recalls. "But that was OK, at first. I was like, yes! I was excited because I knew I'd hit the mainstream. I had never been a nigger before. I thought, 'These people are cowards.'"

But the letter didn't stop the vicious feedback. One of the trending topics it generated online was "Things Better Than Awkward Black Girl" and, most memorably, "the smell coming from Trayvon Martin's dead body." Issa Rae says that stopped her cold. "That's when it stopped being funny." The episode made her sympathize more than she already sympathized with Obama and the massive resistance-cum-resentment he fields all the time. She appreciates now how, in many ways, he's a performer like her; simply in being who and what he is, he models a blackness more subtle and ultimately more puzzling and/or threatening to white people because it is not what they are used to seeing, not what they expect, especially in the rarefied sphere of the presidency. (She also very much appreciates Michelle Obama, who models a physical ideal of black women—tall, dark, and unapologetically so—that Issa Rae can actually live up to.) His ongoing attempts both to fit in and to exercise leadership have created almost constant crises in Washington and in certain sectors of the public, crises that you could shoot and film as *Awkward Black President*. Issa Rae laughs at the idea—because it is plausible, not because it isn't. The upside to Obama's travails ("the Obama effect," she calls it) is that he has opened people's eyes to the diversity of black men; he happens to be a professional, intellectual, ambitious black man with big ideas. He is not Trayvon Martin, although in the collective sense he is, of course, as he admitted himself. It's the notion that Obama and Trayvon belong to the same tribe that America rejects, because it long ago bifurcated blackness into ghetto and nonghetto, with the latter being not really blackness at all but some good, decent, colorless permutation of blackness that by definition had successfully escaped the taint of race. This is what many white people are thinking of when they insist that Obama is not really black: they are referring not just to his genetic composition but to his orientation to the world, his confidence in his place in it.

It's the kind of confidence that J projects in *Awkward Black Girl*, awkwardness notwithstanding; the message of the series is that it is the larger white world that must ultimately adjust to *her*, not the other way around. It's a radical departure from reality, though such a self-possessed figure is as hard a sell in fiction. "We have a long way to go," says Issa Rae. "This kind of diversity just isn't on people's radars. We still have to feed them these images."

♥ In some ways, this whole discussion of Obama iconography really should have started with my friend Marilyn and her obsession with our forty-fourth president. Marilyn is the real-life Obama girl, that Internet, bikini-clad video sensation whose enthusiasm for Obama was cast as a joke, a semi-snarky comment on his runaway popularity when he first came to national attention. But Obama girl at least put on the table that biggest taboo: sex appeal. This is what curator Christopher Jimenez Y West says gives Obama an edge, his secret weapon hidden in plain sight. Underneath the weight of history and political expectations and the relentless debate over both is Obama the man, who, according to many people I talked to (every woman, and not a few men) is compellingly attractive: suave, cute, fine in that ooh-baby way that Yvonne Hutchinson described in no uncertain terms. A leading man who, if he were not president, would probably do well in Hollywood, which was my thought when I first saw him on television delivering that rousing speech to the Democratic convention in 2004, and again when I saw him in person three years later. Good looks tend to go with charisma and charm, and Obama is no exception, but the media has been very reluctant, almost afraid, to point this out. Part of it is fear of trivializing the presidency, casting it as some kind of beauty contest, but I suspect the bigger part of the fear is wading into completely uncharted territory. Because of our history of degrading blackness, which continues up to this very moment, America has not had a nationally recognized black heartthrob. It has not allowed it. We've had plenty of heroes and figures to admire, from Louis Armstrong to Muhammad Ali, and some of them have been attractive, but that's been a side note; none have been framed as sex symbols. Even official sex symbols such as Denzel Washington (well, there's only one black male sex symbol in Hollywood at a time, if any) are described as accomplished and hard-working and talented before they are described as sexy.

For the media to acknowledge the sexiness up-front would be to violate a deeply embedded social code that prohibits discussion of race and sexual potency in any public conversation at the same time, to say nothing of mentioning them in the same sentence in any given article about Obama. And so we get millions of words about his color, more about "Hope" and its followers and detractors, but almost no words about Obama's physicality and energy, which are such an integral part of his brand. There has been considerable discussion about Obama's charisma, but it's largely confined to his rhetorical skills and political acumen and maybe his intellect; to factor in good looks would apparently make the mix too explosive, grant him power bordering on dangerous. Also it would give him mystique, a highly sexual distinction reserved for white men, much as true femininity is reserved for white women.

Black people are on the other side of caution here: Obama's fineness is so obvious as to not merit much internal discussion at all. We have a tradition of the talented tenth embodying admirable qualities, of being the whole package, and that often includes being beautiful. Nor can we ignore the fact that the talented tenth has historically been a lighter shade of black—think Booker T. Washington and W.E.B. DuBois, the two most prominent black leaders in history—which also makes Obama ordinary in a way; his biracial-ness is not exotic to us but almost expected. I admit, the slave-rooted color hierarchy that correlates skin shade with success and palatability among white folks is still troubling and still very much in play today. But the point is that Obama for black folks is a favored son of the middle class who *of course* will be handsome. He could hardly be otherwise.

And so we exclaim over him but don't gush, instead murmur our approval almost under our breath. (We're also loath to publicly voice what we really think of each other—an inhibition that's part of the black self-definition crisis that DuBois called our "double consciousness.") Black magazines such as *Essence* and *Ebony* put Obama on their covers and proceed from the assumption that our president is gorgeous; that's part of being the perfect black man, a bona fide cover boy. In those pages Obama has nothing to prove or disprove; he is home. The obvious—that his look is part of his perfection and always has been—is rarely stated. That's out of respect, but also because there is no need. We know what we think.

Never one to mince words or feelings, Marilyn staked out her Obama crush gleefully from the start, actually from before the start. Before I even had a full sense of who Obama was, she was telling me that he was incredibly smooth, dreamy, the kind of man who could turn ordinary women—women like her, smart though not terribly political, with kids and responsibilities and some ambition left to realize—into mindless groupies. This was welcome magic to Marilyn, and it's fueled an obsession for seven years. Part of that obsession is collecting favorite video clips of him, which she showed me one day on her computer. Going through the collection, she sighed and squealed, like a teenage fan of Justin Bieber. Yet Marilyn is no ordinary fan; she's a learned, almost scientific one. An actor and former dancer, she's certified in Laban Movement Analysis, a language of body movement that describes and interprets how people move. Obama is Marilyn's favorite case study so far, of course. Though he's had plenty of awkward political moments, there's nothing awkward about this president's movement, which Marilyn deems remarkable for its consistent ease and sense of empathy toward others, even under great pressure or clear hostility. "Flow" is a word that comes up a lot in her conversation, which is part Laban, part star-struck—but well-informed—groupie.

"When I look at Obama, I feel a whole man," she says, her eyes glued to a video clip of Obama on her computer screen. "He's got body connectivity—his body moves like an orchestra. You feel his attention to his physical self. It's an animal thing. . . I don't think he's conscious of it. When you have a smile and eyes like that, you use it, but he's not affected by it." That lack of self-consciousness is what makes Obama so appealing, she explains, so sexy. And yet he's very aware of what he's putting out, and how much. "He feels his sensuality—feels the feet in his shoes, the pants on his legs—but he's also very contained, what we call 'bound-flow,'" she goes on. "He lets out just enough of himself, then pulls back. . . Really, he's kind of a tease. You can reach him, he's accessible, but he's not reactive. He can be passionate and forceful, but he makes choices about how he's going to act. He makes choices, but he doesn't manipulate."

Against my will, I am fascinated. Marilyn is describing, in charged but validating language, what I've seen black people in high positions do all the time with similar ease: shape-shift. They are being who they are fundamentally, but they are also being deliberate and staying attuned to people and being the part of you that they need you to be at a particular moment. It is the skill of a great politician, and also the skill required for black people to successfully navigate nonblack settings, to assimilate and maybe even con-trol a situation without anybody noticing that's what's happening. Obama necessarily has both skill sets. But he also has something more, and that is the ability to project an essential, immutable self through the suffocating dictates of what he can and cannot let out. Love him or not, he is always Obama. He doesn't let a hostile world do him in, drive him off-center into a kind of reactive, defensive stance or the soul-killing, body-warping rage or paralysis that I have watched consume many black folk, including my own relatives.

Obama knows what this madness is; he's described it in his book. His resilience to it is therefore not merely heroic, it's sexy. He doesn't just survive the assault, as most of us do, if we're lucky; he rises above it like a plane above storm clouds. He doesn't get stuck. He doesn't panic. He controls the flow no matter what, even if the politics go completely off the rails, as they did during the government shutdown. This is what Marilyn is saying, though I don't think she realizes she's saying it. She's white, which means she's doesn't look at Obama through the thick historical and political lens that I and other black people look through, a crucial lens that can none-theless dull or minimize his obvious sparkle. I do see and appreciate that sparkle—I was more than aware of it in '07—but I confess that I never felt as free to embrace it as Marilyn does. I have to say that it's refreshing, and empowering, and more than a little overwhelming to focus on Obama's eyes, or his bound-flow—some aspect of him that is purely physical. It feels delicious but trivializing. Do I have the *right?* It's a question that doesn't occur to Marilyn. Her responses to Obama are as uncensored as mine tend to be considered, especially in front of white folks (Marilyn excepted—most of the time). I'd prefer not to be so careful, so measured, but I am. I am Obama, all right. All black people are. Marilyn is saying now, spreading her hand across the computer screen as if it were an oil painting, "There's light behind his eyes. Those eyes say, 'Somebody's home.' Beautiful smile, gazelle-like physique, and he also has humor, intelligence, wit, warmth—it's the whole package. What's not to like?" She glances at me a little guiltily, which takes me by surprise. "I don't know," she says. "Is it *wrong* to be in love with the president?"

♥   The window around the corner has lost Obama. One morning in April 2014 he was simply gone. I decided not to ask about his whereabouts; I don't want to know what happened. Even if there's an innocuous explanation—the window shade is being replaced or the family gave the cardboard figure to someone who needed or wanted it more—I don't want to know. I prefer to believe that it moved on to a higher place, a more elevated position. I prefer to keep the *mystique* of Obama intact, to steer very clear of the scenario of the cardboard cutout being thrust head first into a dumpster or cut up and put in a box. I don't want to imagine any end for Obama, only beginning and possibility and endurance. Only permanence. I am feeling a little abandoned, and not a little angry at the family (who I don't know and never tried to meet) for taking Obama away without consulting the neighborhood. He was all of ours, after all. He stood for everyone. He still does.

3 Obama Leads

Obama is not a revolutionary. He's for slow, incremental change.
Deep down I hope that he's more than willing to be a revolutionary.
Lots of people go into politics with ideals. He's one of them.
—*Samarrah Blackman*

In spite of Obama's debt to the civil rights movement,
the ideal of American exceptionalism is only as valid as the standing
of people who have just as often been seen as exceptions
to America. —*Jelani Cobb*, New Yorker, *January 2015*

When I was about nine, I asked my father why there had never been a black president. The question was philosophical; by that age I understood very well that black people were not considered legitimate in many ways, as a president least of all. The idea was a joke, not slapstick but absurd—white people putting us in the White House, when they just got through finally giving everybody the right to vote? Never. Because a black president seemed so far-fetched, adults didn't discuss it as a viable or even particularly desirable goal. My father was deeply involved in the Movement, and his work for racial justice was more or less street-level: building coalitions, pushing for school desegregation. I'm sure he had no objections to a black president, but it was hardly an issue on his radar, or anyone else's. I knew all that. The real purpose of my question was to startle my father, to get his attention so that he would talk about his work and the state of the race to a nine-year-old who was curious but shy about asking big, important questions. So I posed the black president question pointedly, dramatically, gazing into the mirror above the mantelpiece in our living room as if it were a crystal ball. It was almost as if I was asking if there was a god.

My father paused and answered me in the solemn, even tone parents use when they're giving the facts-of-life, birds-and-bees talk. In some ways he was. He told me briefly about the realities of race and racism that had shaped his own life—pedestrian but occasionally ugly stuff. He said that having a black president was one thing among many that *could* happen once we as a people had gained some measure of true equality. The lack of a black president in and of itself wasn't important, he stressed; it was the journey to justice, a path blazed a bit at a time by the kind of unglamorous work my father did every day, that mattered. A black president would simply be confirmation that we'd arrived at a certain point, not the only confirmation, of course, but pretty compelling. Electing a black president, if it ever happened, would be one outcome of a more equitable country.

History has not unfolded that way. The order in which my father assumed things would happen for black people happened in reverse: we got a black president before we got anything resembling racial equality. The reversal has been both exhilarating and confusing, sometimes maddening. On the one hand, the election of Obama to two terms in the White House is black history nonpareil, clear cause for a celebration that, despite all the turmoil of his two terms, still reverberates. The role of Obama as a black leader has been much less clear. Certainly he is black and a leader, but whether he's a black leader in the vein of racial justice advocates such as Martin Luther King, to whom he's often compared, is another question entirely. Obama has not faced the same battles King—or my father or anyone of the Movement generation and before—had to face. That doesn't mean there are no more battles; it means they have been reconfigured, diffused, and must be fought differently. How effectively Obama has fought those battles, whether he's fought them at all, and whether he *should* fight them—or fight some and not others, given the constraints on his own political capital—are all pieces of a complicated debate that only seems to get more complicated.

The complication and ambiguity are built into Obama's role as president. As we are often told and often tell ourselves, Obama is president of all Americans, not just black people, so in an occupational sense he cannot compare to a Martin Luther King or Malcolm X or even to a whole tradition of black elected officials such as Adam Clayton Powell and Shirley Chisholm, leaders representing districts that were predominantly black and historically neglected. They were what we used to call race men and women, people whose full-time job was furthering racial justice, regardless of what they actually did for a living. Race work has always been the primary charge of black leadership, which has included, but certainly has not been limited to, electoral politics; some of the best-known race people besides King were journalists Ida B. Wells and William Monroe Trotter, actor/singer Paul Robeson, educator Mary McLeod Bethune, scholar W.E.B. DuBois, writers James Baldwin and Gwendolyn Brooks, composer William Grant Still, any of the more notable Black Panthers. The list goes on.

Obama is a paradox of black leadership, the first of its kind. Though he's a former community organizer on Chicago's South Side who certainly did what amounted to race work, he is not a race man—not publicly, anyway. But he is indisputably black history. He has achieved in electoral politics what had long been considered impossible for a black person to achieve, fulfilled a dream in a way that might have made King himself weep. Yet it was mostly an individual achievement, not the outcome of struggle or a grassroots demand by black people for some measure of the kind of justice my father described to me years ago. Obama has moved us tremendously, and still moves us, but he is not a movement. His district is not the South Side or Brooklyn or South Central Los Angeles, but the whole nation, a nation that hasn't seen a serious black movement in some fifty years and that assumes Obama is the conclusion, not the continuance, of any such movement. Obama is therefore a black man who is certainly of us, but he is not principally *for* us because, as both his supporters and detractors have argued, that isn't technically possible. The nature of his particular full-time time job ensures that. However much he identifies with and understands us, articulating any *support* for us as president is a political high-wire act that he either can't stomach or doesn't feel is necessary.

Intellectually, politically, psychologically, black folks understand all of this. Yet to have a black president who does not or cannot significantly speak on behalf of black people makes no sense either. That feels like a monstrous injustice, insult added to far too much injury that we have borne and still bear. To have Obama mean nothing for us would be an absurdity much greater and more painful than the absurdity that for so long characterized the prospect of a black person becoming president at all. The new absurdity could officially become a joke, but a cruel one: Obama finally beat the odds, but not much else. He is president, but prisons are still full of record numbers of black men, black employment lags behind every other group—a crippling, long-standing reality that the Great Recession, with its regular scrutiny of employment numbers, made suddenly obvious—and black wealth is roughly half the wealth of whites. In these and too many other ways, the needle of progress has not moved since the '60s; the four-hundred-year journey to justice, far from over, limps along in the long shadow cast by Obama's brilliant career. That career may have been cause for celebration, but practically speaking, it is small consolation for the majority of black people who in one way or another still live at the margins of the American dream, even as the viability of that dream has diminished severely. Still, we put Obama next to Martin and Malcolm not so much because he's earned it but to take ourselves out of his shadow, and also to send a message to the president, prick his conscience: you *should* be there.

The Obama paradox of being the first black president who is not necessarily a black leader also shifts black history off its foundation. Black history, which has always been segregated from "regular" American history but which has also stood proudly apart from it, is suddenly a muddle, an existential question. If the first black American president isn't a black leader, if we regularly find ourselves counting all that he hasn't done to directly address racial justice rather than all that he has done, then who is he to us? Who are *we*? If his electoral victories, which resounded around the globe, don't help to mitigate black troubles at home, or at least represent a turning point in our fortunes, what's the point of striving for the top, as we have always been told to do?

And if the mountaintop isn't all that, where do we go from there?

♥ Defining Obama's place in black history and in the annals of leadership has been a parlor game from the start, not least because black folks' expectations of him are not uniform and never have been. They're all over the place. At one end of the spectrum, the expectations are zero: Obama is simply a fellow black American doing his best to make his way and meet his goals in a hostile and oppressive system, and whatever he does within that system is the best he can do. That's the purely folk-hero view, the one that holds that as long as he's standing with dignity in the face of all the forces intent on breaking him down, he's winning. *We're* winning. At the other end of the spectrum is great disappointment, even disgust, that Obama did not immediately claim his place and his interest in black America and then forge some kind of agenda to help it, per the historical dictates of black leadership and the unfinished business of racial justice; to embrace that tradition is nothing less than his job both as a black man and as president.

In between these two views I've heard infinite variations, many of which draw on both ends of the spectrum and often wind up being both idealistic and pragmatic (like Obama himself), as in: the brother isn't doing what he *should* be doing, what needs to be done, but his hands are tied by definition, so expecting more from him is useless, defeating, counterproductive. Feel good about what you can, and leave the rest. That's the coping strategy we've always employed, or deployed, for the fact that, politically speaking, we almost never get what we want. But the irony is that for some black people, Obama has been responsible for animating progressive ideals and expectations that they eventually accused him of flouting. The stakes of not meeting expectations are high this time. According to the scholar Cornel West, a one-time Obama supporter turned chief critic, history needed a leader to show a new way and stake out new ground, not always seek the middle with the deluded rhetoric of One America. That sort of public relations–minded idealizing serves nobody in need of justice, black folks least of all. West maintained that it was not only ineffective, it was insulting. "We ended up with a brown-faced Clinton. Another opportunist. Another neoliberal opportunist," he told Salon.com columnist Thomas Frank in 2014. "It's a sad thing. It's like you're looking for John Coltrane and you get Kenny G in brown skin."

West's words have the sting of truth, but such an indictment from a black figure of his stature is relatively rare. That's ultimately because unlike West, many black people simply don't have a clear set of expectations to which they've been holding Obama, individually or collectively. The lack of consensus on what a black public figure ought to be doing or saying on our behalf is nothing new, it's just that Obama, by far the most public figure we've ever had, has exposed that lack as the crisis that it's long been. The collective black demoralization since the '60s has been such that we have not expected very much of anybody, black or otherwise. The arguments that Obama is failing us by design or that he's doing the best he can under the circumstances are passionate, often eloquent, and even correct. But ultimately they are all intellectual exercises. Black people have not held any public figures accountable to their interests and concerns for years, mostly because we don't agree on what to hold them accountable to, and in 2015 there are too many things wrong and no single principle unifying them all, as fighting to end Jim Crow or desegregating schools unified black people in the past. The great expansion of the black middle class since the '60s means we have the biggest pool of potential leaders in our history, but we have relatively few. Race work just ain't what it used to be.

The decline of leadership was inevitable, in some ways. In his sobering 2009 essay, "System Values and African American Leadership," political science professor Robert C. Smith explains the deterioration of black leadership since the '70s as a troubling but predictable outcome of integration, which he calls co-optation. Beginning in the late '60s, as leaders of black protest movements were absorbed into the system through jobs and appointments, black agendas and demands from the outside withered. Black elected officials and appointees, especially in the executive branch, became less beholden to community interests and more beholden to the Democratic Party, to which the vast majority of black people belong. That would be fine if the Democratic Party embraced or at least supported black demands, but it doesn't. In fact, much of what the party actually does is antithetical to black interests, especially in the last thirty years, as corporate interests have increasingly shaped the agenda for both parties.

Smith says it's therefore up to individual blacks within the system to force change, but that hasn't worked because too many blacks who ascend the ranks sincerely believe that it is their job to shed the "narrow" interests of black people and represent something "bigger," more universal and inherently more important. The most radical thing they can do is enact Democratic policies that will benefit, say, small-business owners, a group that *includes* black people. But Smith says that such modest and indirect policies have simply not been enough to restructure economies, dismantle institutional racism, and do the large-scale things that need to be done if we are to attain that level playing field that remains so elusive, almost a myth. Obama is part of this pattern of co-opted black leadership, more so because he's ascended the ranks politically as high as any person could go. He's at the top. Yet it is *because* he's at the top that we have such hope for him and what he might do for us; as head of the system, he alone has the best chance at impacting the large-scale stuff, or at least challenging it in a way that it hasn't been challenged before.

So far, Obama has been most effective as a mirror. Whatever we project onto him is reflected back to us ten times, from our deep collective pride in *him* to a deep uncertainty, sometimes anger, about our own shaky prospects as a people in the ongoing American experiment. Obama may be a Rorschach image for whites who see in him what they want to see, but he's a Rorschach for us as well, a particular kind. For us, he's as much a fantasy of what could be as he is a confirmation of what is, a measure of where black folks are now. We always prefer the ideal, but the subtle reality of now that Obama illuminates is actually more instructive. In him we see the payoff of the '60s, the shackles of black ambition finally cast aside. But also we see the price paid for our middle-class success, a limited success at that. Obama has made it to the top, but to what effect? Perhaps the price has been too high.

Obama does have a choice. He could shrug off the whole black leadership paradox of his presidency by doing something racially unequivocal—appoint a black issues czar, something like that. But he hasn't done that. Christopher Jimenez Y West says it's not because Obama believes in post-racialism or doesn't believe blacks have issues that need attention; it's because by nature he's a "Lincoln pragmatist" trying to figure out how to fix the color problem as practically and efficiently as possible. Unlike Lincoln, he's trying to carry this out as president among people whose ancestors owned people like him, which complicates things. And Lincoln's pragmatism was driven by a powerful ideology that kept evolving, principally the idea that slavery had to end; Obama does not appear to be driven by a similarly powerful ideology. That could be part of the reason that Obama doesn't have anyone in his circle who really represents him and his interests, a proxy or a fixer in the way that Karl Rove was for George W. Bush. This has always mystified West. "Egoism is a part of it," says West. "Aloofness is a part of it. He is charismatic. But he's detached." In other words, Obama is a compelling figure, but not necessarily a compelling leader. As Obama nears the end of his second term, West complains that he is looking "more like Jimmy Carter, reduced to reading policy briefs instead of managing. What looks like mismanagement is weariness. The joy has drained out of it for him." Worse, West believes that our first black president, our great symbol, has distanced himself too far from black reality. "He can't go to the river anymore," he says, almost wistfully. "But he let it happen."

Obama has always needed to do more than go to the river: he needs to make the river run, tend to it, be of it. Geneva Smitherman, a distinguished professor emeritus of African American studies at Michigan State University, said she initially saw rekindled in Obama some of the fire that shaped her own views of the American project in the '60s. In his speeches, he invoked Martin Luther King, but also Malcolm X—something that Smitherman says not even political hopefuls of her generation did, especially those aspiring to Washington. She admits to also being enamored by Obama's presentation, his look, the easy way he wore his blackness; what clinched her vote in 2008 was not any articulation of principles, but watching him swish a three-pointer during a basketball game. "I thought, 'This might be a real brother!'" she recalls. But the spell was broken the next year during the epic fight over Obama's health care reform, when he quietly scuttled the public option (though it didn't much matter; the fight remained epic). Smitherman was incensed. To her, creating viable alternatives to big business is the whole meaning of reform. It is the whole meaning of change. "Capitalism is kicking everybody's ass—black, white, everybody!" she says emphatically. As for the enormous racial antipathy toward Obama, Smitherman waves her hand. "White folks are always angry," she says. "Racism wouldn't have been a problem for my Black Power generation. You can't be kumbaya."

Ulli Ryder is forty-one, a generation younger than Smitherman. She also has her political reservations about Obama, though she thinks that expecting him to fight capitalism is generally expecting too much. "Why would he do that? I think he likes money, likes his lifestyle," she says. "I know black people are seen as the moral vanguard, but he's not that." Yet Obama did encourage all Americans to believe in that vanguard, which is partly why Ryder admits that "we expect it to be like the '60s, like the rainbow coalition. I'm not sure what black leadership should be in the twenty-first century, but it can't be that anymore." What can it be, then? Ryder isn't sure. "That generation of the '60s did change the laws, got the signs taken down," she says. "That was the easy part. What we have to do now is change hearts and minds. I have no idea how to do that."

This is the dim, at best uncertain view of where Obama's folk-hero journey is headed, where it is likely to end up. But his story, his unfolding destiny, never fails to hold me. It holds most of us, even supporter/pessimists like Christopher Jimenez y West. The obstacles that stand between Obama and pressing black matters are many, but I'm convinced, like West and so many others, that Obama knows what needs to be done. He *could* lead. He's articulated the problems himself, studied them. Doing for black folks was viewed as nothing less than a moral obligation by his own family. In *Dreams from My Father*, he admits that "it was into my own father's image, the black man, son of Africa, that I'd packed all the attributes of Martin and Malcolm, DuBois and Mandela . . . the voice of my father said, 'You must help in your people's struggle. Wake up, black man!'" Granted, that was articulated before he had presidential aspirations, in a book published before his stint as U.S. senator, and is hard to detect in Obama now; whether the admonishments of his father have gone underground or have just gone is hard to know for sure (though I stubbornly cling to the hope that it's the former). Whichever, in the vacuum of our modern leadership, black people continue to loudly voice their own ideas about what's wrong with us and how to fix it, which means that assessing Obama as our leader has been like the fable of the blind men seizing one part of an elephant and, based on that part, describing the whole elephant differently. I think we would all like Obama to make it easy for us, to sort out the whole atomized mess known as the black crisis (formerly known as the Negro problem) and dictate from his perch at the White House his agenda for fixing it and what things matter most—be the Superman to rescue us from our own confusion and inertia.

My cousin Harold Doley, Jr., is a veteran of Wall Street who thinks that Obama's real leadership problem is that he refuses to embrace his inner Superman, or at least some inner authority figure who swiftly and unapologetically takes charge. That's important for any president, Harold says, but especially for a black president facing white people who are eager, who perhaps even feel duty-bound, to challenge his authority. Harold knows something about this because he's made a bit of black history himself. He's an investment banker who in 1975 started Doley Securities, L.L.C., the country's oldest black investment firm, which still operates in New Orleans. In 1973 he was the first African American to buy a seat on the New York Stock Exchange. He lives in Irvington-on-Hudson, New York, in the palatial former home of Madam C. J. Walker, the black hair-product entrepreneur who in the early 20th century became the nation's first female millionaire. Harold is also a Republican—almost unheard of on both sides of my family—who served in the Reagan administration as financial ambassador to Africa. He's Republican in the old-line Colin Powell mode, conservative fiscally and in other ways, but unabashedly supportive of black folks getting ahead. He says he contributed money to the first Obama campaign, "when I thought he had a shot." He means more than Obama simply having a shot at winning the presidency, he means Obama having a shot at really running things in Washington, making his presence felt.

Harold's been most disappointed not by any particular policy of Obama's but by what he sees as Obama's chronic lack of aggression and his distaste for retribution in the face of adversity. "If we're going to have a black president, let him be strong—a good man but strong," he says. "When somebody shouts at you 'Liar!' during a State of the Union address, you're supposed to *destroy* that person. Obama's not really a fighter, not confrontational. He's an appeaser, basically someone who's not prepared to become president."

He says that two-time California governor Jerry Brown, a Democrat with whom he disagrees on many things, is someone he admires for his resolve and single-mindedness. "He's a fighter," says Harold of the famously quirky Brown. "He'll give you a punch."

I suggest that the virulent, often racist anti-Obamaism that now defines the Republican Party might have something to do with that tendency to appease, and then I can't resist asking Harold how he can even justify being Republican these days, given how the party has done pretty much everything within its considerable power to emasculate Obama, to ensure the total failure of a black first. Harold doesn't disagree with me, but he doesn't answer. He instead criticizes Obama as a kind of badly miscast actor, noting that his black community base—the source of his grassroots power—was created by his close friend and adviser Valerie Jarrett, Michelle Obama, and others. Harold believes this has had implications for other, bigger aspects of his presidency. "I would have to label him a Manchurian president," he says. "I'm a Republican, but I'm first an American—I want us to prevail, I want us to be the most powerful and richest nation in the world. I don't want a president who's an apologist. I want one who's a leader."

Granted, Obama is no Superman. And yet some version of that fantasy (perhaps not the take-no-prisoners, frankly Republican version that Harold favors) feels possible to me. Obama has the goods, in other ways. He is, after all, smart and thoughtful, a man whose writings clearly demonstrate his knowledge and concern about the black crisis and about race overall, knowledge that's produced some startling, little-known insights. In *Dreams* (which I really don't think the white right read closely, if at all, or they'd be truly up in arms), Obama describes the black struggles of the '60s as his political and spiritual rock. Though painted as post-racial, he is, like so many of us in that first post–civil rights generation, still drawn to the unfinished business of black justice. It oriented him. He studied the history of that justice and its heroes, and as a younger man, he engaged in the struggle through community organizing, which gave him a place in the black community that's not just physical. That place is never just physical. Obama writes that the iconic images of the Movement, including students sitting at lunch counters, became a form of prayer for me, bolstering my spirits, channeling my emotions in a way that words never could. They told me that I wasn't alone in my particular struggles, and that communities had never been a given in this country, at least not for blacks. . . . I saw that African-American community becoming more than just the place where you'd been born or the house where you'd been raised. Through organizing, through shared sacrifice, membership had been earned. And because membership was earned—because this community I imagined was still in the making, built on the promise that the larger American community, black, white and brown, could somehow redefine itself—I believed that it might, over time, admit the uniqueness of my own life.

Here is a total inversion of the integration paradigm: it is the black community, or the ongoing promise of it, that defines and accepts all of us, makes us whole. We must all earn membership. It's a radical and profound idea, the opposite of believing that black folk always have to play on the white man's court; what Obama is saying is that the court is really ours. But insight is one thing, reality another. As president and a black man with theoretically unprecedented power, Obama still does not control the court. It is not his. On matters of racial justice, he has been, as he was in his memoir, a more trenchant observer than leader. He long ago defined the issues and placed his own experiences firmly on the map of black experience and need. That's empathy and identity. It isn't leadership. But it is as far as he is willing or able to go. This shouldn't surprise or even necessarily disappoint black people, because many of us are like Obama; we, too, have a full and empathetic view of the black crisis. We tend to see ourselves as latter-day race men and women. But ultimately, we talk about problems more than we take action, either because we're weary or feel powerless to solve them. And the context of taking action has shifted with the times. These days, merely empathizing and identifying with the conditions of the black masses—not simply with the poor or non-elite—is itself a radical position for a black public figure. Obama's racial hesitation partly reflects an almost hysterically conservative era in which all black people are expected to soften, minimize, or completely scuttle a black identity with its suggestion of pursuing racial justice. As has been the case since the end of slavery, blacks are being told in no uncertain terms to set aside our self-interest to accommodate the racial anxieties of white America; we are expected once again to bear the burden of expansiveness and forgiveness and moving on.

We need Obama to stand for us, literally. How thrilling it would be if Obama could plant his feet, Superman-like, and refute this expectation of forgiveness, turn that tide back in our favor, but he doesn't. The fact that he doesn't makes him not evil or less than; it makes him ordinary. This is why we can't let him go, why we "give the brother a pass," as one young man I talked to emphatically put it. Rejecting Obama for his own reticence in claiming a role in black leadership would be tantamount to rejecting ourselves. And hasn't he earned his place in the community? Isn't it far better to have this black president flawed and among us than to have him out there in the wilderness of America, alone?

♥ During his time in Kenya, where he goes to unearth his father's roots in *Dreams*, Obama has more epiphanies about race, especially about the complicated nature of black solidarity. Being in Africa, as compared to America, was "a revelation, socially and psychologically. Here the world was black, and so you were just you; you could discover all those things that were unique to your life without living a lie or committing betrayal." At the same time, he sees how colonialism, including slavery in the states, has wrought black self-hatred and low expectations over time to the point that they seem endemic. And Obama realizes again that a handful of middle-class blacks getting over—what passes for integration in this country—isn't enough. It is not justice. "Without power for the group, a group larger, even, than an extended family, our success always threatened to leave others behind," he writes. "And perhaps it was that fact that left me so unsettled. . . ."

Ironically, Obama unsettles many of us for just this reason—he's in that middle-class handful—but we accept him as such. Acceptance of him as a leader is not nearly as uniform. Samarrah Blackman, the Ph.D. student, resists judging him as a black leader in the modern sense; she sees him more as a symbol, by definition too far removed from the business of black leadership to qualify. That's logical in one way. Presidents tend to function as leaders in the macro sense, advancing ideas rather than the kind of specific action agendas that have been the traditional core of black leadership. Few people I talked to, including supporters, even called Obama a black leader. I get it. Obama as black history is one thing—we're still digesting that—but black leader doesn't compute yet, and it may not for years. It may never compute. Yet Obama has changed the relationship between the very words *black* and *leader*, separated what had once been indivisible; he is a new chapter of our leadership that we don't have a name for yet.

The late writer and critic Albert Murray would say that Obama is living the blues, which isn't to say that he's depressed—I don't think that's in his makeup. What that means is that as first black president, he's been following the musical structure and cultural purpose of the blues: improvising, riffing, extending and elaborating on the story of the presidency as he goes, above all, projecting a sense of ease and triumph over hardship. (Murray always complained that people fundamentally misunderstand blues as an expression of being defeated by life; nothing, he said, could be further from the truth.) He called this "vamping till ready," and he saw it as not just a black thing but a wholly American thing. For his entire presidency Obama has had to vamp like crazy. It's something he didn't quite foresee but that he must have imagined as a possibility, especially given his own early doubts about whether the success of a few black people in high places could ultimately benefit the black community as a whole, whether that success would shore up the community or leave it stranded. Maybe he put those doubts aside, as he seemed to do in the first campaign, when he caught fire as a black man promising to heal our fractured past and damaged ideals of democracy without the specifics of black redress. But I don't think the doubts ever left him.

In *Dreams from My Father*, Obama recalls the cautionary words of Frank, his grandfather's longtime black friend, as Obama prepared to leave Hawaii and go off to college on the mainland. College is the course of every black striver or talented-tenther, but Frank warns him of its dangers: "All you know is that college is the next thing you're supposed to do. And the people who are old enough to know better, who fought all these years for your right to go to college—they're just happy to see you in there and they won't tell you the truth. The real price of admission. . . . Leaving your race at the door. Leaving your people behind." What he says next is soberingly prescient:

They'll train you to manipulate words so that they don't mean anything anymore. They'll train you to forget what you already know. They'll train you so good, you'll start believing what they tell you about equal opportunity and the American way and all that shit. They'll give you a corner office and invite you to fancy dinners and tell you you're a credit to your race. Until you want to actually start running things, and then they'll yank on your chain and let you know that you may be a well-trained, well-paid nigger, but you're a nigger just the same.

I truly wonder if Obama recalls those words now, on days when he's besieged with particularly nasty hate mail and death threats and the open, almost gleeful Republican attempts to undermine his foreign policy, all of which are at least partly a response to the fact that a black man is now "running things." Counseling young Barack, Frank couldn't have been thinking about the presidency—a thought that must have been as fantastical for him as it had been for my father. But his warning about the narcotic effects of black ambition and the illusion of belonging stands. Black people knew what Barack's ambition would be up against, especially since his ambition was staked clearly on those slippery notions of equal opportunity and the American way. A dangerous combination. We just hoped—some prayed—that he would prove the exception and succeed on his own terms. His own terms: we hoped there was such a thing.

But those terms may be a moot point as far as black liberation goes. Well into the age of social media, which has coincided with Obama's tenure, it's becoming clear that we may no longer need black leaders, from preachers to presidents, to spearhead movements for racial justice. The revolution will no longer be centralized: what happened, and in many ways is still happening, in Ferguson, Missouri, in 2014 has made that obvious. Thanks in part to the still-simmering aftermath of the Trayvon Martin incident, and to an entire history of fatal encounters between police and black men that was reaching a critical and dangerous mass in the Obama age, the fatal shooting of Michael Brown by white officer Darren Wilson in August that year birthed a protest that went national. The symbolism is unmistakable. Brown was, like Trayvon, not a hero or an exemplar but an ordinary, working-class black man who also happened to be dark-skinned and bulky, making him especially vulnerable to police suspicion and abuse of force. It was his ordinariness, and the fact that he died in a way all too predictable, that broke the complacency even black people had developed about such shootings. Hell broke loose, and then it began to be organized; street demonstrations grew into continuous protests that I call Occupy Ferguson. They took root all over the country and became the closest thing to a sustained black movement that I've seen in my lifetime.

After Michael Brown, almost on cue, other fatal police shootings of unarmed black men, one as young as twelve, happened in other cities, seeding similar protests that continued to enlarge the scope and meaning of Ferguson. A curious thing developed: not just Obama but traditional black figures such as Al Sharpton began to look increasingly irrelevant in the face of a movement that was clearly driven by events and by a certain zeitgeist, not led by any particular person. The closest thing to that is the movement Black Lives Matter, founded by three young black women who remain much less famous than what they created in 2013 during the criminal trial of Trayvon Martin's shooter, George Zimmerman. Black Lives Matter swiftly became the twenty-first-century edition of Black Power, simultaneously a call for racial self-affirmation and a battle cry against the dehumanization and disrespect of black people of all circumstances and identities—male, female, straight, queer, disabled—not just unarmed black men profiled by police. Described by its cofounder, Alicia Garza, as nothing less than "a tactic for our ultimate liberation," Black Lives Matter applies to all of us in some way, including Obama. He did not lead this movement, but he is in it, whether he admits that or not. It is a strange but timely dynamic: *we* are leading *him*.

Yes, Obama as president seemed very far from the center of Ferguson. Nor was he trying to make his way closer in; no doubt still smarting from the backlash that followed his remarks about Trayvon Martin and the arrest of Henry Louis Gates, Jr., he reclaimed his caution. In November 2014, after a Ferguson grand jury refused to bring any charges against Darren Wilson, Obama called for calm and avoided saying anything that could identify him explicitly with restive black protesters, though he allowed that black people had a right to feel the way they did because the American ideal clearly has not been realized when it comes to police and equal treatment under the law. The response was inadequate, of course, but I felt Obama knew that; once again I saw him laboring for balance where he knows none exists, not yet. That knowledge was at least starting to show more. In an interview with BET anchor Jeff Johnson a month after that grand jury decision in Ferguson, Obama was measured, cagey. He spoke in a low tone, almost a monotone. ("People were saying that I should say, 'This is what the outcome should have been.' I can't do that, institutionally. . . . I'll leave it to others to speculate what Michelle and I say to each other at night.") But as the interview wore on, both men lost a bit of their self-consciousness—or more accurately, a bit of their double consciousness—about the fact that a black president and a black journalist were talking in public about matters crucial to blacks but unfamiliar or unnerving to many whites. For all his caution, Obama couldn't help but let his mask slip a bit. "Black boys get less margin of error," he said to Johnson at one point. "It's not that we want perfect boys to be treated well. We want ordinary, 'confused' boys to be treated well. That's the measure of progress."

The treatment of ordinary black people, not the heroes, as a measure of progress—I was startled by the subtlety, the specificity and humanity, of a statement like that. I had not heard Obama say anything quite like it before. Then I was saddened. It would have been wonderful for every American to hear this straight from the presidential pulpit, in the mainstream press. We all needed to hear it. It spoke directly to the notion of beloved community that King championed, and that Obama tried to revive in '08. But we didn't all hear it. The fact that it was only directed to black people watching BET spoke more to the utter failure of the notion of beloved community in modern times, or perhaps to Obama's failure of nerve. One has so often been a reflection of the other. And yet the job Obama gave himself early on was to assure us that the specifically American ideal of beloved community lives among us, if not within police departments that operate on very different ideas about black people's place in the American family. Obama tried to do this job in a black context that was safe in one way but risky in another, because his stance could have lost black people in significant numbers. That hadn't really seemed possible until Ferguson gave black people an issue on which they had to take a side, no indifference allowed. Ferguson and the issues of equal treatment it raised galvanized us in the way that civil rights did, demanded something of all of us. What Obama gave satisfied some black folks—what more do you expect, was the familiar refrain—but not others. After all, Ferguson was *the* racial matter of his tenure, and growing. We had expectations this time. "I wanted more from him on Ferguson," says Michael Oneal, an insurance agent who lives in New York. He was among the millions who watched Obama's television appearance in the aftermath of the grand jury decision's not to bring charges against Darren Wilson for the death of Michael Brown. "He gave this kind of 'don't riot, no excuse for violence, the law will come down on you' speech. It was tone deaf, and also disrespectful. All this concern about *us* staying in line . . . you would think there would be empathy. That was a real moment of disillusionment."

I understand the moment. It was confirmation of what Oneal had resisted believing for six years, that when push comes to shove, Obama will not, or cannot, take our side in the ancient battle that pits black folks against any state authority, especially police. I was frustrated by his reserve. But I admit that I also loved Obama for his attempt to bridge this particular gap. He failed again, but he did so in a way that inadvertently—or deliberately— illuminated his own political struggles with the racial reality so harshly illuminated by Ferguson. At more than one point in the BET interview with Jeff Johnson, Obama looked downright unhappy, not resolute as he normally is with the press and in front of crowds generally. That moved me. Dennis Tyler, a professor of English at Fordham University in New York, says that Obama's inertia over Ferguson, and the fact that the anti–police brutality movement is proceeding nicely without him, is encouraging in one way—it shows us how for too long we've clung to a model of black leadership that's outgrown its usefulness. "I like the fact that the [Ferguson] movement is dispersed and diverse, though that's always been the case," says Tyler. That's true, but the truth has been obscured by the traditional charismatic-leader model, with its perpetual reliance on the emergence of The One who will deliver us from the evils of the system. Oprah Winfrey, an early Obama supporter, famously anointed Obama The One at a rally in South Carolina in 2007. Though she didn't use the word *black* or even *color*—Oprah, a black maven of literate-to-lowbrow pop culture who has a significantly white following, is expert at that—it was clear she was talking about black deliverance. (Oprah prefaced her anointing by quoting a scene from the Ernest Gaines novel *The Autobiography of Miss Jane Pittman*, in which the protagonist, an elderly survivor of slavery and the Civil War who is still seeking full justice, asks the black children she encounters, "Are you the one?") Tyler says that the obvious problem with The One is the problem with the charismatic-leader model in general, times two: "When they don't meet our expectations," he says, "things fall apart." But Ferguson and Black Lives Matter have not needed any expectations from Obama or anyone else in order to grow. Either Obama was not The One or he's a different sort of One, a Greek chorus rather than the lead actor. Or black folks are beginning to move on.

Twenty-two year-old Gabriel Hercules was one of several young black men who met then-attorney general Eric Holder when he visited Los Angeles in 2014, post-Ferguson, to talk in depth about racial profiling and how it disrupts community. Herc, as he is also known, respects the whole Obama phenomenon but has never been transported by it. He says he was impressed by Holder ("He seemed very calm, cool, and collected—knows how to run a show"), but in the long run, he doesn't expect much change from him or the president. Obama to him is a common-man folk hero—a black man like himself who happens to be president, not the other way around. "They're guys doing their jobs," he says of Obama and Holder—nothing more, though certainly nothing less. Nor does he see those jobs extending to such things as eradicating racism, vis-à-vis Ferguson or any other event. To Herc, eradicating racism is less about doing a job than about effecting a spiritual conversion, and he thinks that a black person is perhaps even less qualified to bring about that conversion than most other people. "What can he *do?*" he says with some exasperation. "People want Obama to voice the problem of racism, but he's living the problem himself. He walks into it every day. He understands it's a problem, he can see it for what it is. But Obama talking about racism won't change it."

(Coda: Eric Holder's Justice Department conducted its own investigation of the Michael Brown shooting in Ferguson and found in 2015 that although there were no grounds to charge Darren Wilson with civil rights violations, there were startling patterns of racial injustice and exploitation within Ferguson's law enforcement and its largely white civic infrastructure. In other words, the notion of institutional racism, so notoriously hard to prove, was made visible by the investigation, and that felt like a victory. A *job* well done.)

♥   During the '60s, "civil rights" was synonymous with racial justice. To-day, "civil rights" suggests that justice without naming it, leaving room for deniability in an age profoundly uncomfortable with putting blackness and justice in the same sentence. Najee Ali has been an activist in Los Angeles for twenty-plus years and is called a civil rights activist by the local media, not because it believes in black justice but because that's what any black person who raises his or her voice in protest of anything is called by the media. It's lazy terminology, though not always incorrect. Najee has always promoted black justice, which has chiefly meant lending his voice over the years to a whole host of Justice for Trayvon Martin–like causes in which black people have been wrongly profiled, arrested, accused, slandered, or killed without sufficient public outrage. His first big campaign was justice for Sherrice Iverson, a seven-year-old black girl who was molested and brutally murdered in a bathroom in a Nevada casino by an eighteen-year-old white man, Jeremy Strohmeyer, in 1997. (Strohmeyer went to prison for life, and California later passed a law, known as the Sherrice Iverson Child Protection Act, that requires those who witness the sexual assault of a child to report it promptly to the authorities.) Another one of his causes was trying to shore up the diminishing black presence in Los Angeles, including an effort to rename a street in black middle-class Leimert Park Malcolm X Boulevard (so that it would cross Martin Luther King Boulevard). Another was to designate Leimert Park Village African American Village, officially branding it as an ethnic enclave, like Koreatown, Chinatown, Little Ethiopia, or Little Saigon. Neither effort succeeded. Najee himself is a Malcolm X–like figure in that he spent time in prison, where he converted to the Nation of Islam and to a new consciousness about racial justice and how reforming his own behavior might help the cause.

When Najee got out of prison, he started a food bank called Project Islamic Hope, and from there, he expanded into activism. This coincided with the 1992 unrest, when Los Angeles was the center of a national discussion about black frustration with the justice system and the state of things in general. (It didn't dawn on me until much later that it was the last such discussion of the decade, really of the last twenty-two years. There wasn't another until Ferguson.) In the new millennium, the focus of civil rights has moved on from racial injustice to immigration and marriage equality, while black crises have been largely reduced to Internet discussions about insults—eruptions from the celebrity likes of comedian Michael Richards, cooking maven Paula Deen and NBA franchise owner Donald Sterling. When it comes to racial issues, bad systems have been replaced in the public's mind with bad actors, even with the Trayvon Martins and Michael Browns.

This has actually worked in Najee's favor, because despite having an organization, he was for many years essentially a one-man show with little ability to do anything other than publicize an incident or injustice with a press conference or two, maybe bring some pressure to bear on a legislator before moving on to the next crisis. It's the freelance, media-driven, frequently self-serving model of activism that has flourished in the absence of credible black leadership and a consensus about what's to be done, not just about individual tragedies such as the murder of Sherrice Iverson but about the collective tragedy of black injustice that make them possible. Freelance activism takes the postmodernist approach to race work: virtually anyone can do it, and it's whatever you decide it is. Not everybody appreciated Najee's presence on the scene, and his press conferences were frankly not adequate to the task, but that hardly stopped him. Over the years, as black justice fell further out of political fashion, he mellowed, but he's still a gadfly, still frames conversations with a kind of old-school black revolutionary zeal. But things have certainly changed, or matured. (Najee himself is close to fifty.) Once a critic of aging, establishment leadership, he now counts many veteran elected officials as his friends. Obama is among them, although "friend" might be too strong a word, more like a kindred spirit. In '08, many blacks in Washington didn't warm to his candidacy until he started winning primaries in white states like Iowa; even though the tide turned and black folks united in the black pride that for them undergirded "Hope/Change," it's useful to remember that was not their first reaction. Najee sympathizes with Obama as he tries to win over black skeptics, and as he negotiates the delicate task of winning the support of white voters while staying authentic to core black voters. That isn't selling out, Najee insists; it's a strategy essential to making any inroads at all. There is certainly little else one black man aspiring to represent the whole country—a freelancer, if you will—can do. "He had to play the perfect campaign," says Najee. "I get it."

He now works for the National Action Network, the New York–based organization headed by Rev. Al Sharpton. Sharpton was an early black supporter of Obama, and though he kept it low-key, that support never wavered. Najee says that early in Obama's first administration, when other black leaders were complaining that Obama was ignoring them and, by extension, ignoring black people, Sharpton said nothing and was rewarded with access to the White House and Obama's ear. Najee first met Obama when he volunteered to help his U.S. Senate campaign in Chicago in 2003; four years later, he supported his bid for presidency. "I'm proud to say that Sharpton's among the very few [black people] who did support him from the beginning," says Najee. He's also more than a little proud of himself. "The whole black establishment was against him. But I always believed in supporting young black leaders, though I didn't know too much about him—he seemed very personable, very friendly." His most resonant memory of Obama so far is movingly simple, and it captures the essence of Obama's appeal among black people who are first and foremost moved by Obama being president; everything he does in that capacity takes on an aura of magic. "At Coretta Scott King's funeral in Atlanta, he smiled and said to me, 'Hey, there's my homeboy from Chicago!'" Najee says with a laugh. He looks delighted, like an eight-year-old at Christmas.

I'm reminded again of my own moment of conversion, of falling in love. How many people has Obama called his homeboy or homegirl, trained that gaze on him or her, and flashed that smile? Like Bill Clinton, Obama has the ability to make whoever he's talking to feel special, partly because he really does remember them—that isn't faked. It is seductive, and much more persuasive than mountains of statistics and reams of policy analyses. If you are black and have connected with Obama, it can fill the room you would ordinarily reserve for legitimate concern about the economy and drones and Guantanamo and the national security state. Ridiculous, maybe, certainly bad politics, but it makes emotional sense. For the first time in our long American struggle, Obama gives us the freedom of not caring about those things because now we have the option of only supporting *him*, and supporting whatever it is we want him to stand for. Though a long way from the group euphoria of 2008, the embrace of Obama as a kind of personal totem still matters greatly. We still need that embrace; we still need him. The race needs him.

Najee says he never bought into the angst in some quarters about Obama's lack of black bona fides. "I was always struck by his authenticity," he says. "All that 'Is he black enough?' is rhetoric. Michelle embodies blackness at its finest, he attended Rev. Wright's church—I never bought into that smear that he wasn't truly one of us. Obama has always clearly identified as a black male—juxtapose that to Tiger Woods! He's *proud* of his heritage. His racial neutrality was a political choice that he had to make." Najee forgives Obama for distancing himself from Al Sharpton and Jesse Jackson during the first campaign; Sharpton especially has always been tainted as too black for prime time, even after he was given a show on the cable news channel MSNBC in 2011. In '08, Najee says, "we were fighting for the Democratic nomination against Hilary Clinton, who had more relationships and more money. He *had* to run the perfect campaign, essentially, and he did. Sharpton to his credit didn't let his ego affect him, like other black leaders did." So that campaign was, to Najee, a form of black leadership in and of itself—the tactical victory *was* a realization of justice. Najee thinks that Jackson and other black figures who've criticized Obama, notably radio host Tavis Smiley and scholar Cornel West, are miffed because they don't have

White House access. When I ask Najee if he thinks Obama is sufficiently addressing black issues—his critics' main complaint—he answers immediately with a sentiment that's become almost stock: "No. But he's not the president of South Central."

I've never liked the belittling of South Central (or Harlem, or Ferguson) implied in that answer—isn't that exactly the problem? I understand Najee's point, and I don't argue with it, but my question is not why Obama doesn't put black folks first; it's about where we are on the national agenda. It's about priorities. Najee credits Obama for responding to pressure from below, as he did with gay rights and immigration reform. In that way, he's more flexible and less imperious than many black elected officials in lesser offices. That is progress, he says. "He spoke about Trayvon because leaders applied pressure—he didn't want to say anything, but he had to give us some play," he points out. Najee was part of National Action Network's demonstrations in front of the Justice Department, urging Eric Holder to appoint a special prosecutor in the Zimmerman case; it was the National Action Network that publicized the shooting in the first place. Justice for Trayvon Martin, with its presidential imprimatur and global reverberations in the Internet age, is clearly Najee's culminating campaign, the moment toward which he has been moving throughout his career. "This is our generation," he says. "It was trending. It was international. We weren't going to let up. This murder is part of my activist generation, not Emmett Till's. We stayed in the streets and forced the president to the microphone." Najee sounds proud; a one-time outsider, he now has a sense of personal influence and inclusion in the process. This, to him, is how things are supposed to work. That doesn't mean black leadership isn't dysfunctional overall; Obama and anything he's accomplished have not solved that problem. But Najee now sees the benefit of old-fashioned race work, which was always built on a common vision of change. That's a strategy he says we have to resuscitate—without Obama's help. "When Obama addressed the problem of homophobia, those groups applied pressure—they knew exactly what they wanted," he says. "Immigrants did the same thing. This is *our* task."

Not all tasks are equal, nor are they necessarily doable, even when there is pressure. Given the political realities around race, Najee admits that indirect leadership on black issues is perhaps the best we can expect from Obama. Eric Holder has been much more forthcoming in that respect, which is why, during his six years in office, he was widely seen as Obama's proxy, the sharp-tongued black lawyer who could argue for things that a black president could not. In 2012, the Justice Department modified sentencing guidelines for drug-related convictions, something that has fairly enslaved black people for the last thirty years, and it was Holder who called for a federal investigation into the controversial and fatal shooting of Michael Brown by Darren Wilson in Ferguson two years later. You could argue that the Affordable Care Act is racial justice, given that black people are the sickest demographic and have the worst health-care outcomes in the country. And then there are the jobs bills that Obama couldn't get passed at all, for blacks or anybody. "His critics say that he isn't addressing black needs, but his hands are tied," says Najee. But how tied is tied? Can't he lead regardless? Couldn't he look out over the landscape and loudly say, here's what's wrong and here's what needs to be done? Isn't that within his power as president to do, what he should do: represent ideals and hopes and elevate the needs of the common man (more common than the 1 percent, anyway) that he campaigned on? Najee answers the question with a recommendation. "We need to organize and plan and do an agenda before he's out of office," he says. "Sorting out those things that are wrong and addressing them—that's not Obama's job."

Najee is right that it's not Obama's job, or more accurately, he isn't wrong. Taking responsibility for our own change isn't unreasonable. It's necessary. But it's remarkable coming from a former prisoner turned activist who made a local name as a keeper of black causes that were being strangled by government, who saw himself as going against a tide of laissez-faire racial politics that was drowning us all. While Najee doesn't agree with all that Obama has done, or hasn't done (and he can't afford to incur the wrath of his boss, Sharpton), he fundamentally can't bring himself to find serious fault with a man roughly his age whom he admires like hell for becoming president of the United States. It's very hard to get past that admiration. And for Najee to be called a homeboy by the president, to be recognized and heard, is too good a feeling to sacrifice to the progressive critiques of Obama, however on point they are. And I truly believe that he sees Obama as ideologically purer and better-intentioned than the lot of black politicians who never really showed him anything, never stood on a solid foundation; Obama is standing on that foundation and Najee is not interested in moving it. Too much has moved in his life already. Yes, there are some gaps in the logic of his robust defense/embrace of Obama, but I leave it alone, because admittedly, I have those gaps myself, though the difference is that I recognize them. Sometimes they trouble me. I don't think they trouble Najee. For him, the circle has closed; the long search for black integrity in the modern age is over. Obama is doing the best he can, responding in the best ways he knows how, asking for nothing more or less from us than any other president would ask, neither ignoring us nor granting us favor. This is as good as it gets.

Although if black folks could ever get our *shit* together, even modestly, Najee is suggesting, Obama would be much more likely to respond to us than past presidents, including Clinton. It isn't that he's blown the opportunity to help black folks; we've blown it for ourselves. Obama arrived in the White House ahead of history, and we never caught up to him. We threw all our support *to* him, too starry-eyed to see or care that it was always a long-distance romance between him and us, and fairly one-sided. But if we had really gotten his attention, had made Obama feel indebted to us for our love instead of merely appreciative of it, the relationship might have turned into something less possible and more real. We were waiting for him to make another move, as he was probably waiting for us, and in the meantime, the Tea Party stepped into the breach, the recession ground on, and a string of foreign crises developed that are still in play—Iraq, Afghanistan, Syria, Yemen, Nigeria, Israel and Palestine, Iraq again. The world of trouble expands, and the Negro problem recedes more and more into the distance.

There are occasional, conscious interruptions of that distance, such as My Brother's Keeper, a national initiative meant to shore up efforts to help young black men survive the crisis of being young black men and become— well, become Obama. Of course, My Brother's Keeper is a corrective effort that's not at all commensurate with the well-documented problem of being a young black man—the very word *initiative* suggests a tentativeness that we should be long past. But the visuals of the press conference announcing it in 2014 were stirring, reminding me again of the sublime quality of Obama's black empathy. He stands at the podium with all these black boys arrayed behind him like a choir, solemn but giddy; they look like they would have jumped into a lake if the president had asked them to. Obama looks moved too, in spite of himself. He watches intently as a boy named Christian nervously introduces him—one thing Christian says is that he was incredulous, and then inspired, to learn that Obama as a teenager struggled with self-affirmation "just like me." As he talks, he glances over at Obama, who nods encouragingly. It is a lovely dynamic, poetic and unprecedented, exactly what I'd hope to see with a black man in the White House, and it strikes me that here is the beloved community Obama spoke of in his book, the one to which all black people owe something and to which we all must earn membership.

At the press conference for My Brother's Keeper, Obama seems gratefully aware of the simple power he has with the black folks who have been so politically removed, and he is also aware of their power over him; we are mutually dependent, travelers on a single path. Behind him are Trayvon Martin and Michael Brown, and at the podium are Trayvon and Michael— Obama himself—and the group looks entirely synergized, content. It looks as if it needs nothing and no one else, no approval ratings or strategists, not even an audience. And then the press conference is over; the boys disband, and the synergy evaporates. But that supreme moment of identification and self-containment lingers, along with its bittersweet message from the president to us: I am of you, I can affirm you. But I cannot lead you. That you must do for yourself. Take *initiative*.

♥   In the end—or even for the moment—how are we to feel about a black president who is not chiefly a black leader, not looking to be one, but could still entertain the idea of being one? Is it enough that he's a fellow traveler, though on a path he now walks alone? We deal with irresolution on many fronts, but this irresolution about the nature of *our* president is not a parlor game or an idle question—the uncertainty nags. It often hurts. Not being able to feel definitively about our most definitive electoral victory in modern history borders on humiliating; not knowing exactly what we're dealing with stings like an open wound that refuses to heal. I understand why Elaine Gills, a professor and educator who once ran a school in Los Angeles called the DuBois Institute, looked so devastated acknowledging that no, he isn't much of a black leader, he simply can't be when he talks down to us that way. That kills the whole deal. And yet, like Samarrah Blackman, she *wants* Obama very much to be something, mean something. Gills confessed her disappointment right away but still clung to that possibility of some encouraging truth; she didn't quite close the book. But the conundrum is painful. For stalwart race people like Gills who have devoted so much of their lives to bettering the lot of black folks, Obama is cognitive dissonance at an ear-splitting volume. He is first a black man trying to cope with fierce white resistance, which Gills understands; that's a given. But within the black sphere, he's telling people to stop bitching, to get off their duffs, "put on their marching shoes," stop complaining and get to work. To Gills and many others (including me, I have to say, on low-point days), that's disrespectful and disingenuous, coming from an obviously deep thinker whose essential understanding of politics and American dysfunction—and American promise—was forged in the poorest and blackest neighborhoods of Chicago.

It hurts too that along the way to the top, and even while there, Obama has argued against rote conservative dismissals of black problems; in his rather modest way, he has stood up for the least among us. By most accounts, he was a dedicated community organizer, a voice of conscience (and yes, also of compromise) in the Illinois State Senate, but apparently felt he had to abandon that once he crossed over into presidential politics. However much black folk understand and even condone his pragmatism, the question we have to answer for ourselves is this: can he be a black leader without directly representing a black desire for change that, fifty years after the Movement, is very much alive? Does the fact that his "Hope/Change" campaign was more a matter of brilliant branding than anything else diminish the fact that hope and change are exactly what black folks need, more than everybody else, more urgently than ever before? And even if he was fully sympathetic to that desperation and that need, could he do right without being black, as it were? Could he lead consciously from a distance?

Washington is a long way from South Central Los Angeles or Brooklyn or Atlanta; in some ways, it's farthest away from the black neighborhoods of D.C. itself. The distance Obama would have to cover to truly lead all of us is not just geographical, it's psychological. And it's enormous: he would really have to be Superman to leap that distance in a single bound, or two, or even a hundred. He is, alas, just a man. That's always our default position, the easy chair into which we sink when things become too complicated, unanswerable. "Just a man" has the benefit of being both true and illusory, of always allowing us to bask in the glory of a black man's extraordinary accomplishment without decrying the office of the president itself, which has disappointed or betrayed us time and again. For deep down, we know that Obama can't *really* be president; the system won't let him. Those of us who had wildly hoped that he might change the presidency itself, change the system, were disabused of that notion in the first year or so, and Superman quickly became journeyman. New York state legislator Jeffrion Aubry, another cousin of mine, summed it up when he told me, "Blacks have faith in him, but not the system." And it's worth remembering that he's a journeyman who's also head of the system. "He's still the president," says Jeff. "He can still send your ass over to Afghanistan to get killed."

♥   Before Ferguson there was Trayvon Martin. Nothing so far has illuminated Obama's black leadership paradox more clearly than the controversy around the fatal shooting in 2012 of the black Florida teenager and the trial of his murderer, George Zimmerman, in Sanford, Florida. (Florida, that historical hotbed of racial oppression, is to me worse than Mississippi; Miami has always been a distraction from that fact.) After that shooting, the face of Trayvon was everywhere, the biggest black icon since Obama himself in '08, though the contrast between them couldn't have been greater: Obama the singular Great Black Hope; Trayvon the martyr for all the faceless, feared young black men who, as Najee often pointed out, too often wind up unjustly imprisoned, profiled, or dead. When the story broke and national outrage started to mount, Obama, looking tormented, told reporters, "If I had a son, he would look like Trayvon." It was a statement of the obvious that nonetheless asserted his own blackness to the entire country in a way he hadn't asserted it—had been very careful not to—up to that point. The following year, after Zimmerman was acquitted of the murder and national outrage boiled up again, Obama (looking even more tormented) went one further by telling reporters that he also had been criminally profiled as a black man—white women saw him and held their purses closer, crossed the street. He added that twenty years earlier, if he had been walking through the Sanford complex that night, he might have been killed too.

In other words, Obama wasn't just identifying himself as black, he was identifying himself as Trayvon; he was speaking not as the fortunate son of wonderfully polyglot America but as another potential victim of the ugly and sometimes fatal racial paranoia directed at black men, whatever their age or station. It was a bold, emotional move, with Obama laying himself bare while struggling to look presidential and in control. He failed rather miserably, but that was his point, that we can't wall off the tragedy of blackness by class or job description or anything else. I have to say that I was moved, encouraged, that my heart leapt to see his attempt to calmly explain what I instantly knew would be misconstrued and used against him. It was the most heroic thing he'd said in a long time, and in failing to cover this confession with his usual equipoise—failing on our behalf—he moved closer to all black folks.

And yet, alas, he *did* give himself cover. He prefaced his confession by saying that the justice system had spoken, that it had worked the way it was supposed to. I know why he said it, but it was outrageous—justice *hadn't* worked, that's why everybody was up in arms. I could be generous and say that Obama was actually critiquing the system by saying with a straight face that it "worked"; for certain people who are not black and frequently profiled, it does work, he was implying. Certainly, those people thought it worked this time. But it came off much more like Obama touching all the bases as usual, voicing his personal concerns and trenchant racial analysis while simultaneously ducking a critical black leadership moment that he fears will sink his presidency and the ambitions tied to it. He doesn't want to lose himself, to commit openly to black justice and then be tarred as sociologist-in-chief (it's bad enough, I suppose, that he was a *community* organizer), especially a black sociologist-in-chief. Instead, he did the dance. He is sympathetic. He agrees with us. Briefly, gloriously, he is one us. And then he has to exit the stage.

In this case I did what a lot of black folks did, what we almost reflexively do with well-meaning black people in high-wire places: applaud Obama for what he did or said right, and minimize the rest. But that's hardly universal. Pam Ward, the graphics designer who is roughly Obama's age, called Obama's Trayvon moment "very strong"; Issa Rae, who is twenty-five years younger, thought it wasn't strong enough—not too surprising, given her own experience with racially vicious remarks about Trayvon. Issa Rae believes that the case had historical proportions, in a league with Emmett Till, and that Obama, a former professor, blew a critical teaching moment for all of us, to say nothing of a black leadership moment. She believes this even though she, too, fully understands his position; she defaults to that understanding as part of her Obama consciousness. We cannot help but understand. Though for Issa Rae, acceptance of what is seems to coexist peacefully with an expectation of something different. Unlike older people, who have seen too much and hope too little, she gives herself the right to expect real change. And it's a permanent right; if Obama doesn't fill that expectation, someone else will eventually.

Pam Ward is already satisfied, and isn't looking to be dissatisfied; while Obama is not *the* answer, as an answer he is more than sufficient. Light-skinned enough to pass for white, she was fiercely Afrocentric as a kid—she grew up in Watts, sported a huge afro, and wrote school reports on the Black Panthers—and sees Obama not as a contradiction of values (black and American, revolutionary and integrationist) but as a natural progression of Afrocentrism. He wears the clothes and speaks the language of the establishment, but the fundamental peril of being black in a white world is the same for him as it was for the Panthers, and for virtually all black people in American history. That peril, which can't be divorced from Obama's capacity to create change, has defined his presidency. "I know it's hard for people to look at the drones, to look at why he doesn't do this thing or that thing," says Ward. "But the tightrope is one that he has to walk. I have a friend in the South who says she's seen bars with calendars on the walls that count down the days [to] when Obama gets assassinated. That's illegal for sure. But isn't it illegal to lynch James Byrd [a black man killed in 1998 Texas by white men who tied him to the back of a truck and dragged him to pieces]? To shoot Trayvon Martin?"

Brandon Brooks says that his generation, the one between Obama's and Trayvon's, is frankly too lost to think much about justice or anything beyond claiming a place in a world that is still indifferent, if not outright hostile, to the well-being of black men. While the Zimmerman verdict disheartened Brandon—it was announced on his thirtieth birthday—it didn't exactly galvanize many of his friends. Nothing has for a long time. "My generation has no guidance, no compass," he says. (He prefaces the whole conversation by saying that he's "really nervous to talk about this" and that "I feel a special responsibility to articulate things, but feel I fail sometimes.") For many of his friends, the Trayvon Martin case was less cause for activism than just another brick in the wall for black people, specifically young adults whose self-image crises are more subtle than but as destructive as the street violence and wrongful murders that get all the media attention. Brandon says that many of his peers are still drifting. They emerged from adolescence and never found their footing chiefly because they never found fulfilling or compelling work. That's economic, and something else more complicated. "They're not willing to work at McDonald's at jobs being filled by Latinos, but they're not willing to work a modest job of any kind," he says. "They want the bling; they want what they want. I have friends who are out of jobs, in jail, ballplayers and hustlers. There's no consistency. It kind of hurts for me to see." Obama, he suggests, soothes that sense of disjointedness—he certainly sought out and found *his* place in the world. It can be done.

Luckily, Brandon found his own niche in the family newspaper business, though he admits to having drifted before that. Most black men do, he says, to one degree or another, whether they're middle-class or poor or something in between; in an effort to find himself, he used to rap, perform, play sports. Obama himself drifted, to me a more revealing admission than the admission that he smoked weed and did drugs (though that certainly bears on black men's lives in a certain way). "Obama broke the mold—he shattered it," says Brandon. "He's proof that his sophistication is such that he could become president, being on the path to Harvard and all that. But he's focusing on a generation that doesn't give a shit." For black people at large who overwhelmingly support Obama, Brandon says he sees "a fifty-fifty split" on the question of what he stands for and whether he's impacting their lives at all. "Half of black people get it," he says. "The other half are still struggling to connect with Barack, or with anyone." The political battles lost, the stagnation with Congress, the routine insults of Obama that tip very close to "nigger" and that he is actually powerless to stop—those things have also reduced Obama's luster among blacks, if not the loyalty they feel.

"There's been a comedown of Barack for sure," Brandon says. "He's not the rock star anymore. I see him as Uncle Barack." Meaning not as cool as before, but still family, and still potentially cool, a point of inspiration if or when he wants to be, when the occasion arises. Barack can always be Barack again. Issa Rae says something similar. "He first struck me as a good, upstanding, genuine black man," she says. But she also saw him as somewhat naive; Obama's efforts at bipartisanship with Republicans, which she watched with increasing distress, were a "complete waste of time." Somewhat like Brandon, however, she remains willing to believe in change, or more accurately, in *him* changing. He's no longer the rock god, though he never was for Issa Rae. She's realistic, not romantic: "I'm defending an uncle who means well."

The belief that Obama does mean well, or that his presidential tenure augurs well for black people in the future, runs deep. Ishmael Reed says that the test scores of black kids in public schools have been rising, in part, he believes, because "Obama does expand possibilities for them." The symbolism is unimpeachable, even if presidents are not. But if nothing turns dramatically or even moderately in our favor between now and the 2016 presidential election, what has been the point of Obama being president at all? The possibility that we as black people really might be shut out of any largesse of the Obama years started to sink in early for me as I watched, with growing numbness, the white right trash or oppose him on a regular basis. It became a new American blood sport. From day one, anti-Obamaism established itself as a full-time endeavor that snuffed out in stages the deep satisfaction I felt about him getting to the top. The Opposition (it deserves to be capitalized) has been unrelenting, never stopping to taking a breath, and it began to dawn on me that if Obama couldn't lead America, if it wouldn't let him do his primary job, then he certainly couldn't do his secondary job of leading black folk, if he was inclined to do it at all. The two kinds of leadership had to happen simultaneously—one couldn't happen without the other—but that synergy is clearly not possible at this point. It is a gap that Obama can't close, the one compromise that can't be had at any price. Over the years, his attempts at compromise have actually polarized things more by more brightly illuminating a divide that we all knew existed but that white folks would have preferred not to see, and the Opposition is furious at the exposure. The more he reached toward compromise, the deeper and uglier and more visible the gap became, and the more the Opposition attacked. (When Obama extended the Bush tax cuts in 2010, much to the chagrin of even centrist Democrats, the right voiced tepid approval for about a week before resuming its chief business of decrying all things Obama, notably his health care law.) Black people have watched all this and almost pitied Obama's position. We all know that it's a precarious position, that his presidency stirs violence, and we have known violence. It isn't a position we'd wish on ourselves. The bottom line is that the matter of Obama's leadership has never rested and probably never will, for black or white, which means that I can't rest either. Uncertainty begins at the top.

Sometimes, when my political doubts about Obama threaten to become overwhelming, I have to retreat into the purely positive end of the spectrum, wallow in it while knowing it's not entirely good for me, like chocolate or retail therapy. It's a form of escapism, but I know that I need it in order to come back to the serious questions at all; I have to look again into the bright light or risk mistaking everything for darkness. Obama is not the darkness, though I've had grave questions about the direction of his journey, and infusions of light—his move to normalize relations with Cuba, his executive order to enact a measure of immigration reform—give me regular assurance not that Obama is faultless but that my original love has not been in vain.

For this kind of assurance, I turn often to Michael Anderson, one of the most realistic but relentlessly positive people I know. Michael is a fifty-five-year-old architect and developer whom I've known since 1992, when the inner core of Los Angeles went up in the flames of civil unrest. Michael saw it as a great opportunity, not just for his business but for the great unfinished business of black justice. "I am 100 percent proud of him," is the first thing he says when I sit down to talk to him about Obama. Michael grew up in St. Louis and is considerably streetwise, a combination of high ideals and high energy that's always trained on the goal of growth and prosperity—as opposed to decline—for our people. His great professional ambition for many years was to remake riot-scarred Crenshaw and South Central in the prosperous image of more hip, brand-conscious cities like Santa Monica or West Hollywood. The renaissance he shopped around didn't happen, partly because of cautious and intransigent elected officials who, as it happens, were black. Michael complained bitterly about the limited imagination of black leadership at the time, though he's slowly made peace with it. After twenty-plus years, he still holds out hope that South Central's fortunes will turn, and he'll have a hand in it. He's very good at holding out hope.

"It was an uphill battle from day one," he says of Obama. "Winning the presidency shows his intelligence and belief that he could accomplish anything." As for black leadership, Michael says, "he's done things for black people that are subtle, that don't just benefit blacks." But blacks have certainly benefited from things Obama has done, he says—health care is a favorite example, student loan reform is another—a fact routinely underacknowledged because those benefits aren't flashy. (Brenda Jackson, the Los Angeles county worker whom I interviewed, made this point too.) They aren't specifically black, nor do they constitute a renaissance. But they help. The needle moves a little, maybe a little more than that, and in Michael's experience with black leadership, that isn't nothing. Michael believes that Obama has actually *changed* the whole tenor of the black leadership crisis, down to local leadership that he says has been less prone to the nepotism and general apathy that have paralyzed it for the last generation. "There's more of a focus on quality people doing jobs," he says. "Achieving a modern lifestyle in black communities is the goal"—as opposed to justice being the goal, at least publicly. Justice is fuzzy, abstract. Building or rebuilding something is so much more concrete. "Things are looking up," Michael says. "Places like South Central and Inglewood now have to be the places where you stay."

In other words, they have to be places you don't leave, which middle-class black people have been doing for decades, as a corollary of white flight. Black flight has been just as crippling, draining away the resources and motivation required for the kind of upgrades that Michael still dreams of doing. The crisis created by black flight is something Obama notes more than once in *Dreams from My Father*. Fresh out of Harvard and working a brief stint at a corporate firm in Chicago, he recalls a black security guard warning him away from the community organizing work he was thinking about leaving the firm to do. The guard says a promising young black man like Obama should instead "make him some money" and stop fooling with the "rhymes and jive" of black folks who don't want to help themselves and wouldn't appreciate him trying. The working-class guard is talking not just about leaving the hood physically, but emotionally and spiritually—total flight. It confirms Obama's own troubling definition of integration: going away from the black world toward something better. (That Obama himself went on to become the pinnacle of successful integration is more than a little ironic, although almost inevitable.) But whatever Obama does or doesn't do in office, far away from the hood, Michael says that he is not a panacea for what ails us. Even if he were absolutely in our corner, he would not be enough; history needs too many correctives for one person to effect, especially one of Obama's temperament. He needs company, or contemporaries. "We would have been better off if Martin and Malcolm and those guys had lived," Michael confesses. "No leaders afterward had that same determination or vision. Jesse had the platform Martin had, but not the spirit."

Obama did tap into the spirit—that's crucial—but he lacked the lived experience and community connectedness of a Jesse Jackson, at least of earlier iterations of Jesse. Ultimately, Michael sees Obama as a manager, more talented as a business leader than as any other sort of leader. That isn't inherently negative, but it's different from what most black people want, or need, Obama to be. Michael concedes that. But he insists that Obama represents great progress. "Business leaders are not politicians, not justice seekers," he says. "I think Obama is results-oriented, and *that's* good for us. That's precedent-setting." He compares Obama as president of the United States to Michael Jordan as once the most popular player in basketball: talented for sure, but popular with whites also because, for all his dominance in the sport, he was racially nonthreatening. Jordan was known for his conspicuous lack of politics, racial or otherwise. Adulation for him came at the price of personal expression.

But sports and politics are two different worlds, with different things at stake. One represents ideas, lifestyles, feverish fantasies of greatness on both sides of the color line; the other represents everyday people. It is reality. The insecurity among whites about who Obama might *really* be underneath the accommodating Michael Jordan exterior, what he believes and where his loyalties lie, therefore persists. Michael Anderson understands this. But he is impatient, almost angry, with a similar black wariness of Obama, which he attributes mostly to a dim view blacks tend to hold of each other, from pauper up to president. It's that learned distrust—the bruised side of Obama's beloved black community into which he said we all earn membership—that undermines the potential of all black leadership. We have all suffered and still suffer the effects of distrust. It is not incumbent on Obama, Michael says, to be the missing link to a cohesion and collective vision of change we have steadily lost over generations to co-optation, as Robert Smith calls it. Obama's reluctance to support us unreservedly is not individual, it's cultural. We are simply not very practiced in supporting each other unreservedly, as other groups are. "Jews don't just support each other, they make other people support them," Michael says, voicing a sentiment I've heard from plenty of other black people over the years. "Our leadership hasn't done the right things; it needs to create our own thing." Obama has at least done that for himself, created his own thing, because unlike so many of us, he learned how. "Obama's mother instilled in him individual drive, which was a good thing because he lived in racially isolated places like Indonesia. Because of that drive he didn't wait his turn in Chicago, he found his own way," Michael says. "The bottom line is that Obama is very focused. I admire that."

My cousin Jeffrion Aubry is a veteran elected official, a state assemblyman who has represented Brooklyn for the last 22 years. (I didn't know this until fairly recently. Jeff's grandparents were among the relatively few Aubrys who broke away from the motherland of New Orleans early on and, instead of heading west like the vast majority of our family, made their way north. I found him—or he found me—on Facebook.) Jeff agrees with Michael Anderson that Obama needed to go his own way to fully realize his ambitions. "Frankly, Obama kind of leaped on the scene, and that's a good thing," he says. "Are our traditional black structures good enough to produce a presidential candidate like an Obama? No." We simply aim too low. Jeff says that "we have been victims of our own skepticism," citing as evidence the still-quoted remark that Michelle Obama made, during the first campaign, about being proud of her country for the first time in her life. Idealism of any sort is understandably a hard sell for black folks, says Jeff, and in some ways always has been. (Barack has modeled a way out of that endless skepticism with his idealism and his confidence in that idealism, which he couldn't have possibly gotten from us—it had to be his own. For us, idealism has always been a necessary tonic to racism, but idealism about our country, starting with the notion that we belong, has always been a luxury.) "Black people are still on the ground fighting survival battles," says Jeff. "The height represented by Obama didn't make the ground swell and change—theoretically, maybe it never could or would." That Obama's idealism has fallen short doesn't change Jeff's view that Obama has led us in other, previously unimaginable ways. "The magnitude of his achievement, the symbolism, is great. You may be defeated and you may not achieve it, but it's possible. No goal is unachievable. That is his message." But, he adds, almost reflexively tempering his optimism, "We didn't die and go to heaven. We're still here in reality." Meaning that the symbolism, and the message, of Obama is wonderful and maybe inexhaustible, that it advances black folk in a spiritual sense. Advancements on the ground have been much harder to come by.

Jeff's father was an avid watcher of up-and-coming black leaders and was the first person who predicted to his son that Obama was "going all the way." The son thought he was crazy:

I said to him, "No way, Pop, this is America." The same America—the
South—that wouldn't hire my dad in the chemical industry even though he
had a Ph.D. We thought it was the greatest injustice in the world. [His father
wound up working in the post office, a good job at the time for thwarted

black men.] But there was something about Barack, something about his generation. Because of what my dad's generation went through, this one had a certain daring and style they had that was in how they carried themselves. For my dad, maybe you couldn't get jobs but that's one thing you could do, you could *carry* yourself.

Obama did that splendidly. But as his star as presidential candidate was rising, Jeff was in the middle of New York politics, which was rallying around its senator, Hillary Clinton. That, and his conviction that race always matters negatively, made him very skeptical of Obama's chances. "America was not going to choose a black man over a white woman," he says. But he confesses that "the nonpolitical side of me sided with Barack, the symbolism of what it meant." After the primary breakthroughs in '08, he was free to indulge that nonpolitical side in the new political landscape created by the possibility of Obama, which promised, among other things, the chance that black folks could have a real living hero in their midst, albeit one we did not produce in the usual way.

Exactly who and what we do have in our midst won't be sorted out for a long time. Roughly a generation ahead of Jeff is Bob Farrell, a former Freedom Rider and a Los Angeles city councilman in the 1980s. Bob was born in Natchez, Mississippi, and lived in New Orleans. He and my father worked closely together starting in the '70s. He's nearly eighty now. and is spritely, though a little stooped because of a bad back. But he's still very much in the fight, with more than a little revolutionary zeal left; like my father, he's retired but very busy on many fronts with the unfinished business of black justice. He is sitting in a tidy cubicle at the office of One Source Fiduciary Solutions, headed by B. J. Hawkins. One of Bob's gigs is advising her organization, which offers various financial administration services or, as Bob artfully puts it, "works to build intergenerational wealth amongst black families." The office is in deep South Central Los Angeles, in an industrial zone south of downtown and east of USC, next to a county probation office.

Bob is pretty much on the negative end of the Obama opinion spectrum, the doubting end, though he'd prefer not to be. As a former elected official and unabashed race man, he can't help measuring Obama by his actions. "He and Bush are interchangeable," he says, looking more than a little pained. "He's a superb maintainer of the status quo. You can make incremental changes, but look at what he's reinforced, the changes he's actually made—increased drone technology in warfare, the level of secrecy government." That last thing really gets Bob; it baffles him. "It's not just the privacy issue, it's the secretness," he says. "Not in my wildest dreams did I think that a cell phone would be an instrument of privacy invasion. I was once deemed a Negro agitator. If I tried to be that today, to challenge the social order, I could be picked up immediately and called a terrorist." He scowls. "Is this the same world I got into and tried to change, could see the landscape of? Now, I don't know what the landscape is. It's like a great cataract has come down over people's vision. I can't blame Obama for that, but we had high expectations that he would set stuff straight."

"Stuff" goes well beyond individual actions such as closing Guantanamo Bay or any other still-unfulfilled Obama campaign promise of '08. By "stuff," Bob means restoring people's faith in government as an instrument of good. He means turning attention back to the campaign for racial justice that is the political and spiritual foundation of many other campaigns, from corporate reform to justice for overheating Earth itself. For all this stuff, we need not merely an enactor-in-chief but a leader, a visionary—not Superman, but certainly someone with extraordinary resolve. Expecting Obama to be this someone is perhaps less fantastical than practical, because we need nothing less. The expectation also has a certain logic. The black leaders roll-called every February, during Black History Month, all had to make extraordinary things happen as a matter of course. They had to defy social strictures and call into question the legitimacy of the entire American narrative about freedom and democracy just to get such fundamentals as integrated toilets. Bob was hoping that as president and a presumptive black leader, Barack would at least be able to raise the visibility of black stuff, if not actually set it straight. Over the years, Obama has addressed race only when circumstances more or less demanded it—the Trayvon Martin moment, the rolling countrywide protests against police brutality, the Donald Sterling racist rant that got him banned from the NBA. (The public outrage over Sterling was so widespread and wide-ranging that Obama's response, in which he invoked not only race but the *s* word—slavery—didn't really stand out that time.)

Though disappointed, Bob doesn't personally blame Obama for his dearth of actions; while the president is a resonant symbol of our possibility, he's as resonant a symbol of our fear and our shortcomings. He reflects us but doesn't transcend us. Bob accepts this folk-hero status, though reluctantly. He'd prefer a Superman. But Obama is useful. "He reminds us of what we've learned about politics, that we have to apply pressure from below always," Bob says soberly. "We still have to register to vote because Obama won't save us, the system—flawed as it is—will save us. If we can get these things done for black people, everyone will benefit. Racial justice *is* social justice for all."

That's true, but if the system considered racial justice so critical, it would work very differently from how it's been working. This is the problem that Robert C. Smith describes and that Obama could not overcome: a political system that was designed with slavery and inequality in mind is going to resist change that makes it anything different, especially change proposed by a black person whose every ask is perceived as threatening the natural order of things. This is what black people mean when they say that Barack is a hero for trying to do anything at all; it's why white opponents call him a socialist when he is so clearly a gradualist, what some black people used to derisively call an "accommodationist." In the roll call of Black History Month heroes, Obama most closely resembles not Malcolm or Martin but Booker T. Washington, the pragmatic, decidedly unfiery race leader of the post-slavery era whose own compromises with white notions of black progress make him controversial to this day. But Booker T. got Tuskegee Institute (now Tuskegee University), which is still a symbol of the kind of black progress he strove to make. What has Obama gotten? What does he *want* to get?

While the more progressive black set decry accommodation—a more passive but less complicated idea than integration—most of the middle class now sees itself as having no choice. It hasn't had a choice for a long time. Accommodation, a fighting word from the '50s and '60s, is now just called getting over, or getting yours, or just plain succeeding, or even excelling. Doing your best. Doing what needs to be done to finesse the system and get you where you want to go, and if you can do it without hurting or stepping on anybody too hard, so much the better. The rise of the black middle class, and the faster rise of the incarcerated class, has made the original moral and political arguments against accommodation a luxury that nobody can seem to afford anymore. In fact, the longtime lack of an argument over which is the better course for Negroes to take, resistance or accommodation, and the nature of each—the lack of an argument over any crisis bigger than the latest insults by a Donald Sterling or Paula Deen—is more proof of just how far the notion of black leadership has fallen. Obama cannot pick it up alone.

Bob has an idea. He thinks we might be able to start rebuilding that notion with a truth and reconciliation committee that would bring to public attention the full extent of the injustices perpetrated against Native Americans and blacks during and after slavery, like the committee that South Africa formed after apartheid. "But of course that will never happen," he says, as if fearful of giving himself reason to hope. He's already begun imagining the next chapter of the presidency—maybe Hillary, he says. She would be better, a tougher compromiser at least, and maybe in that way a more effective negotiator for black folks. It's a little ironic to hear this from Bob, who in his own time in city hall was the idealist, the lingering energy behind black protest in the '80s who sought to infuse that protest into the system. For his efforts, he was tolerated but frozen out of the inner circle of Tom Bradley, Los Angeles's first and only black mayor, a political moderate and former cop whose election in 1973 was nonetheless hailed as a revolution, much as Obama's was hailed in 2008. Bradley ran for governor of California in 1980 and lost, despite being comfortably ahead in the polls throughout the campaign. The only thing the experts could figure had happened was that a substantial number of people who had said they would vote for Bradley got into the voting booth and changed their minds, or they hadn't been quite honest with pollsters all along. That closeted racial unease that couldn't be detected by any polls, especially in politically correct California, came to be known as the "Bradley effect." Obama supporters, myself included, feared his presidential bid would be sabotaged by the Bradley effect. It wasn't, but his victory fueled open attempts at sabotage by Tea Party members and

Republicans that started in earnest almost immediately afterward; maybe *that* will one day be known as the "Obama effect."

Bob says that Obama has given him hope in one way—he's proven that a white electorate will actually vote for a black person, curing him of a certain cynicism that he had carried for a long time. And he gives Obama credit for his ambition and his political acumen. "In retrospect, Bradley lost touch with that [black] electorate," says Bob. "Not Obama. But Obama just wanted to win. That's why he became president." He admits that what he admires in Obama also troubles him. "Was there no other vision? Other people believed he could be a change agent. It was an opportunity, and he took it. In the ultimate test of mettle in the U.S., the presidential contest, he won. The best the other black men like King could do was to influence policy, but in the biggest game in the world, he won—the first time out. *And* he won a Nobel."

Bob is suddenly caught up in his own spontaneous encomium of Obama, impressed in spite of considerable misgivings. I've seen it time and again: while Obama is tough for some of us to swallow, it's tougher still to re-nounce him completely, to leave him to the ruins of history rather than to any glory that he might deserve. We'll be damned if we're going to leave him. "That's another good thing—in terms of motivating us, he's absolutely magnificent," Bob says. "He's put truth in the term, 'You can grow up and become president.' And it wasn't his Harvard degree that got him there either; it was his people smarts. It's a classic American story, and he got the brass ring." Now he's looking a bit awed by the story, as if he's hearing it for the first time, and also as if he desperately wants that magnificence to infuse black leadership, to fill it a little, even though Bob is one of those people who avoids explicitly identifying Obama as "black leadership." The president hasn't really earned it, though Bob implies that it would be nice—magnificent, even—if he did at some point. It might still be possible, but Bob doesn't say that. He has seen too much in his life, been let down too much. He's taken stock of Obama and must move on.

As a coda to the conversation, he says ruefully, "I thought we'd have more time." I think I know what he means, but later I'm not sure. Does he mean that he assumed the '60s generation would have more time to complete the revolution? Is he casting the black body politic as a terminally ill patient running out of chances to be revived or running out of opportunities to get it right? I have a feeling that if I ask him to clarify, he won't remember the moment at all.

In talking with Bob, I discovered—or I was reminded again—that black people are a strange but logical combination of well-earned skepticism and hard-earned optimism. Both qualities are necessary to survive and have been since the days of slavery. Sometimes the two work in tandem, and sometimes they're pitted against each other, as fluctuating attitudes toward Obama have shown. David Dawson is a therapist who comes down on the side of eternal second chances; he believes in the kind of invention and reinvention that is quintessentially American, and very black American. He thinks Obama's genius has been inventing himself not simply as a black president but as a *black* president of American *inclusiveness*, which we really have never had a chance to be because blackness for so long has been the very definition of non-inclusiveness. In order to be inclusive, one must be another color. But in being black, Obama has changed that, shaken up the usual hierarchy implied by the presidential "we." That is utterly new. It is risky. For a black man to seize the moral authority of inclusiveness is, once you get past the massive historical irony of it, radical. Jesse Jackson argued for inclusion, kind of pled for it in the way his mentor, Martin Luther King, pled for it, with hallmark eloquence. But Obama acts as if inclusiveness is *his* to bestow, to distribute. When I mention Obama's lack of a black focus, David emphatically says that Obama is an all-inclusive president, meaning that he isn't ignoring us, only made inclusiveness his own thing, a black thing. He's redefined it. It's up to us to see it that way rather than sit around worrying about which of his actions qualify as black agenda–worthy and which don't. To David, this kind of vetting is the wrong approach. "He definitely had *us* in mind when he put together the health care law," he's fond of saying.

David is from Evanston, hard by Chicago. He is seventy-one, with a raspy voice and a deliberate way of talking. He favors jeans and baseball caps. A stroke that happened years ago has semiconfined him to a wheelchair. When he does stand and walk, it's with difficulty but with more than a little triumph. He reminds me at moments of a Mafia don, a benevolent one. David is unequivocally happy about Obama being in office. "In 2008 I was very proud of his achievement, the way he ran his campaign especially," he says. "He'll go down in history as changing the way we campaign. It's only one of several changes." To the criticism that Obama isn't focused enough on the needs of black folks, he says simply, "We'll see. The jury is still out."

Change for David means not just policy but methodology, and methodology is where he says Obama has broken ground, chiefly because he's had to. But he also says that Obama rises to the occasion on a regular basis, something he thinks the president doesn't get nearly enough credit for. "He's governing on the fly. He makes more right decisions than wrong ones," David insists. Like Brenda Jackson, he's irritated that Obama gets so little slack, particularly from black quarters:

By 2011, some people were discouraged, saying he hadn't done enough for us. I heard this conversation at a car wash that made me want to slap this black guy, who said, "He's done nothing for us." Truth is, the election of Obama heightened black expectations to an unrealistic point. As racist as Congress is, how can folks feel Obama has reached some kind of pinnacle or assume he doesn't deal with the resistance to him being a black man? This [he gestures to the television screen behind him, which is airing an afternoon news show featuring the latest Republican flap over Obamacare] is some 1940s *bullshit.* The man wants to govern, he wants to *help,* and despite the Republicans' resistance, the country is still moving forward. I truly believe that what's motivating the right wing is the fact that *that man* was able to come in and pass health care reform, and then have the Supreme Court uphold it.

David is glowering now, looking like a less benevolent Mafia don. "His legacy is assured if he doesn't do another damn thing. Clinton couldn't do health care reform, Ted Kennedy couldn't do it, and then this *nigger* comes along, gets in office—that was the first violation—and does it. It's much more monumental than people believe. It's changed America. He's writing *history.*" What I hear David saying is that black people are looking for change, when it's been staring us in the face all along. "We expect the wrong things from him, and he expects the wrong things from us," he adds. I agree with him, but I have to say that I don't really know what Obama expects from us as black people, his most loyal constituency; David doesn't say either. It's strange that as absolutely connected as we are to Obama, we are also ships in the night: we don't know him, and he doesn't know us. Neither side has felt the need to probe because from the start we've assumed a mutual kinship; as estranged as we might be from Obama economically or geographically or experientially, he is our brother. He gets us without us having to say too much. He is on the river.

Still, he is in some ways as unknown to us as he seems to be to white folks. He is opaque. The difference is that the opacity doesn't bother us because we're used to it. We live it ourselves. Habitually focused on survival, we don't see much use for self-examination for its own sake. We might expect from our leaders a black focus on certain issues, but we never expect, or even necessarily want, emotional transparency. Obama, who has mastered the art of public intimacy without revealing himself, is in this tradition. He is also augmenting the tradition by allowing himself to be vulnerable in ways we have not seen a black public figure be vulnerable before, and for such a sustained period of time.

Many people I talked to are greatly relieved that after six years, Obama isn't cracking or breaking down under the pressure of the office, that he isn't lashing out or otherwise showing any strain—remarkable, given his inexperience and the ferocity of the Opposition and the fact he isn't exactly insulated from the constant shit by a team of advisors and proxies, as Bush II was before him. Opaque is what he needs to be and what we prefer: not Teflon (that's a privilege black folks have never known) but tough, resilient. His resilience is setting a precedent for how a black leader of nonblack America can be, or can't be; week to week, with each new crisis, he is tinkering, adjusting, bearing the consequences of chaos and his own flawed decisions but always, so far, recuperating, which is something David greatly admires. It is mostly what he admires. Disasters and even embarrassment come and Obama keeps on going, sometimes quietly prevailing in the end or at least partially redeeming things initially pronounced failed or unfixable, like the health care reform rollout, or the deal involving Russia to purge chemical weapons from Syria, or negotiating nuclear de-escalation with Iran, or even the bad economy. Since Obama has been in office, David has often said to me, with forgivable smugness, "You watch. Obama is going to come out of this smelling like a rose."

I suppose if David were Obama's therapist, that's what he would tell him. David would build him up so that he could keep on being Obama—cool, compromising, contained, yet eager to be loved—instead of some cowed or incomplete version of himself. I always hope David is right. I always need cause for optimism. Looking at reality never makes me optimistic, especially in Obama's case. To love him, you have to believe in something else, something besides reality or the facts. You have to be looking in another direction completely. David is not a romantic, like me (to a degree), but he's a believer. He's not evangelical about Obama, but he's willing to spread the gospel to nonbelievers. "If you learn to accept what he has to offer—it happened for me," he says. Of black leadership, he says, "We've put Obama in black history, and he belongs there. Why not? He has gone where no one has gone before. I believe that whatever decision he makes is the best he can make at the time. He's careful, but he's not a sellout. He's too passionate for that." Ultimately, David is among those who say that Obama leads most by being himself. He demonstrates that black folks can hold sway with the power of self, that we do not have to justify our existence with informed opinions on affirmative action, mass incarceration, voter suppression, and all the issues that collectively loom so much larger than we do. These things are very important, but the truth is that we exist without them; we precede them.

Obama long ago gave himself permission to be himself. Even in the middle of his young-man angst, he knew exactly who he was. He was never undeclared. It's this self-assurance that rankles the Opposition, which needs to render him vague, unknown, and therefore dangerous. All the name-calling and put-downs are tacit acknowledgment of Obama's self-assurance (as any schoolyard bully knows), which gives him real power and informs his stance on affirmative action, abortion rights, immigration reform, and everything else. He can detach from all that and simply be. David believes it is this being, not any particular action or ideology, in which Obama excels, modeling something that could shift our whole trajectory as black folks, not just politically but in a deeper and more enduring way. "The man feels," David says. "He bleeds."

♥   Obama successfully being Obama is also what impresses Thomas Sayles, a vice president at USC and, like Obama, a graduate of Harvard Law School. Though he'd been aware of Obama for years, Sayles started closely following him after his speech at the Democratic convention in '04. He says that what Obama is doing—or more precisely, being—takes a certain courage. "He's not afraid to express the breadth of who he is," is the way he puts it. "I'm always impressed by the breadth of all the things he talks about. He thinks very broadly, partly because he's lived in so many places." In the popular Obama life narrative, that global experience is assumed to make his blackness irrelevant, smaller, nearly canceled out. Sayles rejects that. He says that Obama doesn't emphasize or downplay blackness or any other aspect of himself; everything has its influence, its place. That seems to be part of his equilibrium. People have sometimes accused Obama of "becoming" black in front of a black audience, as if blackness were exclusively about performance, something that tends to be true in politics. But I always see blackness in him, even when it's not obviously in play, because it's who he is, not how he acts (though it can be both things at once, as he says at one point in his memoir after considering various meanings of color and concluding that "blackness is what you *do*").

Sayles has heard Obama get "preacher-ish" in front of a black crowd—we all have—but, he says, that doesn't mean it isn't him, nor does it make him unique. "He drops his black very deliberately—not always, but at moments. But all black people do," he says. "We do it naturally, and he chooses to do it." (Yes, but don't we also choose how and when to be black or not, to codeswitch? Don't we all consciously choose how we're going to sound before we open our mouths to a particular audience, whether it's two people or two hundred? In this way, all black people are politicians, chameleonic and authentic at the same time. It's no contradiction in our minds and never has been. And we're damn good at it; we've had centuries of practice.)

Sayles says it's all part of Obama's sense of inclusiveness, which starts with embracing all the elements of his life experience. Far from appearing uncertain or self-conscious about being expansive *and* black, erudite *and* black, he seems proud of it. In fact, he reflects a sophistication you would expect of anyone in the educated middle class. Obama constantly reminds us of how the relatively young, black middle class is not unique or exempt but ordinary. He is just one among many in this group whom Sayles describes as "marrying a lot of things and fusing them to a unique style. Obama is the best of both traditions, being black and being intellectual. He's both, he's all that. *We're* all that."

He pulls at his tie in agitation. "Nothing pissed me off more than that first campaign question, 'Is he really black?' or 'Is he black enough?' I hate all those litmus tests."

He adds, as an afterthought, "If the question is, 'Does he care about black people,' that's a different question." He's right, but the reality is that we tend to collapse the questions, and the answers, too. For many of us, being black *means* caring about black people, it means doing for them. This is part of leadership. Identity and action are inseparable and insuperable. Certainly, we have to embrace our own blackness, which is part of the essential self, before we can lead or even hope to lead black people or lead anybody. The lack of that fundamental self-embrace is why Clarence Thomas is of no use to us. He won't name himself, claim himself; he sees blackness mostly as problematic, regressive, obstructive. To say he has provided no leadership or even empathy as a Supreme Court justice, the judicial equivalent of president, would be an understatement.

Obama is no Clarence Thomas, but neither is he Huey Newton, as many black people are fond of saying. That leaves an awful lot of terrain as to who or what he is exactly on the landscape of leadership; it leaves a lot to our imagination. That's a good thing. That's part of his function as a folk hero. But even with that leeway—actually, because of it—there persists an uneasiness about whether Obama panders too much to the conservative politics of black responsibility, which too often passes for leadership these days. Black responsibility stresses improving individual behavior as the best and most practical way to counter systemic racism, and its advocates go all the way back to Booker T. Washington. It's an idea that's never gone away, especially as the black middle class grew to historic proportions in the '70s and '80s. So it was galling but also fitting that comedian Bill Cosby, the pioneering black middle-class TV dad of the '80s, reignited the call for black responsibility with his now-infamous "pound cake" speech delivered in 2004 at an NAACP dinner marking the 50th anniversary of the *Brown v. Board of Education* Supreme Court ruling that struck down public school desegregation. Among the things Cosby said was that education was no good to us if we as black people were going to just throw it away, and that a black man jailed for stealing a piece of pound cake shouldn't have been stealing the pound cake in the first place.

Obama, though more balanced in his remarks and not nearly as strident as Cosby and some others, has taken a page from the black responsibility playbook on more than one occasion. Starting with what came to be known as his Father's Day speech in '08 at a church in Chicago, in which he admonished black dads to be more responsible and accountable—in essence, to be men—he has, when speaking to predominantly black audiences in a preacher-ish mode, repeatedly defaulted to this traditionally conservative view of racial improvement. The twenty-first-century version is that in order to succeed in opportunity-rich America, black folks would do well to turn off the television, read more books, be less consumeristic and more attentive parents.

Lots of black people I know fret that these relatively modest diatribes are Obama giving white folks what they want rather than giving us what we need. They fear he is consciously choosing to do one thing instead of the other. Sayles disagrees. He doesn't think white folks have anything to do with it, and besides, he says, Obama's sentiments are nothing new from black leadership; they reflect the sentiments of lots of black parents who were typically hard on their children because they knew that a racist, Jim Crow–limned society would be much more judgmental and far less forgiving of their children than they were. Encouragement in black circles can often look like something opposite; it was, and still is, a kind of real-world preparation that's always been almost a thing apart from our liberal electoral politics. Sayles thinks that to call Obama's remarks purely conservative or demeaning to black folks is to miss that point. "He panders less than other black politicians," he offers (which doesn't quite sound like an endorsement—more like, Obama is the least of all evils). "Talking about how to raise our kids is legitimate and necessary." But Sayles admits that legitimate in-house critiquing can look and sound wholly different when read as public policy, especially when articulated by a president assumed by many white folks to have a bead on black America. And however legitimate the point, it can sting whenever it resonates with conservatives who are all too eager to consign black dysfunction to individual behavior; the fact that Obama touches on systemic racism too always get lost in the media translation.

Here is the real problem: black people have always been wary of public discussions about black "culture" simply because we don't control the discussions. We seem to only react to them, going on talk shows to mitigate the damage that inevitably follows the public's response to things Bill Cosby says. In the meantime, beneath the culture-war debate, the very real crises of black people persist. "Remember the Moynihan report? We thought it was the most racist thing at the time, in the '60s," says Sayles. "But didn't all those predictions about black conditions worsening come true? What are we going to *do* about all those problems? In speaking to our issues and to our youth, Obama proves that he cares about us."

I'm sure he does care, but I'm more skeptical than Sayles seems to be about the way Obama has chosen to express his concern. (I'm thinking here about comedian/activist Dick Gregory's response to Obama's advice on one occasion to black parents in which he advised them, among other things, to help their kids with their homework. Gregory, raised in the depths of the St. Louis ghetto, said his mama couldn't read or write, that she was a domestic with a third-grade education who couldn't have helped anybody with homework if she'd wanted to. Yet she provided for the family on her own, and she was so conscious of her impoverished appearance that she didn't attend the very special event of his high school graduation for fear of embarrassing him. Gregory is clearly pained as he tells this story before an audience, his voice rising from a whisper to nearly a shout, and he ends up angrily dismissing Obama as "a punk who didn't suffer through *nothing*.") I think it proves that this is the one line of racial inquiry that Obama feels most comfortable pursuing in public, because responsibility is perhaps the one solution to the racial crisis blacks and whites can agree on, though to varying degrees and for very different reasons. It is a compromise, per Obama's style, though it's yet another compromise in which black folks benefit the least, which is usually another way of saying that we don't benefit at all. (While we may say, like Sayles, that Obama is raising legitimate issues, whites who are willing to believe in black pathology hear all this and get permission to do just that. It probably isn't Obama's intent, but that doesn't really matter—pathology, not empathy, is the big takeaway message. Surely, Obama the politician *and* the black man knows this?)

The critiquing is also the one way in which Obama talks at length directly to us, the occasion on which he freely counts himself in the "we" and "us" and the occasional "you all," pronouns that I have to say I find—against my will sometimes, and my better political judgment—thrilling. To feel like we are having a private conversation with our president, *our* president who has forged such history on our behalf, is almost exciting enough to forget everything except that fact. When he looks up at us from the podium and speaks, relaxing that slightly overdignified posture and smiling with a kind of sly anticipation, I am transported; I hardly hear the words. When he goes among young black kids and puts a hand on their shoulder and leans down with an eager, genuine fatherly interest (unlike Bill Cosby, who tends to wear dark glasses in public and stalk the stage, angry and inconsolable, a kind of Darth Vader of black responsibility), I swoon. The rest of the time, in front of other audiences, he will frequently talk in our direction with his eyes, his gestures, with his very choice to not talk to us at all. That choice feels deliberate. It feels intimate, part of a pact of silence that isn't optimal but that we've all signed on to, and it's why so many of us don't take him apart for his silence. It's why he's so forgiven.

♥   The problem is that we've expected nothing in return for our silence. We continually fail to forge leadership out of our own desires and needs, instead channeling those energies into propping up the individual standing before us who holds an exalted but tenuous position. The forgiveness works the same with passing. Generations ago, black people passed as white because other black people allowed it, allowed them to live a lie, because we understood too well what they were doing; we knew the deceit was more about survival, getting over, not self-loathing though certainly there was some of that in there too—how could there not be? And we harbored a certain empathy for their position: if we were light-skinned enough to fool white folks and be treated as one of them, we probably would do the same thing. Keeping a good job with false information isn't a moral issue, it's a practical one—getting over is always the goal to keep in mind, and we have learned already that, like war, getting over can be a dirty business. But if the individual is advantaged, then we all are. Looking the other way becomes worth it, the price of progress that's admittedly getting more and more costly. But progress we must have, or all is truly lost.

Sayles will admit that Obama as leader has not made the structural changes that black people need, changes that are the hardest kind for any president to make. That's a problem, he says. But that's not enough for him to condemn Obama, to give him up; God/Superman himself couldn't make those kinds of structural changes in America, not now. I press him about accountability—those changes are impossible to make, but shouldn't Obama at least *try*? Sayles dodges a bit. "We used to think that 'accountable' itself was a racist term. We have to be accountable to ourselves. Obama does what *he* thinks is right." I guess he's saying that the rest of us black folk should do the same. But leaving everyone to their own opinion doesn't automatically improve the big picture, just atomizes it. If we're all right, then nobody is wrong, including Obama. Bill Cosby is utterly committed to the rightness of what he says. Of course, Cosby is temperamentally a dictator, whereas Obama is a consensus-builder, and that could be his saving grace. "He's a politician, but he can take good ideas from bad people," says Sayles. "I actually think like that too. He's inclined to amalgamate, and that's not inherently bad." It's not, but amalgamation by itself is not a solution. And it's hardly new. Haven't we all been amalgamating for a long time, adjusting and readjusting our goals downward as the black/civil rights agenda has waned? Not to sound entirely cynical, but is seeing our leaders compromising at our expense really anything new either?

Obama actually has more integrity than most because he doesn't sell out a "black agenda"; he didn't start from there. He can be disappointing, infuriating, but he is technically not a deserter because he never pledged to stay put, and we never made him put anything in writing. I do believe that blacks are on his radar, and I believe that he keeps his options open so that he can perhaps pivot toward us when/if the time is right, whether he's president or not. His initiative My Brother's Keeper is clearly aimed at young black men, though it's meant to help Latinos, too. (One of my pet peeves of the Obama era is how we've grown to lump black and brown together in a kind of ghetto mono-experience, with mono-solutions.) Those publicity visuals—Obama posing with a group of beaming black youth clustered around the ultimate black mentor—speak to what the effort is really all about. The story of black struggle and empathy for that struggle, captured by the visuals, is powerful, more powerful for being a story that's been missing from national politics for years (and without a good story, you can't win). I cheered when I saw it. And I confess that I cheered for Obama doing it at all, for so consciously meeting our gaze, even though he debuted My Brother's Keeper three-quarters of the way through his time in office, when he had less and less to lose by doing such a thing.

Something else that bothers Sayles as much as the litmus tests of blackness is the notion that Obama is not just hard to read but cold and unmoved (another way he fails the black litmus test, which presupposes that black people are fundamentally all emotion, no circumspection). The accusation that underneath the public empathy and dazzling smile is a cold, calculating fish has come mainly from the right—when it isn't busy accusing Obama of being too soft or squishily liberal. For black people, the concern about Obama's true character is more complicated and is related to class and the nature of the talented tenth. We all applaud his education and his savvy, and we all admire his cool. But does his intellect put him out of touch with the black masses? Can he relate? Sayles dismisses the idea of a cultural gap as demonstrably false. "Are you kidding? Look at him with his daughters, with his family, with crowds," he says impatiently. "He's presidential but he's cool—not cold—he's both things. Like I said, he's all that." As David Dawson said, he bleeds.

In 2006, twenty-nine-year-old Jordan Vaughn, a political consultant, was not at all convinced that Obama, or anybody black, was going to be president. He saw the prospect of a black president more or less as I saw it when I was nine. Jordan was a big fan of Tennessee Congressman Harold Ford, Jr., a black man with a long family history of politics—kind of the black answer to the Gores—whose unapologetic appeal to white moderates and even conservatives in his Senate race in '06 presaged Obama's one-America approach. Jordan thought Ford would rise high, perhaps not as high as the White House, but high. "I thought he was going to be everything Obama turned out to be," he says. When he met Obama at a dinner shortly after he won his U.S. Senate seat, Jordan felt the first stirrings of a conversion. "I thought, wow, this guy's audacious. He's for real," he recalls. Like a lot of other black people, especially those in politics, Jordan held on to his skepticism until the first debate in the primary between Obama and Hillary Clinton. After that, the conversion was on. "After the primary, we started coalescing around him, our whole generation—I thought, he *is* for real," Jordan says. "He was kind of a mania that swept the country. You have to understand, I grew up in Bush years. The next thing I knew I was totally inspired, doing stuff for Obama, standing in line in Harlem to vote in a line that was around the block. It was a 180-degree turnaround, a dream, a surreal change of fortune. How could you *not* follow?"

Jordan has sobered up, though he hasn't lost the emotional connection to Obama (first loves are like that). He empathizes with Obama running headlong into the maw of Washington, its teeth sharpened by the suddenly increased racial acrimony of the right. Jordan feels bad about that. He says that Obama "probably never in his wildest dreams imagined that things would be as awful and as wonderful as they've been. All these jabs at his character probably hurt him the most. He probably sits down in a room regularly and thinks, wtf? In the Bush years, when bad shit happened, blame went to Bush or Cheney or Rumsfeld, but now it's always *Barack's* fault: It's like there's nobody *but* him." It's been the fate of a folk hero who bears the weight of symbolism both good and bad, and symbolism on both sides of the color line. "With the gridlock in Congress, it's such a difficult time now," Jordan says. "He was such a novice that he didn't know how to wield his capital at first. Now I know he wishes he had those years back. He'd know exactly what to do and how to do it. But he always had humanity and decency on his side."

Humanity and decency. Jordan believes that in 2012, people rallied again to Obama's side after Mitt Romney impugned most of us as the 47 percent of Americans whose poverty and indolence were dragging down the other, more prosperous half; the swipe reminded us that Obama was likely on the right side of the line, that maybe he *was* trying to do the best he could for everyone. But that moment of common indignation was fleeting. "Americans don't see each other as a group—it's always me, me, me,'" says Jordan. The most frustrating thing for him is that Obama hasn't been able to break the fever grip that individualism has had lately on the American political imagination. The tenets of individualism and personal freedom are supposed to conflict with the group terrorism visited on black people by slavery and a hundred-plus years of Jim Crow, but things haven't worked out that way. In the American individualist imagination warped (as so much has been warped) by race, the twain almost never meet, which is why Obama elicits such suspicion from the flag-waving set; the mere fact that he's black is probable cause to seem him in the negative, to label him a socialist and so forth. Obama does his leadership no favors by trying to ignore or soft-focus this racial/ideological paranoia. Yet he also has no choice *but* to ignore it. That's to our detriment.

"If Barack says, 'The loss of the Voting Rights Act is bad for America,' I say, 'No, no, no, it's not bad for America—it's bad for *us*, for black people,'" Jordan says. "But he can't say that, at any given moment, because he has to stay flexible, stay *open*. . . ." He seems at a loss, not so much with Obama but with himself for perhaps knowing too much, for knowing the answers before even posing the question or the hypothetical. Jordan understands better than most the political realities at work, but that doesn't make him feel any better about things or any more empowered. He and Obama are in a similarly uncomfortable place. His only satisfaction, if that's the word, is that they're in that place together. "Barack *knows*"—he knows what's right, and what's standing in the way of right—"but the sad thing is he still can't address black issues," Jordan says. "White folks don't mind equality but they don't want us to get ahead. Ever. We are eighteen generations into the U.S., but we are enslaved. It's a huge stain on the American ideal, on the dream, on everything. The slave trade led to our wealth that we have now, which we never discuss. That's not true in other countries." Despite our individualist culture of personal confession and exposure, Jordan says we really don't care for the truth. That's infected our national well-being. "You don't see any open race discussions here. Not any honest discussions. That's the difference." (This is what Attorney General Eric Holder said back in 2009 when he called America a "nation of cowards" for being so unwilling to look its own legacy of racism in the face; the Opposition never forgave him for that.) I ask Jordan how other people he knows feel about Obama. "My white friends love him, he's still a celebrity. He's still Barack," he says, a little sarcastically. As for himself, "As a young black man professional, Obama helps my brand," he says after some thought. "But what about the young black guy in the street? Does he help *his* brand? Is there the same identification, the same benefit? Not so much."

Jordan is most worked up talking about Obama's forays into the politics of black respectability, which are really about those young black guys on the street. "Why does he criticize us when he does address us? Does he *really* look down on certain folk?" he says heatedly. "Why is segregation still an issue? Why are home prices 50 percent less in black neighborhoods? The juxtaposition between black and white in a city like Baltimore is scary. How can you drive through there and tell me things have changed?"

Jordan is talking not about Obama now but about something bigger, something impersonal but also entirely personal, a hardened set of circumstances that paralyzes the president as much as it paralyzes and diminishes all black people in some way. "I think that there comes a point where people feel they gave you enough liberation," he says. "There is a blatant issue with black equity. But it's not trendy to save the black community. Immigration is trendy, gay rights is trendy. There are no black programs, nothing to close the achievement gap. You don't have organizations that are willing to give dollars to the cause, and black organizations just don't have the capacity." Those organizations include Obama's own campaigns for president—technically a cause for one man, but they were fueled by the energy and belief of many. The campaigns didn't benefit any larger black cause (or any cause, for that matter, except electing Obama). Yet Jordan remains impressed by the sheer *possibilities* of such energy and the fact that Obama marshaled it so successfully. "Campaigns are billion-dollar startups, and this black man pulled it off," he says, sounding admiring again. "He's the first to do this. From Angelina Jolie and Brad Pitt to Bill Gates, he pulled it off. There's something about *him* that was new, hip, trendy, and everybody wanted to be part of it." Part of *him*, yes. But not part of us.

♥ One persistent criticism of Obama's leadership has been that he doesn't stand on fixed principle, that he gives away too much too soon. Tom Sayles sees that as evidence of something quite positive: Obama's eagerness to do, to take action. He'd much rather do something than nothing, "so he compromises and comes close to his original idea," is the way Sayles explains it. "Health care is a good example, which by the way he did at great risk. I would have waited until the second term, but as it turns out, that would have been impossible." (Other notable and less successful compromises—capitulations, really—include extending the Bush-era tax cuts in 2010 and raising the income level for a newly proposed income tax on the wealthy from $250,000 to $400,000 in 2013.) The great risk and political capital spent on that modest reform said to me right away that the cost of accomplishing anything of size targeted at black people was off the charts completely. Contrary to what many people were hoping, Obama addressing matters of black justice is looking closer and closer to impossible, or unactionable, as his time winds down. Sayles doesn't exactly disagree. He thinks it's not because Obama doesn't believe in action but because those problems are of a scale and depth that make the solutions to them hard to formulate and effect. In other words, the many crises in black make health care reform, even the single-payer reform that we didn't get, look contained. Sayles has another theory. "It's easier to create social equality than it is to create upward mobility, which is why Obama responds to issues of gay rights, women's rights, immigrant rights, but finds it much harder to respond effectively to the complicated nature of poverty and income inequality"—in a race-averse age, "income equality" is a term that now fully encompasses the Negro problem. "It's easier to define what's right than to do what's right." It's what I've said more than once: Obama is expert at observing the problem as if he were observing a species of plant, characterizing it, analyzing its roots. Doing something about it is another issue.

Rather than wring my hands over what he hasn't done or can't do, Sayles urges me to look at what Obama has accomplished and to see the glass as half-full—and half-full would actually be tremendous. Black people haven't experienced that level of satisfaction or political attention in a while, perhaps ever. "You gotta be able to read what he does. He pushes small businesses, which is us," Sayles tells me. "At the heart of all mobility problems is education, and he pushes school reform and college access." Yes, but I wonder about Obama's support of specific things such as charter schools us and so-called teacher accountability, which erode the whole social contract of public education that black people believed in so deeply for so long as *the* great equalizer, staked almost 100 percent of their progress on it—where is the black in that? Every president believes in school reform, which since the 1990s has practically become synonymous with privatizing of some sort. On this issue Obama has definitely sided with the middle class, including much of the black middle class, which now sees school more as a consumer product than as an instrument of justice—quality by any means necessary, even if we continue to resegregate or close down struggling campuses fifty at a time, as happened in Obama's base, Chicago. Of course, Obama didn't start the trend against public education, but he's done nothing to stop it. Andrew Sullivan said in 2007 that Obama was going to have to be as radical as the moment that got him elected. No one needed radical more than black folk. And no one is as unlikely to get it.

Despite that, despite everything, Brenda Jackson is a believer. She believes all the Obama-hating (which to her includes the legitimate Obama critiquing) is just a distraction from the real beast of inequality and bigotry, which victimizes Obama as well as the 99 percent. It speaks again to the folk-hero paradox of Obama heading the system and being done in by it at the same time. "As long as what he's doing is kicking down to me, I'm fine. He's doing an awesome job," Brenda says firmly. She has utter confidence in her views, like David Dawson, which I find comforting. We are sitting in Dulan's; it's quiet and largely empty in the post-lunch, pre-dinner hour. Brenda has brought with her a printout from the progressive website pleasecutthecrap.com of the 200-plus things Obama has done since taking office in 2008—proof of what people refuse to admit, that he's indeed *done* things. Brenda is irate about this notion of do-nothingness, because it suggests a stereotype of some lazy or undiscriminating nigger, and Obama is so not that. Dennis Tyler, the professor at Fordham University, felt some of that indignation when a friend of his mother's who had listened to his reservations about the president implored him not to "give up on Obama." He assured her he wouldn't, not yet. "It's a different generation—she has more empathy with him," he says. "The idea that they would have a black president was unfathomable to them. Also, it was coming from the vein of, folks haven't done a very good job of noting all that he *has* done." That vein taps into a bigger picture—a long narrative of black incompetence and can't-do-ism that has long overwhelmed any counter-narrative of success, Black History Month notwithstanding. Building that counter-narrative is nothing less than a battle, which Tyler and others understand.

Brenda says that Obama also prevents bad things from happening, a more subtle form of doing that is no less important (Tom Sayles would agree), but that gets no recognition at all. High on the list is the passage of the American Recovery and Reinvestment Act, which effectively kept the Great Recession from free-falling into another Great Depression during Obama's first years in office. Also on the list—though in no particular order—is $15 billion allocated to stimulate small-business lending, establishment of a $10.10 minimum wage for employees of federal contractors, and the Credit Card Accountability, Responsibility, and Disclosure Act, known as the Credit CARD Act.

The sheer number and steady pace of these accomplishments are what impress Brenda. She insists that, overall, Obama "puts some stops to what big money is doing," not as many stops as people have wanted, and not exactly splashy or destined for history books. But Brenda refuses to get on what she calls the "Obama ain't shit" train. She recalls angrily some of what she heard during the first campaign, when she was on the streets selling

Obama-wear, in the midst of all the flowering of hope and change: "I went to all the barber shops and beauty salons selling my shirts, and some people said, 'Why should I vote for a black man; what's he gonna do for me?'" (The implicit question being, what *can* he do for me? I get Brenda's indignation, but what sounds like an insult may also be recognition of our own limitations in fixing a system designed to work against us.) Brenda continues, "I get angry at blacks who can't support their own people. That's why I tend not to talk politics with black folks; we can't see our own impediments. We don't think well of ourselves." And this means that we can't possibly think well of Obama. Perhaps we'll support him, buy a T-shirt or cast a vote. But won't trust him because we can't. As a people, we have few good models of that trust. Brenda doesn't think that's a good excuse. "We have to have faith in him to do things in his own time, in his own right; otherwise we oppress him too," she says. "We become oppressors of a different nature."

I hear in Brenda's comments the enduring tension between two views of black leadership vis-à-vis Obama—the laissez-faire view that if we black folks love him and let him do his own thing, it will benefit all of us, and the view that we must apply pressure from the bottom like any other constituency, and "make him do it," as FDR once said (and, by no coincidence, Obama has said too). It's the leader enacting the will of the people. This is what Najee Ali said. But the truth is that in the absence of a clearly articulated collective ask, black folks really do have to rely on Obama's individual vision, which continually shifts. It's been a precarious ride. No wonder Brenda chooses to appreciate what Obama does and to more or less ignore what he doesn't do; no wonder she decides to see the glass as more than half full. That might be the only way to feel triumphant, to feel something commensurate with the great, inimitable phenomenon of Obama himself.

Brenda is nominally middle-class, but she's an unabashed critic of the American project. Like Bob Farrell, she has lots of revolutionary zeal that never got absorbed or co-opted. (Her uncle was the civil rights photographer Ernest Withers.) I know a lot of middle-class people like this. "I feel about Obama like I feel about Angela Davis and Bayard Rustin: he's working within a framework that none of us recognize and is doing a good job at it," says

Brenda. "He's not a revolutionary; he's the president. His job is different." She's right; the framework that Obama is working in isn't something we recognize or even see. Perhaps the most heated and consistent argument I've heard about Obama and leadership concerns his fundamental job description—what it is, how he fills it, how we even compare his job to any other. Even the most casual exchange about Obama tends to end up as some version of this argument. Mostly, it's a friendly argument; sometimes it's not. It's never resolved. I was at a friend's house one evening with a small group of other friends and family that included my older brother, a writer and musician, and his good friend, a veteran music producer. Toward the end of the evening, Obama came up in general conversation, and suddenly, my brother and his friend were having that argument about Obama's professional and historical obligations to black people. What are those obligations? How much attention does he owe us? What is reasonable to expect? My brother thought that Obama should honor the race-conscious tradition of black leaders who came before him; his friend said that simply wasn't workable. Their views diverged with spiraling intensity and would have spiraled infinitely if the friend, exasperated and ready to call it an evening, hadn't shouted over my brother with a charged finality: "Man, he can't *do* that! That's like expecting a bulldozer to be a forklift operator, and Obama's not a *forklift operator!*" That resolved the particular conversation but not the tension between who Obama should be to us and who he actually is. That tension will be with us a long time.

Brandon Brooks has a prediction. "The day Barack stops being a black president is the day he'll start being a black president," he says. "That's when his legacy as a black man will begin. He'll go out and be the possible person he was before the election. He might join the front lines with Jesse and Al. Or maybe his kids will be that new generation of young leaders. I see a lot of Adam Clayton Powell in Barack, but I see him doing things to make sure he isn't just left with Harlem." After his time in Washington, Obama will be free to be black, and free not to be black. What Brandon doesn't address is the question of which state will be more liberating. He implies that a serious legacy, whatever it is, must necessarily be broader than being black—"beyond Harlem," as he puts it. That's always the caveat, the out we give ourselves, the flight enacted in our mind's eye. We never seem to be enough for ourselves, and even the more ardent latter-day revolutionaries agree with that. No one ever says Simon Wiesenthal was overly focused on bringing Nazi war criminals to justice; that endeavor was plenty big enough, more than resonant. But for the last fifty years, nothing we've done for ourselves has been big enough.

Dick Gregory lamented in his 1964 autobiography, *Nigger*, that helping black people always carries a stigma, and carried it even in the '60s, at the apex of the civil rights movement, when racial justice was as urgent and as trendy as it ever got. What bothered Gregory was not the stigma the spirit of the Movement carried among whites—that was a given—but the stigma among blacks. In Greenwood, Mississippi, he was taken aback when black locals asked him if he had come south not to march for voting rights (which he did, at considerable personal and physical cost) but for the publicity. "And it dawned on me that any time you help a Negro in America, even the Negroes will question your intentions," he wrote. "I could have quit show business and joined the Peace Corps and gone to Vietnam and no one, white or black, would have questioned why I did it. But to help Negroes . . . I was just beginning to realize what a long, hard row it would be."

It still is. The hard bottom line is that Obama can't help black people without diminishing himself in the eyes of the public. That has become a standard political calculus, voiced over and over by just about everyone I talked to, though they did not use words like "diminish." They stuck to the politics and process in a way that sounded not racial but eminently logical, almost neutral: he's the president of all, not just of us, and therefore he can't say or do certain things. It sounds very reasonable. But underneath it courses the still-awful truth of black exclusion and marginality that even a self-possessed black president with impeccable grammar, a peerless intellect, and a more than legitimate claim to inclusiveness can't erase. The truth is that instead of leading black folk, Obama is trying not to be consumed by us. His presidency has proven that you can't do both things at the same time. You have to choose. However sympathetically Obama glances in our direction and however much it thrills us, we feel the weight of that choice every day. And we bear it largely in silence, as we've always done.

4 Who Is This Guy?

Who is Obama? We don't really know. Who are his friends, who can
vouch for him? He's like the spook who sat by the other side of the door.
Nobody connected to him can really illuminate his character.
—*Cheka Abubakari*

Obama is inspiring, intelligent, charismatic. But he's not transformational.
He's not a freedom fighter. He's just trying to make this place
better for everybody. —*Cara Taylor*

One of the most memorable things about the first Obama campaign, in
2008, was the growing swell of recognition among all his supporters, black
and otherwise, that we were vying for the same person. This was new. Almost never do presidential candidates strike black people the way they strike
everybody else. This was true of Bill Clinton, a Southerner who staked out
his singular appeal to black folks in 1992 when he campaigned on Arsenio
Hall's talk show. He was a rarity. Though pundits mused about the populist
charms of Reagan and even Bush II, many black people saw those presidents'
overtures—or saw through them—as so much white-man tricknology.

There have always been perceptional gaps. But with Obama, good feelings
on both sides of the color line had a real moment of convergence. Maybe
we all didn't feel exactly the same way about Obama—blacks loved him for
his blackness, whites loved him for transcending it. But the core excitement
about the victory we were helping to put into place, primary by primary and

poll by poll, was roughly equal. Obama needed all of us to make it, and we answered the call. His color made him hugely symbolic from the start, but he was also one of all of us, or how we imagined our best selves: dynamic, attentive, imaginative but level-headed. He was an extension of us, a brother or an ideal neighbor or a smart friend who was also heartily sick of Bush and had raised his hand to volunteer to do something about it—because, you know, he's that kind of guy—and we all agreed. We knew him as he didn't quite fully know himself or his purpose yet; we the Obama dreamers had an inside track on this president-to-be. For this and other reasons, black and white and Latino and Asian lifted him up in a single motion and with the same sweeping expectations, and the synchronicity felt almost effortless and empowering in a way electoral politics had never felt in my lifetime. I first voted for president in 1980, when I was eighteen, and after thirty-eight years in the wilderness of Reaganism and neo-Reaganism, Obama was a sharp upward trajectory breaking the surface of murky waters with a light I had never glimpsed, or even knew existed; he was quite literally dazzling.

The appearance of that light assured me that something new was at work in this 2008 election that felt not like more tricknology but like a kind of deliverance. Obama was not a savior, but he could be a facilitator, a co-conspirator in the various dreams of change that he sanctioned and that Obama dreamers readily believed in. His diverse supporters had not achieved the unity he was singing about. But the fact that we were all coalescing around a man who truly seemed to understand *our* need to be understood felt breakthrough. It felt like enough.

But once Obama became president and started doing things (or not doing things), the racial divisions and perceptional gaps swiftly returned, and with them a stubborn mystery (no more mystique) about who he really is. The questions and grumbles ranged from practical to existential. Was he a conservative who had posed as a liberal, a centrist who had made noises like a progressive, a successful black man most at home with the white power structure enshrined in Wall Street, a Zelig-like character who was whatever and whoever he needed to be in order to accomplish his own agenda, which was unknown to everyone else? (And underneath it all ran the paranoid, sarcastic question of the Tea Party/white right: is he even an

American?) The unifying good feeling about Obama the man that had fueled the campaign was replaced by a creeping wariness about Obama the president, and we've heard little about the man since. Over the years, the media has tended to describe him not as a man first but as a set of attributes or poles. Opponents have more or less made him the devil, intrinsically flawed and totally irredeemable. The disillusioned, mostly white left sees him as a placeholder for empire, what health activist Gary Null called the "perfect messenger" of corporate interests.

Black Obama supporters have their own take. They are largely satisfied about who he is, because they judge him not primarily through the lens of political expectations but through the lens of black respectability and representation. As far as most of us are concerned, Obama is an upstanding young(ish) black man with an impeccable education, solid career, family values, church membership, and a discernible black consciousness. He more than passed muster long ago; there's nothing else he has to prove, or to be.

But lost in both the loyalty to and leeriness about Obama—or deliberately ignored, I think—is any real curiosity about Obama himself, not as a black folk hero or icon or a failed political savior but as a person. The man endlessly photographed and written about is almost never examined as a complicated individual whose persona says as much about where we've come as a nation as Kennedy's did in his time. Certainly, times have changed. Kennedy, the man and the folk hero, was forged in the good tension between his dynastic past and his vision for a different American future, a tension that said much about the nation in the early '60s. Whether we support Obama or not, few of us see him beyond the bright but rigid boundaries of the symbolism that he brought into office; he does not stray far beyond them. It's the clearest evidence yet that we as a country have been too warped by our history with race and racism, both as victims and as perpetrators, to really evaluate a black public figure on the basis of character alone. By "character" I don't mean having skeletons in the closet, or not—the political definition of character. I mean character defined by more affirmative, intimate things such as the kind of books Obama reads, what he dreamt about as a child, what his excesses and weaknesses are, and how all of it makes for a man whom we admire anyway, or at least one whose narrative speaks compellingly to our own life and times. To not explore these things is to deny Obama his real place in history because it denies him his full humanity—which, of course, we've denied to black people forever.

Not that black supporters see Obama as less than human or ignore his gifts; quite the contrary. Our affection and loyalty are real. But we tend not to analyze him too deeply. For one thing, it feels politically unnecessary—white folks will take him apart, and they certainly have. Another reason is that we simply are not in the habit. For us, it's always been less important to measure our inner lives, and those of our leaders, than to keep an eye on what the world is doing to us or saying about us; such vigilance is how we've survived in a country that's been mostly hostile to our well-being, to our being here at all. Yet in the moments when I do shake off the vigilance and think of Obama only *as Obama,* minus any political or historical context, it feels illegitimate somehow, as if I were breaking some law of physics or aiding the enemy. Character scrutiny also feels reductionist (as opposed to the uncritical scrutiny of a love object by fans, such as Marilyn's scrutiny of Obama, which makes us both happy and hurts nobody).

I encountered similar reticence in other black people. When I asked about their purely personal opinion of Obama, many expressed puzzlement, even distaste—what did it matter what they thought? To contemplate Obama as a *person* would be like zeroing in on a pixilated photo, which on closer inspection only disintegrates, dissolves, and why do that? Leave Obama be, they seemed to be saying, keep the picture big, defined. Obama detractors didn't care much for the question either, because to them the answer was self-evident—his actions (launching drone strikes, amping up the security state, maintaining Guantanamo, etc.) tell them everything about the man that they need to know. At both ends of the spectrum, there's been an unlikely consensus that none of us need any more information on who Obama *is.* We all know enough to suit our purpose.

The irony is that Obama has pretty much already told us everything about himself, at least the things that matter. *Dreams from My Father* actually put to rest things that we're still arguing about now—how black he is or isn't, and where his racial sympathies lie. In the book, in the deliberate, detailed style that's become familiar, he describes his awakening to blackness from virtually every possible angle; he raises the big questions, probes his own motives for feeling this way or that. He is blunt and unequivocal. Though he seeks to refine the meaning, he never waffles about his blackness and how it defines him, separating him at points from his own family; he doesn't soft-pedal race or try to pass as white (he couldn't anyway, biracial-ness notwithstanding. He himself once said that when he walks down the street, people don't see a half-white man, they see a black man). Throughout the book, Obama observes with vested fascination how race works, initially in his own household in Hawaii, and then in Indonesia, in California, at Harvard, on the streets of Chicago, in Africa. The experiences in each place all reinforce his early recognition that being black is a special condition with a special history to which attention must be paid; to do otherwise imperils us all, not the least himself.

So the race question, rather than being a source of confusion, was a light that guided Obama to his authentic self and clarified his ambitions. In Edward McClellan's *Young Mr. Obama*, he says in a Hyde Park interview shortly after the publication of *Dreams*, speaking about the post-Africa period, "I came home to Chicago. I began to see my identity and my individual struggles were one with the struggles that folks face in Chicago. My identity problems began to mesh once I started working on behalf of something larger than myself. Through this work I could be angry about the plight of African Americans without being angry at all white folks." It's these kinds of connections that interest Obama; he's more comfortable examining the nature of race problems, more at home with pondering rhetorical questions than advancing any particular solutions. He is a philosopher at heart, as this book makes clear.

Not that philosophy isn't provocative. Obama's unsparing analyses of the troubled state of the race in *Dreams* should be disconcerting to us, even a little dangerous; though often brilliant and on point, they lack any prescriptions for progress, and prescriptions are what we've been trained to expect from someone in Obama's position. Solutions, even unworkable solutions, have always been our north star. James Baldwin, another philosopher, was also an unsparing analyst of the race problem; in the '6os he was our designated messenger and conscience at large, who frequently shocked both black and white folks with his intimate but ominous visions of America. (They were ominous *because* they were intimate—it couldn't be otherwise.) But Baldwin, like Martin Luther King, had a remedy—love—about which he was totally serious. Obama has touted the same remedy, in a fashion, assuming that red and blue states melding into purple and members of Congress reaching across the aisle are a form of love. But is he serious in the same way Baldwin was, or was he just sloganeering? Did he hold that true cause of love and then lose it, put it away as impractical? All of which further stokes the question, who is he?

One question I sensed black people had but held on to was how much being black has messed with Obama's mind and his own notion of himself. As Baldwin surely would have said, for any black American, especially a black man, being messed with is just a matter of how much ("To be black and an American," he once said, "is to be in a constant state of rage"). Part of what drew blacks and whites together in the single hopeful vision of Obama in '08 was the possibility that he had not been damaged by his black American experience, that he had emerged from the hole *he* was born into relatively unscathed by white supremacy, with his confidence and self-esteem intact. That in itself would be miraculous, and worth voting for. But it wound up being not very relevant, because we were all reminded very soon after the election that racism is imposed from without, and no matter how unscathed and confident Obama is, if the Tea Party sees him as a nigger, which by definition is an insentient being, then he is. He is not a person, to say nothing of his own person. As such, he can't project himself and his feelings about his country onto the national psyche the way Kennedy did because he isn't allowed to; love depends on a certain reciprocity, an equality of feeling. Obama has the love of black folks, but he's always needed more than that to make the presidential relationship work. Black people knew that. We have watched him try to make that bigger relationship happen over and over, watched him compromise and explain in depth and give stirring speeches at critical moments, and we privately shook our heads. If Obama truly didn't know that love and acceptance wasn't forthcoming, if he was *that* confident, he might have been better off, certainly as a black president, if in his life he had been a bit *more* scathed by white supremacy. The ideals that he held so close and that depended on a certain naiveté that most of us lost early in our lives would have had a better chance of being realized if he had bled more. Yes, many black folks agreed, those ideals needed some scars.

Of course we all want to be recognized for our individual humanness, for our feelings and the breadth of our ideals—that would be true justice. But neither can we fall for the deracinating myth of individuality. In the context of conservative ideology, a black person's declaration that "I am me and only me" is generally a disavowal of blackness and of its history of struggle. It's a fine line between individuality and racial belonging that Barack negotiates well in *Dreams*. Far from the multicultural-friendly, I'm-just-me manifesto I expected, it is instead Obama's frank and focused account of his life as a black American, not as a half-black man or someone unaware of or indifferent to race until some big "aha" moment sets him straight. Barack knows quite early what and who he is and how people perceive him; his white family and the exotic locales where he comes of age are but various settings in what is consistently a black man's story. Being black is what politicized him, what helped him put his native country into proper perspective, and it's also what framed his vision of a good and possible and redeemed America.

His vision of black America, though, is not terribly hopeful. There he sees a long legacy of self-loathing that troubles but also intrigues him. It's a legacy many black folks prefer not to articulate—even to each other—because it seems so damning, and because it remains so unresolved. But Obama recognizes it as an important dynamic that exists not in isolation but as a consequence of a history involving all of us, black and white. From *Dreams*, here's a passing but profound observation on the epithet "nigger," whose meaning and appropriate usage remain a flash point of controversy:

> Often the word *nigger* replaced *black* in such remarks, a word I'd once like to think was spoken in jest, with a knowing irony, the inside joke that marked our resilience as a people. Until the first time I heard a young mother use it on her child to tell him he wasn't worth shit, or watched teenage boys use it to draw quick blood in a round of verbal sparring. The transformation of the word's original meaning was never complete; like the other defenses we erected against possible hurt, this one, too, involved striking at ourselves first.

Obama is talking not as an observer but as part of all these scenarios, as one of the black "we" who suffer, among other things, the fallout of our displaced attachment to the word *nigger*. But Obama is not trying to mine black pathology to condemn or titillate; he is genuinely interested in black folks and what makes them tick, what breaks their hearts, because he's deeply interested in himself: as he understands black people's significance, he understands his own. It's a symbiosis I rarely see in black memoir, especially in this quest for self-knowledge that's much more Socratic than sociological. (And yet later—sigh—he taps the pathology less empathetically in his Father's Day speech by admonishing blacks for not taking care of business, for being indifferent to their deficiencies, and so on. He does talk about larger social forces at work, true. But where is the exhaustive analysis and compassion of *Dreams*, that expert negotiation between self-love and black self-love without selling out either, something that could set a true example of change? Is that simply too subtle for politics, especially presidential politics? Does Obama abandon that subtlety with any regret? One more thing we don't know about him.) More evidence of this interest is his connection with Frank, his white grandfather's close black friend who speaks to young Barack in a very different and more intimate way than he's ever spoken to his grandfather. Frank tells Barack that because of the history of racism, the relationship between black and white is inherently unequal, even in a one-on-one friendship. There is simply no way around it. "He *can't* know me, not the way I know him," Frank says of Barack's white grandfather. "That's why he can come over here and drink my whiskey and fall asleep in that chair, sleep like a baby. That's something I can never do in his house. *Never.* I have to be vigilant for my own survival."

He goes on to say that he doesn't blame Barack's grandmother for being wary of black men (which Obama cited later in his Jeremiah Wright "race" speech), because black men have a good reason to hate. Grandpa may be troubled by her wariness, but he understands it, too. This is the point at which young Barack says he feels "utterly alone," within his family and within society; there's a real grief in the discovery that everyone is pretty much powerless to do anything about the entrenched realities of race and racism. It's a long way from candidate Obama's there-is-only-one-America rallying cry, or maybe the impetus for it. The point is that Obama grew up being entirely aware of who he is, where he fit on the color continuum, what he was likely to be in for. He knew, and he didn't deny or repudiate what he knew. But he preached a new reality anyway.

Obama's own political/folk hero was Harold Washington, the first black mayor of Chicago, elected in 1983. Washington was a bridge between the tradition of black elected officials as the vanguard of black leadership and a new tradition of a charismatic black politician who continues that leadership but consciously appeals to everyone. In Obama's mind, however, Washington seems to have fallen short of being either. He did get more black folks into key positions in Chicago city government, he says. But what did it all mean? Nothing seemed to change for the black folks on the ground. (The same could be said of Tom Bradley, the first and only black mayor of Los Angeles, elected ten years earlier, in 1973.) Obama writes that in the end, Washington was less a bridge than part of a sputtering cause of black justice, an "inheritor of a sad history, part of a closed system with few moving parts, a system that was losing heat every day. . . ." It's an accurate description of the long, slow collapse of the post-'60s black leadership best described by Robert Smith, in *We Have No Leaders*, and lived by all of us, Obama included. Washington's election was an historic event that broke years of racial acrimony for which Chicago is famous, though what Obama sees in hindsight is not Washington's new power but the constraints on that power, all that Washington could *not* do. (He is, of course, talking about himself in the future, though he doesn't know it yet.) Implicit in his critique of Washington is a critique of a black tendency to always celebrate the positive and inspiring at the expense of ignoring the failures and limitations and the lessons therein. This is Obama the thinker and student of history talking, not the reactionary-sounding put-down artist in the mold of Bill Cosby, who has rankled more than a few of us. I believe the thinker is the true Obama, but all that he's realized about the complicated nature of the black psyche and racial progress simply can't be distilled into a few talking points, and so the few we get are, to put it mildly, inadequate.

I think Obama knows this. But he also knew by the time he ran for president (and probably for quite some time before then) that his full critique was a moot point because white folks don't give a shit about the failures of black leadership, and black folks expect almost nothing from those leaders. In that gap, or in that vacuum, Obama had plenty of room to sell the broad, shiny, one-America ideal that only a presidential campaign could accommodate, an ideal that encouraged us to finally come together so that Harold Washington and Lincoln and Kennedy and Malcolm X and King did not die in vain. Perhaps he knew that he was dealing in the fantastic, the historically grandiose, and on some level, so did we. But we needed to believe.

And yet, curiously, Obama does not really seem to be inclined toward belief. He urges *us* to believe, but I think that he prefers reflection—he lands on a moment, mines its epiphanies, moves on. In *Dreams*, he had one such epiphany about the elusive nature of black individuality, a kind of personal Trayvon Martin moment that happened many years before the actual one in 2012. During an encounter with some young black boys who were in a car blasting hip-hop, he realizes that the only difference between those boys and himself at that age is the fact that he grew up in more forgiving circumstances. He feels part of some order; they do not. Maybe they never will. The prospect of *them* not ever knowing order unsettles him. "I suspect these boys will have to search long and hard for that order—indeed, any order that includes them as more than objects of fear or derision," Obama writes. "And that suspicion terrifies me, for I now have a place in the world, a job, a schedule to follow." His terror is knowing that he can't escape the fear and derision that these boys already feel, no matter how hard he works or how solid his job: these lost boys are him, in some immutable way. Their fates are connected. The sense of connection is positive—for lack of a better word—but it's also sobering, full of an emotional complexity that's almost existential and wholly absent from the usual heated but very impersonal public discourse about race and the "race problem." In his memoir, Obama makes the race problem personal, like Baldwin did. Most black folk prefer focusing on ways to fix the brokenness—I know the problem, they say impatiently, now tell me the solution; that's what matters. I've heard it a million times. But Obama sees brokenness as a lesson, a valuable resource we mistakenly treat as a cultural defect or self-hate. Simply wanting to move forward is much too simplistic; only by training a light on the dim, unexplored areas will we be set free.

Another complicated thing about Obama is that he seems to uncynically embrace both American ideals and America's troubled black past, which indicts those ideals. Baldwin also embraced both, but he grappled with them almost physically as he tried to reconcile—wrestle—them into some kind of agreement, if not harmony. King did the same, but he knew that embracing the idealism would extract a price; at the very least, it meant walking into fire. Fifty years later, Obama was (I don't know that he still is) much more confident that the conflict between American ideals and black history can be worked out, and he assumes, or he hopes, that other people feel the same way. This to me is true post-racialism, the idea that black people can finally resolve the riddle of double consciousness, that they can openly claim both their history *and* a sense of national belonging.

It's an optimistic idea that belongs to Obama's generation—my genera-tion—the first to come of age after the Movement. It was this generation that could advance the idea that a black person is not simply trying to catch up after starting from behind—the deficit model—but is also making a way forward and everybody *else* is following behind. It's a radical departure from the tradition of white domination and black acquiescence and the opposite of what we think of as post-racialism—far from being diminished, blackness has fully emerged. It's taken center stage. It models. "Obama is taking us out of the darkness of the whole slave energy, transitioning us to a whole other level of humanity," is how the poet Eric Priestley put it. "He exemplifies the best of what black people have become, and *that* transcends ethnicity."

♥   In the last chapter of *Dreams from My Father*, Obama does get free, in a sense, when he attends Wright's church in Chicago and gets hit by his "audacity of hope" sermon. Obama is officially—spiritually—converted to a new black way of being, which is honest and critical, not tragic or defeated, examining the brokenness up close, sometimes angrily but also with belief in the possible. The Reverend Jeremiah Wright is a philosopher/illuminist like his protégé, Obama, plumbing the dark places but remaining an idealist. They're similar. How tragic that campaign politics intervened in '08 and Obama felt compelled to justify this friendship to the American public, although what he was really justifying was his own inclination toward black justice, and that—not Rev. Wright—was what he was being pressured to renounce. As graceful as that speech was, it was a bad moment for Obama and for us, a public moment of private betrayal. Black people who felt betrayed said little to nothing, instead retreating to the political mantra (he *had* to do it, of course he had no choice but to do it) rather than examining Obama himself and his deepest motives; once again it was more important to claim a victory than acknowledge defeat, and this defeat was particularly stinging for being so subtle. The speech worked in that Obama was ultimately elected, but the victory was Pyrrhic. It was early, rude, but unsurprising evidence that even the magical candidate Obama couldn't overcome the "sad inheritance" of black disempowerment, couldn't really do anything different even though he deeply believed in different. He was already caught in the forces of fate, a folk hero long before he became president.

Returning home from Kenya, Obama does reconnect with the audacity of hope. But Chicago and its urban crises put him back into a certain despair, a keener awareness of an absent community despite his community work. Things on the South Side seem worse to him, less hopeful, more isolated. The caring of which hope is made and that is so essential to young people is in short supply. "All too rarely do I hear people asking just what it is that we've done to make so many children's hearts so hard, or what collectively we might do to right their moral compass—what values *we* must live by," he writes. "Instead, I see us doing what we've always done—pretending that these children are somehow not our own." All the musing and weighing and sifting breaks with the tradition of a black leader/race man as stoic and strategic, eyes always fixed on the prize; not Barack. He lets the nettlesome questions and loose ends and vulnerability show, and he does it with ease and a certain relish. This is him, and it constitutes a new kind of cool. Obama has in fact added something to the trope of cool that people have tried to dismiss as patently uncool—nerdiness, naiveté, or even non-blackness. But it's none of those. It is something that powers straight through all the criticism like a drill through soft dirt: the power of himself.

Nobody in any political or ethnic camp really knows what to do with that power—exercising it isn't done—so they ignore it. Writer Rebecca Walker senses this power in the essay collection *One Thousand Streams of Blackness*, an anthology of musings about what it means to be cool. In the book's introduction, she fixes on one of the more iconic images of Barack, in black shades, stepping suavely out of a limo. Instead of calling it sexy—that's taboo—she calls it quintessential Black Cool, a catch-all description of that innate self-assurance that marks black men from Super Fly to Denzel to, now, Barack. But Walker holds out Barack Cool as something singular and different, because "cool" is exactly what he is and also what he's not, and it's that tension of opposites—or their perfect harmony—that makes her catch her breath. He is both the intellectual, starched-shirt president and the kid who grew up on Philly soul like all of us in that first post-Movement, college-educated generation that always welcomed the opportunity to cast off the degree for just a moment and belt Al Green or the Spinners into an open mike; Barack is, as Tom Sayles has repeatedly insisted, *all that*. Many of us are. And yet *all that* in a figure as famous and as potentially powerful as Barack is almost too much for us to process. Walker betrays her ecstasy over this embarrassment of riches—or more accurately, of menu selections—when she writes, with an almost audible sigh, "He is so, so cool I cannot turn away from the image. I want almost to eat the image, to ingest the cool, but what I really want to know is *what makes him so cool* in this picture."

She knows; she's just playing dumb. I understand. Protocol prevents her from saying what exactly it is she wants to ingest, and why. The nation may still wrestle with the question of who Barack really is, but black women determined early *what* he is: a complete package. He is the man, no hyperbole intended. For the starstruck among us, the "what"—devoted husband and father, educated, consciously black, good-looking, all that—more than answers the "who." But we black folk must temper our enthusiasm by dubbing him "cool," which gets at something more human and ineffable, although vague, and that is the whole point of cool: mystery. But what Rebecca Walker is really taken with is not just mystery but something in the photo that's opposite, something inviting and open despite the dark shades, but because she isn't allowed to say the words, she must instead contemplate ingesting Obama's image. That's as close to him as she can get. She has to keep a safe distance from the photo, avoid losing herself in the pixilation that happens if she gets too close, but she still yearns to *know* Obama. She wants to embrace him and risk losing it all.

Baldwin once said that to love is to dare to know. Loving Obama created in me from the beginning a certain anxiousness (what's he going to do, how will he react now, will he do the right thing?) where there used to be only a well-oiled acceptance of black elected officials and what they do. But he's changed that. Everything matters now. I have no idea what to expect, but that's progress. Even my regular bouts of anger and alarm at Obama are progress, because I am angry and alarmed at *him*. And because I am constantly trying to know him, the fate of everything in his purview as president—not just racial matters, but war and fracking and climate change—has become personal.

One of the first things that Ken Moore, who is originally from Chicago, says about Obama is that he's cool. It is a running theme of our conversation. I met Ken more than a decade ago, when he was operating Howling Monk, a jazz coffeehouse in downtown Inglewood. He had quit a more than comfortable job as an accountant for a movie studio in order to pursue a dream of merging his business ambition with black cultural preservation. Ken thinks that black people are enormously proud of Obama's cool and all that it suggests: resilience, endurance, mental toughness, forbearance, grace under pressure, all without breaking a sweat. Cool is the collective defense of the entire history of black struggle, carried in this moment in time in the person of Barack Obama. Cool is buoyancy, the weightless counterweight to the heaviness of racism. Opponents repeatedly try to drag Obama down with scandal and insult and impossible demands; they try to drown him, but he doesn't drown. His penchant for compromise notwithstanding, he remains his own man. He remains himself. That more than qualifies as an act of resistance. "What they hate about him is that he's an uppity Negro," says Ken. "He's not a card-carrying Uncle Tom—actually, a Tom would not have been elected. He has a proud look. He's smart, he's cool—and if you can't be cool, what's the point?"

Cool puts Obama in the black family, though Ken distinguishes between

Obama's blackness and his own. The president, as we were informed early on, is not descended from slaves (though it was discovered later that he is, in a fashion, on his mother's side), and didn't grow up with the kind of intergenerational anger that Ken felt when he watched his own father defer to lesser white folk. He says that though Barack lived in Chicago, he isn't of it. But that doesn't mean he doesn't belong. Ken is distinctly impressed that Obama community-organized in Altgeld Gardens, which he calls the worst projects in Chicago, where virtually nobody went, including himself, even though he had family there. It took something to spend time in Altgeld. "Obama reminds me of a guy I knew in Chicago, a guy who could be in a bad neighborhood and walk into the middle of some bad dudes he didn't really know, and part the waters without having to say a word," he says. "Now *that's* cool."

For David Dawson, Obama cool is defined by what Obama doesn't do—that is, buckle under intense controversy or criticism. He quietly but steadily keeps going and more quietly recovers, even flourishes. Doesn't say a word, says David admiringly, and next thing you know, Syria is surrendering its chemical weapons and Obamacare is working by inches, and then by feet, and diplomatic relations with Iran are opening up and Cuba is coming back into play. David admits that Obama has always been a centrist managing from the middle—that's always been his plan, politically. But that doesn't diminish what David sees as Obama's core grit and strategic sophistication, for which he almost never gets credit. It is those qualities, not his politics, that will ensure his legacy (though that doesn't mean David ignores his politics or writes them off as immaterial to Obama's character. Back in 2010, when Obama extended the Bush-era tax cuts, David was so irate that he fired off an email to the White House. He's made an uneasy peace with it since. "When I understood the ramifications of extending the tax cuts, I was OK," he says, sounding not quite OK. "But I *still* don't like it.") When Obama did healthcare reform during his first year in office, David says, "He went against much of the advice and said, 'to hell with y'all, I'm doing it first.'" That's grit. He says Obama, though he loves being on stage, is humble, with his feet on the ground. "It feels like you could go in a barber shop with Obama and rap with him," he says. "He's like an ordinary guy who came to the White House. You could *definitely* sit down and have a beer with him."

Over the years, it seemed as though Obama would have liked to have a beer with someone, to shed the presidency for a moment and breathe, let down the guard of cool a bit. In a quirky video that made the email rounds in 2014, he takes an unannounced stroll across the Capitol lawn, eschewing the usual limo or very private mode of transport. It's a clever and effective PR move. (At that point, he was mired in the scandal surrounding the dysfunction of the Veterans Administration, among other things. Why *not* go out and take a walk?) But it's still startling for its unscripted quality. In the video, Obama strides easily, no jacket, loose-limbed, presidential but eager to reach out to people he passes, to shake their hands and gauge their reaction to his casual greeting ("Hi! How are you?"), in which he offers neither his name nor his occupation. He looks almost hungry to recalibrate that connection of '08, in which so many people responded so overwhelmingly to him and to the *possibility* of him. In this brief, quirky outing, it seems as though he wants to know if the possibility still exists, if *he* still exists as a folk hero, not just for black folks but for everyone.

He gets warm but fairly subdued reactions, and then one elated woman, after being assured that he isn't a wax figure, cries, "This is the best day of my life!" Obama seems amused underneath his serious look; at her request, he hugs her and stands for a photo, and she glows. They seem not like president and constituent but like two people at a reunion, each happy to see that the other is still intact, alive, albeit somewhat worse for the wear.

♥ Cool means undaunted, which can mean impenetrable and aloof. It can also mean undaunted in a sympathetic way—unafraid of people and points of view not your own, unafraid to venture out, to take a walk. Obama is both kinds of cool, but he is more of the latter. At one point in *Young Mr. Obama*, McClellan describes how Professor Obama wins over a student with this sort of cool in his law class at the University of Chicago. In McClellan's account, the school's focus is heavy on intellect and legalese; professors in their idle time talk cases and arguments, while Obama prefers to talk about the human consequences of the law. One of his students, a gay man named Jim Madigan, recalls how impressed he was by the way in which Obama articulated the rights of gays in a key sodomy case. In another case, the infamous Dred Scott decision, he talked empathetically from the point of view of propertied slave owners. Madigan was struck by his professor's equanimity and by his deftness in switching points of view as required, but doing it sincerely. Being open and circumspect rather than dogmatic or didactic about textbook court cases like these was, in its way, romantic. Here was a man, and a mind, for all seasons. The experience both confirmed and contradicted Madigan's professed view of Obama as a player—a very straight man who obviously caught women's attention, who was also black.

Madigan implies that Obama could have easily been very full of himself. Instead, he seems more interested in filling himself with other people (ingesting them, if you will). If he was a player, that's hardly all he was, and in any event, he didn't seem to care what people believed about him. That kind of confidence is the ultimate cool because it's not about performance—the look or the limo or the easy strut or the dark shades, or even the coveted mystery. Obama can work all that very well, almost subconsciously, but it's all secondary. He is cool, which means he has many different temperatures but almost no extremes.

It feels counterintuitive that you could live in the bounded middle like that and still carry ideals. Ideals by definition are extreme. Obama has been both lauded and criticized for being an idealist and a naïf (when he's not being condemned for being a sellout and a corporatist), starting with his "One America" campaign of '08 and invoked in everything from his battle to enact gun control after the Newtown massacre to his spontaneous walk on the Capitol lawn. Obama's rather conventional brand of idealism (though it isn't really conventional, because a black president's ideals, however mainstream, are by definition unconventional) does reflect our life and times, says John Quinn. Quinn is a production manager for classical music performances who lives in Berkeley. His father was an A.M.E. minister stationed at a church in Lancaster, a high-desert outpost on the northeastern edge of Los Angeles County's vast suburban grid. Quinn, who's in his '60s, is what you'd call a recovering socialist. Obama's embattled idealism, he says, "is as much an indictment of the '6os as anything else. How to even apply the ideals?" Quinn says that part of the problem is that Obama has no help; he has people who work for him, who are even loyal, but who aren't keyed into his vision of a world sprung not from Obama's campaign promises or his "A More Perfect Union" speech but from his mind and heart. Quinn, like many other black folk, sees the absence of any Obama posse/proxies as tragic, not least because without that context and support—without that extension of himself—Obama as a person remains obscure, his true story hidden from view.

"For me, Barack is actually a Shakespearean character, a flawed character in history," says Quinn. "People were ready to vote for him, but they're not *with* him. The haters have a narrative of Obama's life. Those who want to love him don't have a narrative." Nor will Obama offer that narrative himself—not now, anyway. "Maybe we want to hear him think aloud," says Quinn. "You could fantasize about that conversation, but he's too interior a person for that. Clinton was a total extrovert, Obama an introvert [which makes Clinton stereotypically blacker than his Democratic successor], despite the fact they both have charm and need to be liked. Obama is a creative problem-solver, not a manager. He lives to contemplate." I agree, though I wonder, as I always do, exactly how much of that introvert is Obama and how much is Obama wearing the mask that so many black folk don in our work lives and can deploy at a moment's notice, a mask that is our armor, not our essence. It is vigilance. The mask since the '6os has gotten more sophisticated, with different contours, and it's made of modern, less weighty stuff—fiberglass as opposed to metal or stone. It's not as impenetrable as it once had to be. But a mask is still necessary, and we still wear it. It has never seemed not necessary; nobody ever said that when you become president and represent all the American people, *then* you can take it off.

But the mask creates problems. When most of the people don't know you're wearing a mask in the first place, when they assume that what they see is all that's there, you have a communication problem. You have a problem of intimacy. The Shakespearean flaw that Quinn sees in Obama is misplaced confidence: *he* thinks we Americans see him plainly, understand him. For the most part we don't, either because too much blocks our vision or because history has warned us that this kind of transparency is dangerous. We do not see Obama fully just because he wants us to.

Maybe the whole journey to the center of Obama is a fool's errand, a distraction at best. For Maulana Karenga, there really is no black individual in the American sense; individualism is a flawed democratic ideal based on a more deeply flawed notion of American exceptionalism that never applied to us, has in fact worked against us. It still does. Karenga, founder of the black cultural nationalist Us and creator of the Kwanzaa holiday, has a complex view of Obama, as most black people do. He grants him his humanity and the unprecedented scope of his symbolism as president; at the same time, he sees Obama as an integrationist who has given away too much and repeatedly failed in his obligation to represent the issues and concerns of African-descended people in this country and around the world (a job for which Obama, per his exotic African lineage, did seem uniquely suited). But Karenga takes the symbolism very seriously. "Two important things: in gaining the highest office in the land, Barack destroys the myth that blacks lack the capacity for great achievement," he says. One of the last leaders of the '60s still standing—Organization Us is one of the very few outfits from that era that's still functional—Karenga is wearing his customary African garb and thick-rimmed glasses. Over breakfast at the Ritz-Carlton in Marina del Rey, one of his favorite L.A. spots, he is characteristically intense but genial, almost jovial, which I always thought an interesting contrast to his image as an uncompromising, unsmiling warrior of black cultural nationalism (which is exactly the image projected in the painting of him that hangs in the African American Cultural Center on 48th Street, Karenga's place in the Crenshaw district southeast of here). "Second, we know that his failure is seen as the failure of the race. So we're defending our reputation and our honor and our dignity when we support him," Karenga says. "He's weak about a lot of things, but—here he is. There *we* are."

We are Obama, and he is us. Even though black people are differentiated and distinct, we all reflect on each other, and the higher up we are on the social or professional ladder, the greater the reflection on all of us below. That makes Obama an absolute star in our firmament. What rankles

Karenga is that this great star Obama dims himself, and the rest of us, by almost never sympathizing with black people in the way that he publicly sympathizes with gays or immigrants or women or the middle class or other constituencies seeking justice the way black people have done for decades, and still do. We set the template. Karenga understands the political reasons why Obama steers clear of even uttering the words *black* and *African American*. But in his mind politics should follow ethics: Obama should recognize us and our plight publicly because it needs recognition. Obama has a choice here, Karenga believes, and he has chosen badly. It's a dangerous choice because if Obama hides his color—hides that part of himself—in plain sight, then all of us black folk must struggle that much harder to be seen. Karenga says the long history of black invisibility has in many ways been exacerbated, not reversed, by Obama's hyper-presence. Too much about that presence has been muted, cut off. "A people has got to be rooted in its own culture in order to be itself and to free itself. Black people are always asked to erase ourselves," Karenga says emphatically. "Nobody's over in the Latino community saying, 'Ya'll got to stop being Latino.' If we can't describe ourselves, no solution can be authentic. White people want to impose their conception of us on us, so we can't be confident in our own identity. Can't be self-determining if you're not rooted this way, because you'd be using other people's values to determine yourself."

Certainly, that's just what so many of us have been doing for decades, integrating, using American consumerist values to determine ourselves and our progress. How truly heroic it would be if Obama could be the one to snatch us back from the brink of massive self-extinction with the force of his own ethics and vision, play the romantic lead by reviving our own foundering narrative and giving us back group definition and voice and a sense of ourselves. If only *he* could illuminate our own lives, which we have recently seen grow dim and shadowy, especially after a major recession in which many of us lost the tenuous foothold that we had in the American project.

Is Obama irredeemably middle-class? Black people have a tortured relationship to the condition. Everybody aspires to the middle class as the great social equalizer, the gateway to even higher and more permanent success that really opened up only in the '60s. The middle class is the place we all want to go, at least economically; none of us want to be, or to remain, poor and struggling. We all need to get over that hump. But being middle-class curries contentment with, even gratitude for, the status quo and discourages risk. It discourages empathy. The problem with being middle-class is that it gives us something to lose, not just money but a certain standing in the white mainstream, which still resists black inclusion, however much money you make or don't make. But to even have a shot at that inclusion, you have to be at least middle-class. Those who are working-class and lower might as well be invisible.

Karenga doesn't really offer an answer to this paradox of the middle class and the larger paradox of integration, but he is adamant about identity being the one thing that nobody black can ever afford to lose. Muting identity is like giving away your soul, he says, including any capacity for transformation. "If you don't bring people into consciousness, they won't choose revolution; they'll choose what they're choosing now: comfort in oppression," he says. He chuckles, leans forward, and lowers his voice. "When we talk like this, the middle class thinks we're messing up their chances, getting in their business. They [and here he means Obama] have told everybody they need a good job, money to send their kids to college, and here's Maulana telling them to respect themselves. They say, 'We *do* respect ourselves!' But what does respect really mean?"

I have to say, I don't know. So is Barack choosing to live comfort in oppression and encouraging us to do the same? Is he, however unintentionally, erasing us? Many black people say no; they argue that overall, given the fierce and enduring opposition of the white right, he's holding a line, not erasing it. They argue too that what Barack is not simply can't be as important as what he is. "Barack is *not* an Uncle Tom or a puppet," says Tony Jackson, who manages his wife's veterinarian practice in Inglewood. "He *is* a gift and a message." He says the worst thing Obama has had to do is to hold his tongue, obscure himself. In that way, he agrees with Karenga that Obama deliberately downplays his blackness but is much more sympathetic to the reasons for this. Stephen Townsend is Tony's age—forty-three—an illustrator who's worked at DreamWorks Studios and has struggled to keep a foothold in Hollywood's burgeoning animation industry, with partial success. He has a similar take. "If nothing else, Obama has shown people a good heart and great intentions. Be he can't tell anyone what he's going through on a daily basis," he says. "That's a tragedy."

My friend the retired city politico who never wants to be named, stresses—it is her mantra—that Obama lives mostly as a symbol who, by definition, can't be all iterations of black people. He can only be what he is: black and middle-class, or upper-middle-class. That in and of itself is not inherently evil, she says. "He is *not* Trayvon!" she exclaims. "Obama can't be us because he's not like us. He is *like* Ivy League–educated black folks, though Obama isn't elitist like them, or like the ones I know, the ones who send their kids to prep schools. Obama's blacker than any of *them*." To put it in more personal terms, she describes the president as "like my geeky cousin who went to school and did well. He can dance a little, sing some. That's him." That's as intimate a rendering of Obama as I've heard so far. It is high praise.

Brenda Jackson says the only real difference between Obama and the rest of black people is the extraordinary circumstance of his being president, a circumstance that severely limits his communication with us. She says that we therefore must have faith that there is more to Obama and what or how he thinks than what we see and hear on television, in the papers, or online. It is we who must empathize with him, not the other way around. "We all walk a tightrope; it's just that the stakes aren't as high for us as they are for him," she says. So he must find other ways to do things, and we have to recognize those ways when we see them. "Obama said once during a press conference, 'If I remember correctly, I won the election,'" she says. "That's him cussing everybody out, telling everybody to shut up and sit down. He's not a bully or a yeller or a screamer. He's not kissing white folks' ass, and he's not kissing ours either. . . . but we want him to go for the jugular, to straight-out put somebody in their place. Even I fantasize about that."

Michael Anderson, the architect and enthusiast of black middle-class living—in his mind, *that's* revolution—flatly says that nobody is in a position to judge who Obama is. "Nobody is really being truthful about what Obama's trying to do," he says. "From the beginning were sharks, pit bulls, the KKK, everything coming to the surface of the water. Politicians are like pimps and prostitutes. Obama is in the player's club and knows how to get shit done, but they won't let him, Republicans have made it impossible to pass certain reforms, do certain things. Obama knows what we don't."

♥   In the section of *Young Mr. Obama* chronicling Obama's challenge to Bobby Rush's congressional seat in Chicago, McClellan parses the different degrees of blackness and suggests that they make for different people—biracial Obama is middle-class arrogant and out of touch with the masses, whereas former Black Panther Bobby Rush is more authentic and "real." The conflation of color and character has dogged black folk forever, inhibiting any discussion of individuals. "Bobby Rush understood the struggles and aspirations of the high school dropout or the hotel maid trying to raise three children in a way that was impossible for Obama," McClellan writes. "Obama's blackness had been an advantage with his Law Review colleagues and his New York publisher, Rush's blackness had been another handicap to overcome, like his stutter and his poverty." McClellan makes Obama sound out of touch by dint of his genetics and education—not a "real" black person. He's on the losing side of the old divide between the house nigger and the field nigger, only in this case it's the field nigger (who later evolved in the big northern cities as the street nigger) who has the advantage here; Obama is a tragic mulatto who by definition doesn't know himself. He is inevitably self-deluded.

Karenga suggests that Obama is a house nigger, a servant of white interests, though he bases that view on Obama's actions, not on his appearance or his education. But even this more nuanced view excludes a truth that serves no one to talk about: black people are complicated. The truth is that millions of us have lived in the hood and grown up speaking properly, just as there are hordes of middle-class blacks you'd swear were from the hood if you heard them talk. Blackness is a vital and viable identity, but it doesn't stay in defined spaces and defined people. To assume that Obama can't be compassionate or keyed in to black concerns or feel black himself *because* he is well-spoken and erudite is doing the old racist thing of presuming to know black people better than they know themselves. Growing up in my own hood of South Central I knew lots of potential Obamas, guys who were outwardly cool and definitely black-centric, but they had other dimensions; they were kind or sensitive, or they loved dogs or comic books or glitter rock. And these qualities were not mutually exclusive; they coexisted.

McClellan says, "Obama was never meant to be the voice of black empowerment the way that Jesse Jackson and Bobby Rush were. With his biracial heritage, Obama was born to reconcile the interests of black and white." Obama is assumed to be a born conciliator *because* he's half-white, as if he's got 50 percent more bargaining power than the rest of us black folks merely because of his genes. Of course, it hasn't worked that way at all for him as president. He has turned out not to be the natural bridge builder that whites assumed he would be (though it isn't for lack of trying), and that failure is why they fall away. Obama, alas, could not bring us the meaningful integration that we've never had. But black folks don't see this as failure. We knew all along it was a setup. We already knew the limits of integration. And we know all too well that being half-white, or some other percentage white, often doesn't mean overcoming because, socially speaking, if you ain't *all* white, you just ain't.

That said, it's the half-black set that's been responsible for so much critical black history: W.E.B DuBois, Booker T. Washington, Frederick Douglass, Bob Marley, and now Obama. That's always been the profile of the talented tenth—more advantaged than the average Negro, but not white. Obama must know this, but it's one of the many things that he can't say because it offends the fragile racial sensibility of many Americans that he theoretically represents. A bit later in his book, describing Obama's stint in the Illinois state legislature, McClellan offers a more well-observed comment but nonetheless can't resist a dig: "Obama may not have been the voice of black empowerment, with a raised fist and a copy of *The Wretched of the Earth* on his bookshelf"—though he very likely read that book—"but he was at least in a position to bring the community's concerns to the white mainstream." Yes, though that makes him no different from any other black elected official anywhere—aren't they all trying (or should be) to mainstream black crises? The scenario that McClellan can't quite resolve in his head is that Obama the half-breed is born to build racial bridges, not solve black problems; he obviously can't do both. Color allegiance is at the heart of the question "Who is he?"—"what" being more critical than "who." Not that black folks have this issue; we embrace Obama as black. In many ways, he embraces us back. But we frankly have no more real insight into his character than anybody else because we don't ask, and the president only lets out so much. We are left with knowing him communally, historically, experientially. We fill in gaps because that's what we've always done, how we've always made ourselves and our people solid in a world that would poke holes in our meaning at every opportunity. Black people *know* him, as Brenda Jackson says, by faith.

For political consultants, candidate Obama represented a once-in-an-era opportunity. Gearing up for Obama's presidential run, campaign strategist David Axelrod told the doubters, "I think there's something special about this guy. This guy's the real deal. This is the guy we try to make all our candidates sound like, this really genuine and heartfelt appeal to people's sort of reclaiming their citizenship . . . there's some there there." Axelrod certainly describes what I felt that day I saw Obama and, almost against my will, connected. He doesn't describe what I felt next, chiefly that Obama connecting with the mainstream looking to restore faith in itself was not necessarily an encouraging development for blacks. In 2003, Laura Washington of the *Chicago Sun-Times* wondered what Barack's distinct appeal to whites would mean for black folks in the Senate race, particularly working-class blacks who simply were not part of his more natural constituency of liberals and academics. Those folks are fine, Washington said, but what about her Uncle Leland? If Obama became senator—president wasn't on the table then—would her salt-of-the-earth uncle and other black folks like him be forsaken? The big question was, if Obama is *their* man, can he also be ours?

Interviewing Obama during his senate campaign, McClellan mythologizes him a bit more when he describes him as "gliding across the floor like Fred Astaire playing Abe Lincoln." I get the comparisons—like Astaire, Obama moves with a definite but easy, almost unconscious grace; like Lincoln (one of his great political heroes), he is tall and lanky, with prominent ears and a studious nature. But I miss the lack of any comparison of Obama to other black entertainers (Honey Coles? Nicholas Brothers?), the racial decontextualizing that seems required in order to make Obama special, to really bring him into view as an individual. To be white is to have that privilege of individuality, to not be defined by historical realities that brought your people to this country in chains and methodically decimated any sense of personhood or individuality over hundreds of years. All of which means that while McClellan's comparison may be limited, it's a huge compliment to Obama because even though black people have always been fabulous performers, the root of American music and dance, we never had a Fred Astaire. We were not allowed stature like that. Obama has a stature none of us have ever achieved before. It hasn't meant that he's become a cultural icon to white folks the way Fred Astaire was—he is more a curio, an ongoing event. Being president has not made him white—that is, fully individual—or let's just say that being black has made that regard much tougher to come by. That's distressing in one way but oddly comforting in another. Black folks don't want Obama to be white. For all its social advantage, being white is not always a positive; it's often synonymous with being inauthentic, untrustworthy, mercenary. White folks have had to forgive Obama's blackness, and we've had to do something similar in hoping that Obama's *whiteness* won't do him in, that it won't work against his character.

Tom Sayles, of USC, says that Obama, the first president fully of the Internet age, is as impossible to know as any other famous, routinely overexposed person who makes regular headlines on Yahoo News. His exposure actually obscures him:

> The paradox is that Obama is this individual celebrity, somebody who appears on the covers of tabloids, whose life we treat like Oprah's or Madonna's. It's that rock star thing, which he still has despite what our popularity polls here say. At the same time, he's a symbol of social meaning and history. Americans have to understand him this way before we can understand him as an individual, but we cut out the history on purpose and are left with an incomplete picture. This is why whites seem not to understand Obama, to see him as an enigma, which is how they see all black folks. Black people see his dimensions, but *they* don't. That's why we understand and forgive him his lack of attention to us.

But he adds as an afterthought, "Whites mistake this lack of attention for, 'He's doing the right thing by you because you're not complaining.'" In this way, black silence is actually feeding the post-racial myth that all is well in black America because Obama is at the helm. Silence is the fertile soil in which the whole idea of post-racialism flourishes.

Sayles says there are really two Obamas: aspirational and executive. The first is the idealist, suggested in his memoir and solidified in his first presidential campaign, who would like to remake the world; the second is the pragmatist, always figuring out what's doable as president. Every politician is probably both, or started out as both, but the division between Obama's two sides feels particularly acute, and consequential. Who would he be now if he had not become president? How else might his two selves—superimposed on the two halves of his double consciousness—have been aligned to make a whole? It's one more thing about Obama we may never know.

Jordan Vaughn, twenty-eight, has another, more hopeful view of Obama—as a model of self-actualization for the modern age. And it's a process that's unfolded in real time. "He's developed right in front of us. He quit smoking in office, watched his daughters grow up—he's matured like a real person," says Jordan, a political consultant who lives in Washington and works for Obama staffer Jim Messina. As a millennial, Jordan finds it inspiring that Obama is still a work in progress, a self-made guy who's continually being made. "Barack has really made people feel they can be exactly who they are," he says. "I'm black and gay, but I'm in politics, not fashion. He advances that notion that you're fine as you are—he really believes that." For black people still struggling to establish their full humanity, self-acceptance is an essential notion that is less ethereal than perhaps it is for everybody else.

Stephen Townsend agrees that Obama becoming Obama, missteps and all, models something important that we need to see. But he also says, somewhat paradoxically, "The biggest bummer about Barack is that he's hard to get to know. The fact that he's black, male, and intelligent got my vote—I didn't need to see much more than that." But Stephen wanted more. At Obama's most revealing moment, during the press conference addressing the verdict in George Zimmerman's trial for the murder of Trayvon Martin,

Stephen says Obama didn't reveal enough. The president's conflictedness, though authentic, wasn't encouraging. "He made his stand on the [Trayvon Martin] moment, and then he said, 'OK, leave me alone,'" says Townsend. "I thought, well, maybe *this* is who he is. He doesn't want to wild things up." He shrugs, slipping into an almost predetermined acceptance of Obama that I've seen over and over. "I get it. I'm still a supporter, he's like family . . . though I wish he had a little more Martin Luther King in him."

Townsend is much more encouraged when he takes Obama out of the individual context and puts him in a larger one; then, the president goes from being underwhelming by choice to being unavoidably heroic, like a soldier who falls after deliberately walking into a hail of bullets. This image of Obama as warrior/martyr/folk hero is much more compelling. It gives meaning and dignity to the quotidian struggles of all black folk. "If Barack is under fire, the rest of us [black people] don't have a chance," Townsend exclaims. "We may never get another black president, but he did his thing. We all need that sense of hope that we can do *our* own thing, get to the next place." It's something Obama himself echoed in a lengthy 2014 interview with David Remnick for the *New Yorker*, as he reflected on his eventual place in history: "Everybody gets a paragraph. I'm just trying to get my paragraph right."

❤ Since 2008, I've had a lively running conversation about Obama with Kerry Newsome, the owner of a shoe store and boutique I frequent on La Brea Avenue in North Inglewood. It's a very nicely appointed place on an otherwise unremarkable street, with bright, edgy window displays that advertise Kerry's fashion acumen and years of experience in retail (and as it happens, he is in fashion but not gay—straight, married with children), and it's an irresistible stop whenever I wander over there from my digs on the south end of town. One day not long after the 2012 election, I find myself in his shop having a particularly animated discussion about what's next—what Obama will do or won't do this term, and as always, what he will do for us. Kerry has argued both sides. He's said that Obama owes black people nothing that we don't demand, and he's also said that by dint of being a black president, Obama owes us every bit of justice that we deserve but haven't gotten yet. Today, as I intermittently browse a rack of sweaters, we talk about what Obama himself would like to do, how he really feels about things so far but can't say. We have been at this point in the conversation many times before. This time, post-election, Kerry seems particularly frustrated; after some back and forth he suddenly erupts in a confession.

"I don't *know* the guy!" he exclaims. "I don't know who he is, what he stands for. What does he want me to *do*? If he wants me to go get a welfare check, all right, I'll do it, but tell me something definitive. I can't love you if I don't know you." What Kerry is saying is that while Obama has more than earned his moment in history, Kerry can't fully give him loyalty because he still doesn't know what—or who—he's supposed to be loyal to. Four years after the glory of '08, Obama has put Kerry in extended limbo, and he's starting to resent it. I've felt the resentment myself, though I've felt it more as weariness—the inevitable lapsing of romance—than anger, more of a temptation to give up, break off the relationship that romance has settled into. Kerry's reaction speaks to something I heard film director Justin Simien say in an NPR interview about *Fruitvale Station*, a movie about the last day in the brief life of Oscar Grant. Grant was the twenty-two-year-old black man who was shot execution-style by transit authorities in Oakland on New Year's Day, 2009 (a Trayvon Martin moment, one of hundreds, that preceded Trayvon). Simien described Grant as a black everyman who was many things to many people; he wore many masks that changed, depending on where he was and whom he was with. The tragedy was that Grant was the wrong self at the wrong time, and it cost him his life. Identity fragmentation is a condition of all black people, but especially of black men, including Obama, because they represent the greatest social threat and have to monitor their presentation most diligently. Simien's own movie, *Dear White People*, is also about the treachery of that fragmentation, though from the somewhat surreal viewpoint of the black college set, not the working class of *Fruitvale*. Nobody is shot dead in *White People*, but there are consequences for black people being their wrong selves at the wrong time (and, usually, in the wrong place) or their true selves at virtually any time.

I've always noticed how Obama, however comfortable he appears before the cameras or making a public statement, never seems to quite fit his surroundings; his surroundings always seem to demand that *he* fit *them*. It's why I always hold my breath when I watch or hear him at a routine press conference because I half-expect disaster, a melting down (of the press corps, not Obama) or a sudden tearing apart. It is because with each press conference I'm witnessing up close and in public, in a video feed beaming around the world, the ancient, painful, and inherently private phenomenon of a black man, this one leader of the so-called free world, still living behind the psychological scrim that DuBois called the Veil. And I feel as Stephen Townsend and Kerry do, that if President Obama has no chance of finally dispensing with the Veil, none of us do. Of course, I am always obligated to watch him try; that's part of folk heroism. That's his journey, and ours. But until the Veil falls, the empowerment that we all assume that he grants black folk, the symbolism that's the least and the best thing he can do for us, remains elusive.

Brandon Brooks at the *Los Angeles Sentinel* thinks that trying to examine the inner Obama is looking at things from the wrong end. Obama's private life and past struggles are the things we never see before the cameras, and probably never will. We only need to know that he was once an adolescent with great potential who pulled back from the brink of indifference that submerges many a young black man and chose education, the way forward; the rest is quite literally history. "Often, black men don't know how or where to channel energy, and clearly Barack did," says Brandon. "As a black man, he's become inspirational, everything we needed—upstanding, sparring with power, John Boehner and those guys. He really *is* a man of steel." He brightens. "Plus, his shit is tight! No side girlfriends!" He grins, contemplating not Obama's inner life but his outer, daily life, which feels to Brandon more intimate. "Can you imagine, Barack probably still puts on his wave cap at night, Michelle wraps her hair," he says, chuckling. "Being regular, yet he was still going to school, studying, achieving. He grew us up. A godsend to remind us of the state of our own lost generation."

Brandon admits that as well as he feels *he* knows Obama, he's aware that other people don't. Some, like Kerry, can't figure him out, while many others don't care to find out and never will. "It's heart-wrenching that Obama can't change the world, can't advertise who he really is," he says. "He has to make calculated decisions to better his brand, like Michael Jordan. I almost hate that he had to be a hand-picked Jackie Robinson, kind of put there by the powers that be . . . it diminishes his accomplishments." On the other hand, no one who's been elected president hasn't first passed muster with the powers that be. What Brandon is saying is that Obama probably gave up more to pass muster than he wanted or expected. As Brooklyn's first black player, Jackie Robinson was instructed by the Dodgers never to get angry or respond to racial taunts or threats or even to violence. He complied and was considered a hero at least as much for what he didn't do, what he kept to himself, as for what he did. But his widow, Rachel, said that keeping all that feeling in was partly responsible for Jackie's early death at fifty-three (the age Obama is now, looking somewhat gaunt and less dewy-eyed than when he took office at forty-seven). Bob Farrell, Obama critic, is nonetheless amazed that Obama is in the mix, actually playing the game—not to his liking, but playing it. "To see this kind of amplification of a black man—I'm proud of Obama, very proud," he says. "I am disappointed"—and here he recaps the reasons why, including Guantanamo imprisonment and the escalated security state and Washington's ironclad loyalty to Wall Street. "Though as the first black man elected president, well." Bob throws up his hands. "He is a miracle unto the *Lord.*"

When I press Ishmael Reed about whether he likes Obama or what sort of person he might be at heart, he is reluctant to answer. He finally does— briefly, anxious to return to other questions with which he's more comfortable. "I like Obama, he's a good guy," he says, somewhat hurriedly. "But he's a centrist. He's the pretty multicultural face on the empire. But he won't completely cooperate with it." He adds, as an afterthought: "The talented tenth is out of touch, and Obama is one of them. He's trapped." In this somewhat scattershot critique, Reed does two things a black revolutionary must do—decry Obama's avowed middle-class status, and defend Obama's right to be black and not be shot down by racists and congenital skeptics. That so many white folks hate him is, for Reed, evidence of some character worth defending, perhaps the part of Obama that doesn't or won't quite cooperate with the empire. "The guy went to Harvard, yet he's called a monkey!" Reed fumes. It's hard not to like a black man so obviously wronged, and as I've said before, if black people don't acknowledge the depth of the wrong, who will? Who else will ultimately humanize Obama, make him a person, see him most clearly through the Veil? In *Barack Obama and the Jim Crow Media: The Return of the Nigger Breakers*, the wronged Obama gives Reed the media critic the most fodder by far—the O.J. Simpson murder case, the subject of a previous book (of fiction) by Reed, is a distant second.

And yet Reed hates the Father's Day rhetoric, hates the thought of Obama chiding black people in public for their lack of progress. It's a tradition he links to Nixon and Reagan and the insidious "Southern strategy," which consciously exploited black loathing among whites and reconfigured the whole Republican Party in the '60s. Reed hates it that Obama, a philosopher/ intellectual with a clear black identity and a clearer understanding of black history, would even *appear* to acquiesce to such thinking. It's a waste. Listening to him talk, I'm still not sure how much Reed is condemning Obama and how much he is condemning an Obama constricted by political reality and precedent. They are two separate entities. So does he forgive Obama the Cosby-like sentiments? Is that a deal breaker? His response is typically elliptical, but illuminating. "I still rooted for Obama, even though I *knew* he was a centrist," he says. "Look, I root for Serena, Venus, Tiger Woods—every time they lose, I lose. When Tiger plays, I say all the time, 'I hope Phil Mickelson hits it in the water.'"

The black Superman swooping in and saving us all is one fantasy. I've heard many black people articulate another, more modest version of that fantasy that's at least half-real: behind Obama's degrees and impeccable public speaking is a super-regular black guy, a kind of black Joe the Plumber who is solid and plainspoken but who still stirs fear in the heart of white America, as all regular black men tend to do. (Obama confessed during the Trayvon Martin crisis to his own episodes of being racially profiled, as have many famous and successful black men.) In an '08 pre-election sketch on the video website Funny or Die, the comedian David Alan Grier said that he would prefer a regular black man as president—one who was as "incontrovertibly" black as Don Cheadle or Wesley Snipes, one who would make foreign dignitaries at the United Nations recoil in racist horror. Comedians Keegan-Michael Key and Jordan Peele, whose inimitable Comedy Central sketches give Obama an angry, street-lingo–spewing alter ego named Luther, met the president at the White House; Key said that Obama told him off-mike, "I could use Luther." It's hard to know how seriously he meant that, but I was relieved that Obama was even hinting at a true self that black people would understand without question, a self that needs no translation. But in public he really does almost need a translator like Key and Peele, or a clarifier, because his blackness simply obscures him too much to be understood by everyone in the same way at the same time. Blackness at once elevates and distorts his great symbolism. Blackness represents great American tragedy, hypocrisy, anxiety, faith, and struggle to overcome, but it can't represent where we need to go—that is, hope. It's another reason why Obama can't be a Kennedy or a Lincoln or an FDR, or even a Fred Astaire.

Where does that put Obama in the pantheon of presidential symbolism? What will he ultimately stand for? Even a middling president like Millard Fillmore stood for something, a kind of hapless hopefulness that is, at heart, quite American. Fillmore gets a certain distinction and even empathy for not being quite up to the virtually impossible task of holding together a union that in the mid-1800s was splitting apart over the question of slavery. He was a man out of his time whose compromises with his own beliefs got him and the struggling nation nowhere—but perhaps he tried his best. Obama can't be accorded that kind of context or forgiveness. He is not understood as a man of his time, and since we don't know what *kind* of man he is, being in over his head is never cause for empathy but cause for indictment, for alarm. To say Obama failed justifies the regret of having him there in the first place. In the mind of his opposition, he should never have tried at all. He was always the wrong man at the wrong time.

The far white right made it clear from the beginning what sort of man it thought Obama was. The less rabid, non–Tea Party forces of white conservatism nonetheless helped cast him as illegitimate, not just uninformed but unformed. George Will, in a 2013 *Washington Post* column about Obama's governing "epiphanies," sneers at his intellectual capacity. "Obama, of whose vast erudition we have been assured, seems unfamiliar with Mancur Olson's seminal *The Rise and Decline of Nations*," he wrote. (My initial, admittedly somewhat petulant reaction to that statement was: and *you* are undoubtedly unfamiliar with George Clinton's *One Nation under a Groove*—a serious deficiency in the education of any conscious American.) Did anybody accuse Bush II of not reading Mancur Olson, assault his erudition because of it? Bush's lack of intellect went largely unaddressed by the likes of Will, and sometimes it was even lauded as proof that he was a man of the people, a real American who was self-assured enough—man enough—not to have to be propped up by books and theory and fancy words and big ideas.

In the conservative monde and well beyond, Obama doesn't get a pass of either kind. He's neither a man of the people nor a thinking man allowed to think for us all. He's a cipher, an interloper. The only exception to this was the romantic, emotionally fluid period of the first campaign when a critical mass of people felt good about what they were doing in supporting Obama, which of course was about something bigger than Obama. The long-term relationship with Obama fails because in the light of day-to-day, white folks—especially the chattering class—seem at a loss to relate to him as something other than a creation of their own imagination and goodwill; it's as if he had no life at all before they gave him one.

So, who is this guy? Whereas Obama once embodied transparency, he is now all shadows and uncertainty. For the critics, this is especially true in foreign policy, an area in which they are eager to call his trademark circumspection weak and indecisive. He is not a *real* man, they suggest, in more than one sense of the word. Former presidential candidate John McCain has led the pack in hammering away at Obama's lack of nerve in not sending troops to Syria, or Ukraine, not sending in ground troops to fight the stateless Islamic State the way it should be fought. All this stokes a white supremacist theme that Obama simply isn't masculine enough for the job (or that he's too aggressive and/or too arrogant, another black male stereotype, which underlies accusations of Obama being a dictator for vowing in 2014 to use his executive authority to enact policies that Congress had refused to entertain, let alone pass, for six years).

John Bolton, the Bush-era United Nations ambassador famous for his non-diplomacy, excoriated Obama in a 2013 op-ed that predicted with great certainty failure in the Middle East on three fronts—Syria, Israel and Palestine, and Iran. It's not a matter of if, he declared, but when we will experience another 9/11, which would be the only thing that might finally awaken people to the perils of a president such as this. In Bolton's dire prediction is a pointed insult: "His equivocation regarding Syria's chemical weapons program has provoked giggles or dismay at White House weakness." Giggles? That stokes another, more subtle theme popularized over the years, that Obama is leading us into global disrepute because black people are simply too unsophisticated and unworldly to take the big perspective. Obama, Bolton witheringly suggests, is a permanent rookie playing in the major leagues. He is undeveloped, like the entire colored Third World, and always will be.

Commentator and Obama watcher Andrew Sullivan is known for his relatively staunch support of the president over time, support increasingly framed by his view of Obama as a key advocate for gay rights and marriage equality. Sullivan's support derives chiefly from the quality of Obama's character, his sense of self developed over a lifetime. In a 2012 article for *Newsweek*, Sullivan compared Obama's quest to reconcile his two families, or foundations (black and white), to the eternal attempt by gay men to reconcile their own two, dissimilar families (gay and straight). By 2012, Sullivan's understanding of Obama had evolved into accepting him as a cold, calculating politician who nonetheless wants to do right in the end; part of that is sympathy for gay rights that he has translated into policy. "I have always sensed that he intuitively understands gays and our predicament—because it so mirrors his own," Sullivan mused. "And he knows how the love and sacrifice of marriage can heal, integrate, and rebuild a soul. The point of the gay-rights movement, after all, is not about helping people be gay. It is about creating the space for people to be themselves. This has been Obama's life's work."

If Sullivan is right—and he's on to something, I think—I can't help but wonder, what does Obama believe about helping black people create spaces to be themselves? If he could convince them with policy that they, too, belong, that they're fine as they are, wouldn't that be good for the country as a whole? Wouldn't this move all Americans forward? Isn't this the kind of aspirational leadership Tom Sayles says he excels at? I hear questions like this in all the animated, slightly anguished black conversations about why Obama is willing to help gays, immigrants, women, the Ebola-stricken, and not us. The cold, calculated political answer is that we do not have the money, as Sullivan tacitly admits gay donors do have; but we also no longer have the cultural moment, as marriage equality does. Nothing in the air is making Obama do anything about us or for us. But that answer isn't good enough; he knew this situation going in. He knew that the math was not in our favor, that history was not on our side and hadn't been for a while. Had he decided not to do anything for black folks beforehand? Can he be *that* calculating? Did he decide early on that he could afford to let us down but love us anyway, as many of us have already done for him?

❤   I met Carmalita Jackson in a masters writing program at a university in Los Angeles. She's twenty-five and from a small town in Ohio called Washington Courthouse. Carmalita voted for Obama in '08, the first year she was eligible to vote, and she associates Obama with a personal racial awakening that began that year, when she left largely white Washington Courthouse to attend historically black Central State University, roughly thirty miles away. She and her siblings were raised partly in foster homes, and when she was a teenager, Carmalita was quasi-adopted by a young white couple from her church, who actually steered her to a historically black college, saying it would be good for her. But Obama provided her with a whole new context, and a new sense of family. "I felt an identity with him, with his struggle with biracial-ness," she says. "When I went back home to vote for him that day, I felt very visible. Obama had caused a big rift in my town, a big split. We had never talked about religion or politics before. Now black people were being heard. It felt like one less battle that we have to fight." One less, but plenty of battles remained. "There's nothing he does that's right, even if he does exactly what his opposition expected," she says. "It's never going to be enough."

While Carmalita is more than a little dazzled by Obama as Obama—she greatly admires his cool, which she calls "jazz, smooth, with the most swag, *our* cool"—she says that his winning the presidency, as significant as that was for her, "is actually a small thing. It doesn't matter that he holds the highest office in the land; he can be taken apart in public. Michelle too—she can be taken apart for her looks or whatever. As a black person you have to be twice as good, twice as mannered; you can't misbehave, and it's still not enough. Nothing matters."

Cara Taylor is twenty, a college sophomore at the University of Redlands who is also from the Midwest—from Glen Ellen, outside Chicago. She approves of Obama and, like Carmalita, identifies with him. But she approves in a vague way, or a way that seems vague to me. She has trouble embracing him as a black figure, something that many in her post-racial generation have been discouraged from doing, though her mother and grandmother were very involved in the Movement, she says. Of course, she knows race plays a role in the great wall of Obama resistance. But she seems reluctant to say anything definitive about the scope or nature of that role; she won't, or can't, characterize it. It's as if, when she looks at all the evidence, no piece of evidence is allowed to outweigh another. It's a post-postmodern view of things that shares the laissez-faire spirit of post-racialism: balance at all costs, even at the cost of a larger truth. The notion of a "freedom fighter" or "race man" strikes Cara as a bit alien, anachronistic, especially when applied to Obama, whom she takes at face value and not as part of a black tradition that she's never witnessed. (She has seen no black leaders in her lifetime: no Martin Luther King, Malcolm X, or Jesse Jackson in his prime. She has no one in her living memory to compare Obama to.) To Cara, Obama is certainly history-making, but he is also merely who he is. She attributes to him none of the transporting symbolism or historical call to action that older black people feel and see. In her eyes, Obama is the perfectly nice, potentially great but fairly unremarkable guy who sat in front of her in church one Sunday in Chicago when she was in the eighth grade.

Cara's attitude is a bit troubling to me, somewhat vacant, but a little bit liberating too—she likes Barack chiefly for who he *is*. Nothing else seems required. In a perfect world untroubled by color and slavery, nothing else should be required. I can see that Cara wants to free Obama from history, not so that we can all turn our backs on history but so that we can be fair to Obama. In her mind, there is actually such a thing. "Obama is inspiring, intelligent, charismatic," she says of the first black president. "But he's not transformational. He's not a freedom fighter. He's just trying to make this place better for everybody." I have to agree.

5 Is Obama Bad for Us?

Black people are failing at caring about themselves. Call each "nigger,"
don't create any political pressure. Obama cares about black people, but the
black political pressure is absent. So he may not act in proportion
to how much he cares. —*Ken Moore*

We really don't have leaders, to say nothing of heroes.
We hardly have anybody. —*Elaine Gills*

One day at a black issues luncheon that I attend every month, my tablemate
and I got to talking about Obama. Ron declared flatly that, as the de facto
top black leader of the country, Obama is the king of sellout.

I was startled. I'd heard plenty of reservations about Obama at this point,
some of which I share. But a sellout? This felt like a new level of reservation,
the notion that Obama was short-shrifting our problems not because he's
politically hamstrung or too cautious or overwhelmed but because that's
what he intends. We're being hustled. I tried to object a bit, diplomati-
cally, but Ron was adamant. After six years, he'd seen enough. Look at the
increased security state, he argued, how all the spying and secret surveil-
lance in the name of antiterrorism had only given law enforcement even
more license to racially profile. The constitutionality of such stuff is only
the beginning of what outraged Ron. What really bothered him was that,
in the big picture, this selling out fit into a long tradition going all the way
back to Africa, when blacks sold off other blacks to white slave traders and

fed the trans-Atlantic slave trade. And we give these turncoats a pass, Ron complained. We don't *object* to being sold out. Obama is just the latest one of these people, though Ron admitted that black people have a certain attachment to him that he'd never seen with other black sellouts; when he posted this opinion on Facebook, he lost friends (Facebook friends, some of whom were actual friends), which angered Ron even more because it reflected our dysfunction as a people. What, we can't criticize? Who can? The silencing effect of Obama's presidency alone is bad for us, he said. The best you could say is that he hasn't made things better; the trouble black people were in before he arrived on the scene has only gotten deeper. Overall, said Ron, given what we'd expected and needed and hoped for and all that Obama should have felt responsible for, he's been bad for us. No question.

I was stunned and embarrassed. I could agree with Ron on some particulars, but not on the specific charge of Obama being a sellout. That was undignifying him in a way that was almost pornographic. I would not believe it; I could not believe it. The consequences were too great: if Obama is a sellout, the game is over. I can't look in his direction, let alone love him. Suddenly, it became important to defend Obama's fundamental integrity to Ron, not to win the ultimate argument about his presidency but to preserve the possibilities granted by that love. I say that people's strong reactions to his Facebook criticism suggest that Obama is the center of so much black hope and pride still, which is not good or bad; it just is. I'm cheating—I do know what Ron's getting at, and he's not entirely wrong. Of course, Obama has sold *himself* out plenty of times, modified his positions or abandoned the more liberal angels of his nature in order to get to that equally-good-for-everybody middle ground that never materializes. He's done this on lots of issues—extending tax breaks for the rich, giving up too quickly on the public option of his health care reform, contemplating Social Security "reform"—not just issues that might be reasonably called black.

And yet Obama has received unbroken support from black folks, not really for what he does wrong but for what he doesn't do at all, and what he mostly hasn't done is sold us out outrageously or obviously enough to warrant us giving him up. What's always mattered to black people is the degree to which Obama turns his back on us, not how much he affirms us with his policies or how much he sticks to principle. A low bar, perhaps, but a complicated one that goes back to the lack of clear expectations black people have for any leader who claims to have our interests at heart. And because Obama has had to spread himself so thin politically, much more so than any black elected official before him, as long as he isn't totally spurning us or selling us down river, as Clarence Thomas and Ward Connerly have done, he's got us. For all his blind spots, we know that Obama is not an ideologue, like those men; he's not our grassroots champion, but he can be appealed to. He actually *wants* to be appealed to.

We've also accepted from the beginning that he's a work in progress, like so many black folks who are still carrying forward unrealized aspirations and unfinished dreams, even in middle age—aren't most of us still out there trying to make things happen for ourselves and also for the race, building the car and trying to drive it at the same time, as the saying goes? The most encouraging thing about Obama is that he is not unique in this respect. Like any folk hero, he is exceptional, but he is also not an exception. While that ultimate lack of exceptionalism may be disappointing to some black people, certainly to activists like Ron who need Obama to be exceptional—extraordinary would be even better—it's also reassuring. We are all Obama. We can all claim a tiny bit of his success and much of his failure. On the other side is the view that Obama—whether he's seen as a failed president, a triumphant one, or something in between—has set an impossible precedent for black folks that will sink us, not raise us up, in the future. The symbolism that so many say is Obama's unquestionably positive legacy could weigh us down like lead. "My great-grandparents were illiterate sharecroppers, now we got Obama—it's the end of black history," says Ulli Ryder. "He proves that it can be done. We're back to individualism—if you don't become Obama, then it's your fault. It's looking at systemic problems through an individual lens. That's why he doesn't mean anything at all."

My friend the city hall insider likens Obama to Oprah Winfrey. She says Oprah started out her career as a heavyset, dark-skinned black woman who turned black female stereotypes on their head by being empathetic instead of sassy, literate instead of streetwise, vulnerable instead of tough, and glamorous in a way that is entirely her own. Eventually, she became queen of all media. In turning certain black male stereotypes on their head—he is thoughtful and deliberate instead of fiery or folksy, collaborative instead of cocky—Obama succeeded too, and now, like his champion, Oprah, he occupies a supreme position of influence. Being in such a position of influence when nobody expected you there is absolutely *good* for us.

The black left/progressive/Afrocentric set doesn't agree at all. The grumbling about Obama being negligent of us started almost immediately in '08 and, as time passed, rose to an audible pitch as the perception shifted from negligence to downright indifference. Cornel West, in pointedly excluding Obama from the tradition of what he calls "black prophetic fire"—racial visionaries like King, Malcolm, DuBois—has pretty much called the president a sellout. West is a rarity in that he is a black critic who is also fairly mainstream. Black Obama critiques have always been much less high profile than black Obama support, though that started changing as the Great Recession (for most black people, a Depression) dragged on and a certain disillusionment that had been in the air since 2008 thickened.

The black progressive critique roughly follows the white progressive critique, but with an extra element of indignation over what critics see as a black man's betrayal of the social justice principles on which black people still depend for their ultimate liberation. This makes the critiques not just political but personal and that much more intense. As the most visible and credible Obama critic, West has been the most flayed by black Obama supporters, whose counter-criticism of West and his takedown of the president has often bordered on disgust. In 2012, West's fellow scholar and pundit, Melissa Harris-Perry, blasted him in her column in *The Nation*, calling his opposition to Obama unseemly and mostly petty, an outsized reaction to his not getting tickets to the inauguration and the White House access to which he felt entitled. Most black folks I know side with Harris-Perry: Cornel, they sigh, has lost his damn mind.

Maybe he has. But what's distressing is that there seemed to be no middle ground on this at all, with Harris-Perry or anybody else. Black folks think either that West is a hater out to embarrass Obama and the entire race in its big presidential debut, or (and this is a much smaller group) that West is a black prophet himself and that Obama followers are too besotted with the president to hear him. Nobody much mentions that West has a long history of critiquing power, whoever holds it, and that he has consistently said that he supported and believed in Obama and is only holding his feet to the fire *because* he believes, *because* he's defending the possibilities that in his mind Obama still represents. Technically, West was suggesting, there is still time for Brother Obama to be redeemed, to make good on all that magnificent potential.

Other black critics held out no such faith. In a *Harper's Magazine* cover story in 2014, Adolph Reed, Jr., declared that Obama is most definitely bad for us, bad for all Americans, because he represents not just the collapse of black leadership but the collapse of the entire American left. Reed says that over decades, the left has been dragged steadily rightward, and the only thing standing in the new century is the politics of persona represented by Obama, who he says draws on facile, romantic, but powerful ideas of racial conciliation as some great national fixer. Reed despairs that even the most committed leftists have been duped or muted by the initial campaign of hope and change. "Confusion and critical paralysis prompted by the racial imagery of Obama's election prevented even sophisticated intellectuals like Zizek from concluding that Obama was only another Clintonite Democrat—no more, no less," he writes. "It is how Obama could be sold, even within the left, as a hybrid of Martin Luther King Jr. and Neo from *The Matrix.*" Like scores of other Obama doubters/critics, notably Ishmael Reed, he's also angry about the Father's Day sermonizing to black audiences and how usually sensible white journalist/activists such as Glenn Greenwald and Katrina vanden Heuvel have lauded Obama for being "courageous enough to beat up on a politically powerless group." To Adolph Reed, Obama is bad for us because he's not nearly as radical as the times need him to be, not even close, and also because he actively distorts the already distorted view most Americans have of the black condition. In Reed's view, Obama is, by accident and by a certain design, deceptive, which is more reprehensible than being a sellout.

Cheka Abubakari is another black Obama critic who didn't start out that way. He's a former full-on, if unlikely, Obama believer who became disenchanted by degrees and by the end of '09 had no faith at all. Cheka is sixty-three, an alumnus of the Movement, and an educator who specializes in the history of classical African civilizations. The only difference between him and Adolph Reed is sentiment. Cheka genuinely regrets his break with Obama; he feels he was left no choice. Like Cornel West, he still seems troubled by the idea of what might have been. He had been excited by Obama because he seemed his own man, not as indebted to the American power structure as other black politicians with presidential aspirations, or aspirations to be anywhere in the White House. "I thought he'd slipped through the cracks," says Cheka somewhat wistfully. "Blacks like him are usually rewarded with corporate jobs or foreign relations positions, but he didn't fit the Vernon Jordan–Ward Connerly mold. He wasn't involved in any companies that influence appointing diplomats. He attended the most progressive black church in the country. Then when he became president he got rid of all the white progressives"—to Cheka, a sure sign of trouble—"and brought in the old guard. He's a puppet. He stepped in and served the master." The antebellum image makes me inwardly wince, just as I winced at Ron calling Obama a sellout. What Cheka is saying is that in choosing which white folks would best represent the interests of the people, a black man went with the slave owners instead of the abolitionists. Unthinkable.

"I don't listen to him anymore," Cheka says. "I put him in the same category as Bush. And yes, I hold him to a higher standard because he's black, not the opposite. He has a special charge. Obama should take it upon himself to help those who aren't politically sophisticated enough to help themselves." He grunts dismissively. "He's just another American." That's meant as an insult, I know, but it also rings with an oddly poignant truth, and possibly a compliment. Obama *is* just another American. Isn't that the status that black folks have been fighting for all this time? If he can be regarded as just another American as opposed to yet another spectacularly failed Negro, wouldn't that be progress? And isn't *that* good for us?

Professor and author Michael Eric Dyson has been that rarest thing of all, the most impassioned Obama supporter who is also his most impassioned critic. His oft-declared love of Obama is both personal and cultural, as it is for so many of us, and he makes no apologies for it. His criticism is poetic, sprawling, and unsparing but firmly rooted in that love. He too has gotten plenty agitated about Obama's political treatment of black folks. At a particularly charged moment during a 2010 black agenda forum, he called Obama a "pharaoh" to whom we must appeal to let our people go. But he has not renounced Obama or crossed the line from critical to bitter, as many say West has done, including Dyson himself. (In a 10,000-word essay for the *New Republic* that appeared in 2015, Dyson charted in searing detail the intellectual decline of the man he once called a friend and mentor, a decline he says was hastened by what he sees as West's consuming, deeply personal, and frankly undignifying animus toward the first black president.)

Dyson doesn't see Obama as useless or deceptive because he first sees him as a black man with agency, like himself, and more important, a black man with a clear affinity for other black people. Obama is worth holding accountable, just as a good friend is worth getting mad at and making up with; indifference simply isn't an option. Engagement is essential. But Dyson also views Obama as a symbol, a folk hero mostly wrought by the historical moment whose individual meaning only goes so far. He compared the president to Jackie Robinson. Though certainly gifted, Barack is not necessarily the best that black people have got or will produce. Jackie Robinson was a gifted athlete, adept in several sports, but not the greatest black ballplayer by far, only temperamentally the best-suited to break major league baseball's color line. It was Robinson who paved the way for Willie Mays and his ilk, says Dyson. Obama will do the same, however much he frustrates us during his own time in the uniform.

Damien Goodmon is a public transportation activist, at thirty-two years old a seasoned community organizer and political consultant who, among many other gigs, worked on Obama's 2004 Senate campaign. Damien is soft-spoken but fast-talking, not in the way of an operator or hustler but in the way of a restless intellect whose drive is such that he once worked on a political campaign from his hospital bed as he recuperated from a serious illness. Damien's been in search of legitimate black leadership his whole career, something on which to hang his growing concerns about the fortunes of ordinary black people whom he sees struggling simply to be heard, never mind being granted a place at the table. Though he worked for the up-and-coming Obama of '04, Damien confesses he never bought the

"We are one people" speech—"That's what white folks wanted to hear," he says succinctly. He says he preferred Al Sharpton's much more politically challenging but now largely forgotten speech at that same convention. Nonetheless, when Obama's star rose, he joined the team in Los Angeles and helped to coordinate the 2007 rally where I showed up. It was, he admits, a heady time. "Working for him was fun. I loved it," Damien says. "Yes, it was more about personality than policy, but I was excited about being part of something bigger than me." The prospect of the kind of leadership he had long sought—principled, dynamic, *and* with a national platform—was growing before his eyes.

And then something happened for Damien, as it did for Cheka, the jarring inverse of an "aha" moment. During the campaign, Barack and Michelle appeared on the *Oprah Winfrey Show*. In the midst of a discussion of about the deep political divide in America, Obama said something to the effect of, "Both sides are wrong; you've got to find a middle." That's been Obama's mantra all along—from the beginning, really. But it was only then that Damien says he was forced to acknowledge that, for all his electricity, Obama was not going to provide the black leadership he was looking for. "It gave me pause, pushed me back. Where was the ethical basis for that idea, a *middle ground*?" he recalls. "There's a political basis for it, yes, but not an ethical one." Later, he saw the millions Obama was raising from Wall Street, and his wariness deepened. But he didn't turn his back; he went to the first inauguration, he says, because he was still excited, anticipatory, willing to "give the brother a chance." The willingness didn't last long. The mortgage crisis that devastated black homeowners, quickly fraying a middle class that's held up the hope of a whole race, shifted Damien's view of Obama for good. It also rekindled his anxieties about a black future.

"Black people were dying, and he failed to do anything of substance, and that was unforgiveable," he says. "He's just not for working class people. I'm worried. The state of black leadership is so poor, now we're projecting to our young people this type of leadership that's so unconcerned with poor people, to say nothing of black people"—because if you can't talk about the poor, you can't talk about us. "It's problematic. It's disappointing."

I ask Damien if he expects anything from the president at this point. He says yes, though "expects" is really the wrong word. "Maybe he'll expand Pell grants, other crumbs like that, something to keep us from revolting entirely," he says, only a little sarcastically. "The problem is, we have this poor class that thinks it's the middle class, and a neutered middle class. Obama will engage moderate Democrats on economic policy issues. That's who he is." I have to agree that moderateness is certainly part of who Obama is. But does this make him a sellout or just a disappointment? Or are the two the same thing? Damien doesn't say, but he raises a question about Obama's legacy that's equally troubling and equally unanswerable. "Is it even better for us to have blacks at that level?" he says. "There is some benefit—more participation in the electoral process, for one. But losing that strongly progressive and ethical basis that for so long defined the African American community and our political lexicon, as far as I understand it—was it worth the cost? Was it better *not* to have a first?" Ironically, it sounds like a question that a younger Obama, the student of American history and astute racial analyst/observer/philosopher might have posed in his memoir.

(Postscript: along with myself and many others, Damien attended a community viewing of the first Obama–Romney debate in the 2012 campaign, four years in and long after he'd officially lost faith. He was still watching; something still counted. He was politically done with Obama by then. But I could see that he hadn't quite extinguished his feelings about him, the hope that things still might change, that as long as Obama occupied the space never before occupied by a black man, something could break. At the viewing, I saw that Damien couldn't entirely squelch a sense of identification with Obama, this wayward but once-promising brother. Damien has known more than a few brothers like that. We all have.)

♥ Carl Dix is cofounder of the Revolutionary Communist Party (RCP) USA and the Stop Mass Incarceration Network. Like Adolph Reed, he doesn't believe in any iteration of Obama-ism and never has. That would go against one of the RCP's core beliefs that anyone of any color who defends a system as broken as American capitalism simply cannot be an enlightened or effective leader. "The logic of promoting Obama's candidacy because it'll inspire more Black youth to succeed carries with it an underlying and wrong view of what is the problem and what is the solution," Dix wrote in an article for the RCP's *Revolution* newspaper in 2008 that warned against the dangers of rising Obama mania. "Black people who buy into this are on the way to giving up on fighting the system that's responsible for their oppression. Whites and people of other nationalities who buy into this can end up seeing no need to join the struggle against this oppression. And it hands the U.S. ruling class further justification for the vicious repression it is unleashing on the masses."

Ideologically, Dix and Reed are pretty much aligned, though Dix's critique is somewhat less scathing; he seems to understand but doesn't take part in the romance black folks have had with Obama, nor does he take the tough-love approach of his friend and frequent collaborator, Cornel West. He sees why Obama has taken hold. "When he ran [the first time], I thought, 'This is a meaningless exercise'—for the people, but not for the movers and shakers," says Dix. He has the confident, remarkably even voice of a veteran organizer used to countering opposition with reason, not emotion. "When the economy declined to where it had been in the '30s, I knew we needed something extraordinary to bring back faith in the system, and Obama was it. People had reached a point of lost faith, not just black folks, but young folks, everybody. Jesse ran to bring people into the system, but everybody knew he wasn't going to win. This was different."

Like other black critics, who range from the center to the far left, Dix cites Obama's Father's Day speeches as glaring evidence that the president's policies, if not his heart, are not in the right place. The fact that Obama has repeatedly acknowledged in such speeches the systemic and historical factors inhibiting black progress doesn't let him off the hook. Indeed, Dix says it only confuses things. "It's a dual message," he says. "He's saying to black folk, 'You've always blamed white people and this is largely your fault,' but he also mentions larger social forces responsible for racism." Tom Sayles argues there's nothing wrong with a dual message. He says that Obama is not equivocating or trying to have it both ways but merely telling the truth:

the root of our stagnation is both personal *and* political, not equally both but certainly both. It's just that we can't seem to hold the two critiques in our heads at the same time. But Dix says that's no excuse for not making black crises a priority. To acknowledge the complexity of a problem is fine, maybe even progressive in the context of modern American political discourse that discourages complexity of any kind. But acknowledgment is not action. Empathy by itself is not justice.

"The message from Obama and Holder, the black faces in high places, has been, 'I understand, we're working on it,'" says Dix. "That's not enough. Obama's post–Zimmerman trial speech was typically double-faced, too. He first said, 'Respect the verdict, our system works.' The second speech was, 'I am Trayvon.'" Dix insists that it's incumbent on Obama and his black appointees in high positions to reconcile these two positions, take an ethical stand rather than a practical one that covers all bases. Doing that would be leadership. "Holder says that as a black man, he has to give his son the speech about the dangers of racial profiling," he says. "The head of the Justice Department is telling me that he can't change the system and has to give *his* son the talk? No, that shouldn't be."

It strikes me that what Dix is describing is not just the administration's shortcomings but the total unworkability of integration itself. How can you embrace a system designed to keep you out of it, hold it accountable for doing something—minimizing and excluding black folks—that it was in fact meant to do? The only real way out of the riddle is to change the system, which Dix says Obama and Holder were in a unique position to do, or to try to do; it doesn't take a Communist to see that, for most black people, changing the system fundamentally is really the only way forward. King and Malcolm knew that. Obama, the trumpeter of change, doesn't seem to believe in the kind of radical change to which those men ascribed. Or he believes in it to a certain point, but can't bring himself to scrap the greatest-country-in-the-world presidential rhetoric that he probably also believes and that's been so essential to his success. "There is this narrative that Obama is an outcome of MLK's dream," remarks Dix. "I'm not into MLK, but the fulfillment of that dream had to do with ending oppression of blacks, peace and justice for all. Clearly, the civil rights movement didn't fulfill that, but to say that Obama is an outcome of the dream, someone who came forward to represent the system, which is responsible for the problems of inequality—it's hard to accept this."

It is. And yet black people have lived with and absorbed so many conundrums and contradictions—social, legal, cultural, political, psychological—that those embodied by Obama and his presidency can seem mild by comparison. Contradiction often seems like just a part of the incoherence and various gaps in logic that still define the black American experience. On many levels, we accept the incoherence. I see that acceptance most clearly in the response—or nonresponse—of many black people to Obama's original Father's Day speech. "I don't have a problem with him telling us, 'Take care of your kids.' He's the president; who else is going to say it?" says my cousin Jeff, the longtime state assemblyman from Brooklyn. He laughs, a little guiltily. "Of course, if white people said it, it would be totally different, but with him I get it." As to the notion that the admonishments of black folks give the white right more fodder for their racism, Jeff almost scoffs. "What do we care what white folks think, anyway?" he says. "How could they *possibly* think any worse of us than they do now? We're in a pile of shit. No white person is coming down to save us. So we've got to do something else, like we've always done. It's what we've done through history, dealing with a pile of shit. Getting out of it is rule number one."

Obama's been stuck in his own pile for years. It's funny—or common sense—but it's only when he was elected president and gained the office with the greatest political privilege in the free world that he earned the distinct nonprivilege of being black. He earned the right of membership in the community, as he himself said. It was only in becoming president that Obama, so famously untouched by American racism, began to feel what it was really like to be stuck in a pile of shit. To really live the contradiction.

Christopher Jimenez y West is a critic, too, but more in the Dyson camp of first claiming Obama as family, although the Father's Day speech and other tough love diatribes stick in his craw. "That's not tough love. Where is *the* love?" he says. "Obama's bigger message is, 'Y'all should be happy that I got here. And leave me the hell alone.'" West admits that Obama's sentiments are not unusual—it is the quintessential black conservative position (small *c*) often articulated by "black churchgoing, middle-class folks sitting around upbraiding black ghetto folks," part of the ongoing internal conversation about the Negro problem and the eternally uncertain future of the race. The we-need-to-get-it-together debate has always been part of the diaspora of opinions, the flow of the ideological river, if you will. But it plays differently when articulated to the general public, especially by a black president whom white people in both parties are perfectly willing, when convenient, to see as the voice of black America. With Obama's permission, a complex in-house discussion about the state and future of the race is thrown open to the country at large, and we don't fare well. We never do. The inevitable oversimplifying of race matters that happens at the national level, on the talk-show circuit and even among ostensibly sympathetic media outlets such as NPR, is always bad for us. The oversimplification is bigger than us and always has been. Obama delivering a dozen more eloquent and deeply nuanced speeches on race isn't going to change that.

Perhaps in the end the oversimplifying won't matter, or not as much as we assume it will. Tom Sayles predicts that Obama's legacy will be defined more by foreign policy than by anything stateside, that he will be the most significant president in that regard since Nixon. As of this writing, Obama is juggling major crises in Iraq (again), Russia, Ukraine, Syria, Nigeria, and Egypt, to name a few places. A nuclear weapons reduction deal with Iran is being hammered out, even though it's been vehemently opposed by the white right every inch of the way. The slowly spiraling conflict with the extremist and murderous Islamic State especially threatens to put us back into long-term war with the same country that Obama promised we would leave.

Obama's legacy on black issues will still matter, regardless of the fact that we haven't quite figured out if he is purely a president, a black leader, a postracial race man, or simply a black folk hero inventing himself as best he can in a brand-new environment with limited resources, like the rest of us. "Is he doing enough for us?" asks Sayles. "No. *He* would say that he's not doing enough. But what is doable?" To Sayles, the question of what is doable is less about what Obama wants than it is about the fastidiously anti-Obama Tea Party, that minority within a minority of Republicans, conservatives and libertarians, that has nonetheless set the political climate for the entire country since 2008. It's been a rightward drift on steroids, enough to sink a whole raft of Obama's better intentions, from a bigger economic stimulus bill to real health care reform to modest gun control, all measures that would certainly have benefited black folks. But wherever Obama has put his hands, it seems, the Opposition has tied them. More punitive than that: it has sought to bind his wrists behind his back to ensure as little movement as possible, which is why, whenever the right starts mounting an attack on Obama, I see it in my mind as a prelude to a lynching.

But even in the midst of the ganging up, Obama has had choices. One choice he made that was notably bad for us but that surprisingly few people I talked to brought up at all was his response to the police incident involving Harvard University professor Henry Louis Gates, Jr. In 2011, Gates, America's best-known and most media-accessible academic, was arrested at his own house in Cambridge after a confrontation with a cop called by a watchful neighbor who thought Gates might be an intruder. It turned out that Gates was missing his key, and he and the black cab driver who dropped him off were trying to figure out a way into the house. Obama speculated later in a press conference (which I watched with great anxiety, as usual) that the Cambridge police acted "stupidly," hardly a controversial view among black people familiar with racial profiling by law enforcement. But it touched off such heated criticism on the talk-show circuit that the president backed away from his remark, finally inviting the arresting policeman to sit down with him and Gates for a beer in the White House garden. What had been a potential teaching moment on race—specifically, the phenomenon of racial profiling—Obama blew all by himself. It was frustrating especially because he started out truly teaching, by calling out profiling for what it was, and then undercut his own lesson by treating a deeply systemic problem as if it were an individual one. The threesome at the White House gave the impression that the whole affair had been just a little misunderstanding between adults.

I know (well, I believe) that Obama knows better than that. I also know that this is his way of compromising, but the complainers are right—at some point compromise diminishes black people, and it diminishes us first. Sometimes there is simply no usable ground between what is palatable and what is right, and that's especially the case with race. Filling that ground with something isn't better than filling it with nothing, and sometimes it *is* selling us out, however unintentionally. The supremely awkward beer-garden moment was not only unpalatable but undignified, for Obama and for us; I desperately wanted him to have the last word, and he refused it. It was Obama who sent the invitations to lunch, but make no mistake, it was a small-town white cop, not the country's first black president, who was calling the shots in the White House that afternoon. That innocuous-looking confab was evidence of our failed American dream of racial equality, and of Obama's inability to fix it. I knew he couldn't fix it. I didn't hold that against him. But I would have preferred not to have seen that failure dressed up as success and so prominently displayed, beamed around the world in black and white.

♥ Samarrah Blackman has maintained her optimism about Obama with a tortured kind of reasoning. She says that because he did not come solely out of black elected officialdom, he is different from other politicians who've let us down. He's consciously black but has never really employed the '60s-rooted rhetoric of self-determination, empowerment, and racial pride, and therefore he can't really violate that rhetoric or sell it short. Samarrah is still troubled by the Father's Day speech, which she calls—reluctantly—white pandering. She also calls it a lack of faith. "I think he always believed in gay rights—he didn't 'evolve,'" she says. "Why can't he believe the same things for us?" She points out what Carl Dix pointed out, that even as Obama outed himself as a black man during his Trayvon Martin moment, he tried at the same time to distance himself from the fray. He tried to have it both ways, to be both things. "So what does he want to *do*?" Samarrah asks, echoing Kerry's question and his impatience. "Does he want to make history? Does he think that helping black people is too small a legacy?" A somewhat painful thought, one I think many of us share but don't fully voice. Elaine Gills, the professor and founder of the DuBois Institute, says, "I thought he'd have enough sense of urgency about our plight to do something big, a paradigm shift. He has to have some gumption. Treat us equally, that's all I ask. I'm not saying get up there and wave black, red, and green flags; I'm talking about something much more sophisticated than that." She frowns. "Like we can't tell the difference between the two." (Like Damien Goodmon and Cheka, with whom she often teaches, Elaine was a believer until she heard the Father's Day speech; she says she can't imagine Obama doing that—scolding, advising—to any other group. My cousin Jeff can't imagine it either, but that's because to him what Obama's is doing is intimate and specific: nobody else *should* get the speech.)

Pam Ward doesn't waver a bit from her sympathy for Obama. He walks a tightrope, she says, and it's both a curse and a blessing—a curse because he must always watch his step, a blessing because he walks it at all. We as black people must take the curses with the blessings. As for the Father's Day sentiments, Ward says that Obama's public remarks about black people have also included remarks about more nuanced, much less sexy issues such as the government's role in ameliorating the legacy of slavery. In his post-Ferguson remarks, Obama put the incident in a wider context of racial and economic oppression that for young black men too often means death by police. "And part of my job that I can do, without any potential conflicts, is to get at those root causes," Obama said. "That's a big project. It's one we've been trying to carry out for a couple of centuries. And we've made extraordinary progress, but we have not made enough progress." He got instant blowblack from the white right for even admitting that racism is alive, and for suggesting it lives at the heart of the controversy that roiled Ferguson. But it was a brief, shining folk-hero moment, confirmation from the top by a black man of what black folks already know, what they have been living a long time. The acknowledgment was symbolic, yes, but it was unprecedented. Obama did not go to Ferguson—Attorney General Eric Holder did—a decision that drew criticism from those who felt he was ignoring a key political moment for black people, perhaps *the* moment of his presidency. I understand the criticism; I would have loved nothing more than to have seen Obama in the streets of Ferguson, communing with dissenters in real time as opposed to being surrounded by rapt young black boys costarring with the president in a staged press conference about My Brother's Keeper. Still, I was heartened: in the tense wake of Ferguson, Obama looked in our direction, held our gaze. Briefly, he was *us*. It was progress. It was good for us.

In 2012, Cornel West and radio/TV host Tavis Smiley took their Obama agnosticism on the road in the Poverty Tour. The tour was a traveling town-hall discussion about the crises facing poor people, a topic that had been virtually absent (and still is) from mainstream political dialogue in the age of Wall Street. The tour wasn't explicitly a critique of Obama and his own rhetorical aversion to the issue of poverty, but that certainly was the impetus for it. I went to the discussion in Los Angeles, at a temple on Wilshire Boulevard. It was lively and well attended, with the distinct air of a media event. Black people were among the poor people being discussed onstage, but they were not the focus of the conversation, nor were they the majority of the audience. Blacks are a minority here in Los Angeles and always have been, but given the hosts, I expected to see more. Najee Ali says there's a definite perception among blacks that Smiley and West—he makes the names sound nefarious, like Bonnie and Clyde—are not truth tellers or soothsayers but haters. "They're worse than [Sean] Hannity or Fox News because we have the first black president in the nation's history—we should at least come together and support one of our own," he says indignantly. "Tavis and Cornel were calling for Obama to take King's bust out of his office—they don't let up." He adds, "Of course, I don't agree with everything Obama's done, but I'm not going to say anything disparaging that the right wing can use to attack him." Ken Moore feels the same way. He says he renounced Smiley and West (with his bushy salt-and-pepper beard and combed-back afro, Ken is often mistaken for West), "because of their deliberate lack of understanding of what Obama's going through."

The audible rumblings about a negative Obama legacy for black folks, which clashes with a very basic presumption that his being in office as the first black president could only be good for us, started before Obama's second term and grew louder as the first term lengthened into an era. By May 2013, Smiley and West were fairly gloating on their eponymous weekly radio program over the fact that other blacks were joining them in criticizing Obama's criticism of black folks in the commencement speech he'd delivered to historically black and male Morehouse College. In that speech, Obama raised the specter of Bill Cosby yet again. But many of his remarks were personal and almost confessional—for example, he said that in his own youth he had as good a chance of going to prison as any of the young black male graduates he was addressing out there. What angered Smiley and West and others was that Obama was encouraging these graduates with advantages unknown to previous black generations not to make excuses for failing or not living up to their potential. Racism and discrimination still present obstacles for blacks, Obama told them, but in a hyper-connected world, nobody cares anymore. Opportunities are not exactly a given, but they are ours to lose. On their radio program, Smiley and West fumed—would Barack talk down to naval cadets the way he talked down to the Morehouse men, they asked?

Ken Moore says no, but that hardly means Obama's a disaster for the race. He says the same thing about Obama's embrace of Wall Street and his relative silence about poor and working people—not optimal, but we can't look at those choices as strictly individual, he says. Moore agrees with Michael Anderson, Tony Jackson, and many others that the president is dealing with multiple factors at any given moment on any given matter, factors that none of us on the outside can see. "Sometimes [black people] have to be taken down, but this isn't one of those times," says Moore. "Obama's got to go to bed with Wall Street, but he's not a whore. I'm not an apologist, but I think it's a matter of degree. He's chipping away at the problems. And he's not been assassinated yet.

"If you're black in America, what the hell are we going to do about it? We're stuck," he adds as a kind of philosophical coda—or as a preface—to the conversation. "What the hell are we going to do about it? Black is the default, and Obama's in it. He's chief of the tribe."

In other words, black-man-in-chief. It's not a position Obama signed up for along with his primary one of commander-in-chief. Publicly, politically, he's resisted being seen that way. And yet there are those inevitable moments when he *is* black-man-in-chief, moments when the presidency and American history and Obama's status as a modern black icon/folk hero/pioneer converge, and emerge, into a single thing that's powerful and intentional. In those moments, such as the one in which he stood on the Edmund Pettus Bridge in Selma, Alabama in 2015, commemorating the fiftieth anniversary of Bloody Sunday and the march to Montgomery, Obama is inspired. In those few moments, he is not chastened by race but liberated by it, unmasked, fully himself. I saw this even in the controversial Morehouse speech—the first ever delivered to Morehouse by a sitting president. That fact alone gave me chills, as well as the fact that Obama spoke to a crowd of black men in which he willingly, at points eagerly and with palpable relief, included himself. He was sharing. He was making poignantly specific the generally bland, all-inclusive presidential "we," a word that he called in his impassioned Selma address, which seemed to rekindle the fire of '08, "the single most powerful word in American democracy."

"We" describes his guiding idea of one America, of course, but in those moments of convergence, "we" also describes black people within that democracy, or outside it, or in the White House. "We" describes the tribe. It's Obama reminding himself, out loud and in public, that he belongs to the tribe and he's glad for it. And he's also reminding us that our blackness, our isolated and marginalized "we," has more power than we've grown accustomed to giving it. Blackness can effect justice, can model expansiveness and altruism that the rest of the world would do well to follow. Here's part of what he said at Morehouse, the part that was specifically absent from the controversy that focused on his advice to graduates to be upstanding black men:

Whatever success I achieved, whatever positions of leadership I've held, have depended less on Ivy League degrees or SAT scores or GPAS, and have instead been due to that sense of empathy and connection—the special obligation I felt, as a black man like you, to help those who needed it most; people who didn't have the opportunities that I had, because but for the grace of God, I might be in their shoes. . . . So it's up to you to widen your circle of concern—to care about justice for everybody, white, black and brown. Everybody. Not just in your own community, but also across this country and around the world. To make sure everyone has a voice, and everybody gets a seat at the table; that everybody, no matter what you look like or where you come from, what your last name is—it doesn't matter, everybody gets a chance to walk through those doors of opportunity if they are willing to work hard enough.

♥ Us founder Maulana Karenga doesn't think Obama is particularly good for us. But he doesn't demonize him, in part because he doesn't publicly disparage any black person if he can help it. Disparagement is bad for building community, something he's spent his life doing and still does. "I don't support Obama," he says bluntly. "What I do is support him against the right wing, because the right wing is not just attacking Barack, it's attacking black people *through* Barack. They don't want him to succeed. Our people *want* him to succeed. Liberals and progressives aren't opposed to his success, but they're not going to lend any assistance whatsoever."

It is therefore up to us to assist. Karenga doesn't give Obama a pass, by any means; he remains disappointed that this favored son has not lived up to his historical and cultural obligation of furthering black justice, which is another way of saying that he's been too much in the thrall of an overwhelmingly white American power structure, which chose him and rewards him in a fashion, but serves *us* not at all. Interestingly, Karenga doesn't say *how* he thinks Obama as president could solve the conundrum of a black presidency, only that he should. "The irony of Obama's ineffectiveness is that this is one of the most intellectual presidents we've had, so he has no lack of intelligence," he goes on. "And he had progressive politics, once upon a time. So what happened? How did someone with that kind of intellectual and mental capacity end up a warmonger, a buck dancer? He keeps being nice to white people even after they're calling him names, and then he gets to us and he's lecturing us on how to raise our children. What is that *about?*"

Jordan Vaughn hews to the middle—he's very Obama-esque—but that doesn't mean all his opinions cancel each other out. To the contrary, they're amplified to the same pitch. "Obama's been so good and so bad for us at the same time," he says. "He's empowered us, given us a sense of pride of being part of a black family, improved and clarified an image of black families in America." But even the great image boost—if indeed that's what Obama has mostly given us, when all is said and done—is problematic. "He's given white America a portrait of blacks they never get to see—middle-class, ambitious, all that. The disservice is that it makes whites think that this is all of us. They're desensitized to the black struggle." That is, more desensitized to it than they were before. Some white folks were unaware of the contemporary black struggle to begin with.

Bob Farrell, the former councilman and Freedom Rider, worries more about the desensitization Obama has wrought among black people: whatever his larger meaning, will he incline us to be not post-racial but post-struggle? Will we, thanks to his high profile, more readily embrace our blackness but further relinquish the idea of a black cause? That second thing feels counterintuitive to me, but then I am of a generation, probably the last one, raised with the assumption that black struggle is a constant, part of our cultural makeup. I can't see a future for black people without it. On the other hand, I often don't know what black people across generations see as our future; like Obama in his presidential journey, we often seem to be making up that vision as we go.

Bob says that in his daily work he can feel excitement from Latinos about the evolving immigration rights/reform movement; they increasingly know their children will be better off. What about our children, what is the basis for a similar kind of hope? "At the very least, Obama could tell stories and anecdotes, the way Ronald Reagan did, to make us part of the national narrative," Bob says almost wistfully. "He does tell stories, but not ours." And he means not the iconic stories about Rosa Parks on the bus, but stories of ordinary black people in modern times being big things, resonating, mattering *as* black people. Obama himself may be a folk hero, reflecting and even affirming the rest of us in intended and unintended ways. But the individual story he's living right now as the first black president—the one America follows so intensely, the reality show—is entirely his own. We can't penetrate that story; we can only watch. *That* is not our story.

The great leftist writer/critic Gore Vidal said in a 2009 interview with the *Independent* that Obama just isn't up to the task of being president—Vidal had high hopes for him, but a year after the election he, too, became seriously disillusioned. A student of the history of the American presidency, Vidal pronounced Obama too intellectual, too "delicate" for these blunt-force Republicans whom he called not a party anymore but hatemongers, "like Hitler youth." He is in agreement with Karenga about Obama's intellectual capacity—in a documentary about Obama's life, Vidal calls him twice the intellectual JFK was—but in the new century, the American people are too corrupted to care. Vidal says that it doesn't help that Obama is inexperienced and overmatched, especially by the military, an institution to which he defers too much; part of the problem is that unlike JFK and others, Obama himself never served in the military or fired a shot. On the other hand, Vidal says that nobody with any conscience can control America, which he calls a "madhouse" that "makes no sense," a declining empire that will soon provide China with its coolies.

Vidal's only slightly sarcastic analysis made me think that Obama in the future might be viewed as a potentially inspiring historical development who simply wound up being on the wrong side of history. Certainly, he and his promise of change couldn't have come at a less hospitable moment; the people, under assault from so many crises, from mass foreclosures to climate change, couldn't rouse themselves to make it more hospitable. Maybe that's why when the party of the first Obama election was over, everything went as slack as if nothing had happened at all. "If there's one big problem Obama faces, it is that people get used to whatever is," remarks Stanley Crouch. "Indifference grows out of survival. We see the same things over and over and simply can't respond." Not even to the phenomenon of a first black president.

Is this all there is? The economist Julianne Malveaux, in a 2013 column on the debut of the My Brother's Keeper initiative, asks the question with almost audible scorn. Is this as much as a black president can do for us, this late-in-the-game, photo-op friendly program that gets on page 12 in the front section of the daily paper? Whatever the merits of the initiative, she says, they are offset (as they typically are) by Obama's less auspicious moves, such as his nominations for the federal district courts in Georgia—one a lawyer who successfully defended voter ID laws in that state, the other a conservative former state legislator who opposed marriage equality, voted for reduced access to abortion, and voted to retain the Confederate insignia on the state flag. Voting rights, gay marriage, and access to abortion are things Obama believes in, Malveaux says. So why do this? Why does Obama continually believe one thing and do another? Is he hopeful that the conservatives will have a conversion, that they'll see the light because it is Obama to whom they owe their fortune? Is this part of his willingness to bring everybody into the tent with the assumption that the tent itself will be reconfigured into a new shape?

Malveaux notes with distaste that the national civil rights organizations have been silent about these nominees—about most of Obama's more questionable moves, in fact—and ends the column with another provocative question: "Are they too frightened of losing the president's good will to speak up? Ten years from now, will we write that the status of African-American and Latino boys and men has improved? That Judges Cohen and Boggs have made rulings that have further eroded civil and human rights? . . . Which is the Obama legacy?" Malveaux is not saying here that Obama is bad for us, but she's certainly proposing that he might be. She doesn't fault My Brother's Keeper for affirming and supporting young black men. But the initiative is not looking at the infrastructural racism represented by institutions such as federal courts; it is looking at the individual. (And nowhere in the White House press conference on My Brother's Keeper, which I found so moving, did anybody talk in detail about the infrastructural racism that most often holds these young men back.) What Malveaux is saying is that the power of the system is no match for the power of the individual; no matter how successful the individual black person—Obama included—that success almost always represents an escape from the rule of the system, not evidence of its change. This is what my father meant when he cautioned me as a nine-year-old against over-measuring the meaning of a black president, if one ever came along. He was right. What he didn't know was how essential that meaning would be for most of us, the lengths we'd go to in order to secure a meaning we could live with.

Georgia congressman David Scott, who is black, shared Malveaux's alarm about Obama's federal bench nominees. Choices like these are where he draws the line at compromise, and where he thinks everybody else should too, including the NAACP and other civil rights and black advocacy organizations. But the interesting thing was that Scott saw no disloyalty or felt any disdain in his opposition. "I love my first black president," he told journalist Roland Martin on TV One. "But the ones you love can hurt you the most . . . we have to save him from this." I was encouraged that a sitting black elected official like Brown would get personal and go straight to the black heart of the matter—Obama, he said, can't do this to *us*. *We* can't let him. He's saying that the whole presidential experiment is a collaboration, or it should be. Scott is saying to all black people (and all people of conscience, I think) that this Confederacy sympathizing should be a deal breaker, a line in the sand for everybody. Yes, we know Obama is president of all, including president of the rednecks. But that doesn't make the rednecks right. This should be one of the moments in which it's clear there is no usable middle ground—and really, why would you want it? Brown was not discarding Obama over a questionable position; he was trying to educate him: that is, after all, our job. If it's political pressure that Obama wants or needs in order to do the right thing, maybe the thing he would do if he had his druthers, let's give it to him. Let *us* as black people uncorrupt ourselves and save Obama from himself in the process.

There really seems to be no way to save Obama from the fury of the white right and/or the Tea Party. Certain people are waking up only slowly to this fact. In May 2013, as the threat of the nation going over the fiscal cliff loomed because Republicans insisted on repealing Obamacare as part of a budget deal, I heard a foreign policy expert on the radio talk with near disbelief about how the Tea Party–driven Congress is willing to burn the whole village of America rather allow Obama to rule it. It wants to destroy Obama at any cost, including lying and withholding from Americans things they're entitled to, such as Medicaid. After six years of a political cold war that sometimes flared into open combat, the foreign policy expert, a white man with no political affiliation that I could discern, was only now accepting the truth. He sounded genuinely upset. He said that he believes Obama is a smart, decent man but that the decency is being smothered by a fierce opposition, and he can't push through it. He is obscured. It's a vicious, exhausting circle: with each new crisis here or abroad, Obama is given all the blame, driving the broader narrative of Obama Is Bad for Us and the determination of Republicans to unseat, or at least disempower, him up until the moment he's actually out of power. "Break the nigger," as Ishmael Reed told me, with not a hint of sarcasm or irony. He didn't need any.

Jackie Robinson had it bad for sure. But his skills as a ballplayer were unassailable; he came to the Dodgers fully formed. Not so Obama. His true rookie status has made him, despite his status as president, the most powerful and the most vulnerable black first in history. Tony Jackson describes it in a sports analogy. "Blacks have been dominating football for decades now—it's our game," he says. "We're quarterbacks now. The presidency is the reverse. Obama is in the arena, but he's not the game. He's remade politics, but his politics will not follow him into the future." Just as our unfinished civil rights past didn't really follow Obama into office, because America would not allow it. All of which makes him a loner in the most unromantic sense—a black man with no context to speak of, disembodied, with only himself to reference.

Some months later, I am again listening to the radio and hear a speech by activist, author, and former journalist Chris Hedges, a well-respected progressive and former Lutheran minister whose books include *The Empire of Illusion*. In this speech, he casts Obama not as the devil or a defining disaster but as the chief purveyor of "Brand Obama." The first black president is a typically hyperbolic American marketing campaign that has the sheen of promise and change but fails to deliver. Obama with his talk of transformation is a bill of goods, Hedges says, part of the ruined landscape of America that Hedges calls the crumbling "empire of illusion." He is right; I know that Hedges is speaking to power the sort of truth nobody wants to hear, including me.

I know we are on the same side. But Hedges doesn't see the entirety of my side. Obama's almost blind, perhaps desperate faith in compromise, his belief that between two bad choices is a good one, is certainly part of the ruined landscape. But Obama is also a black man who came and saw and conquered the seat of empire, and nothing can take that away from him or condemn it to illusion. Hedges condemns the symbolism, as have many others, as meaningless. I don't, quite. Black people are very comfortable with symbolism and gestures; because of our unfinished history of struggle that's still being written in moments and metaphors, symbolism and gestures don't rankle us as they perhaps should. For us, symbolism *is* power; it's the placeholder for real change, yes, but it's what's kept us going all this time. *All* our prominent people are symbols. All of them are folk heroes in that they are suggestions of the great things that could be, that should be. If we had had to measure the state of the black nation solely by the number of things actually done, we would have died spiritually a long time ago. There would have been no Obama, or no one like him.

Obama is our number one symbol, and he will probably remain that for a long time, maybe forever. He is our biggest and brightest, even though he's fallen short and may continue to fall short, yet he's never fallen short of his symbolism. He has sometimes tried to mute it, but he has never disavowed it. In that way, he's more than kept up his end of the bargain, and we won't forget that because symbolism sounds easy, facile, but it isn't. It is not automatic; it must be earned. This is what the progressives can't or refuse to understand (but that conservatives understand quite well, because they themselves are very well versed in symbolism and know its power), that Obama leads psychologically in a way that no one but black folks can see or acknowledge. That isn't to say that Obama solves our problems or completes our history—that's what white folks think and what black people actually resist. What I'm saying is that we have a relationship with this new entity of Obama that has broken new ground and that will probably endure, but it's been rocky so far. The romance has been intense but often unromantic. The relationship has shown us things, brilliant things, but also things we never expected or wanted to see or think about again, and now we have to think about them. We have no choice. It is part of our history. We are changed.

One last thing about that change. Jeff told me a story about Election Day, 2008, in Brooklyn. It is one of many similar stories told around the country that I read about but that I only really got when Jeff told me this:

I went to the polling station. There was a line circling around the park to vote, early in the morning—blew my mind. It was cold and damp that morning, frost blowing out of people's mouths as they talked. I said, "Well, they're doing it for him, but they're doing it for themselves." I'd never seen that before. And it stayed that way all day. We had snafus with space, but people waited and didn't leave. This is the heart of community, not the intelligentsia, and they understand what it means for him to be in that position. Maybe nothing gets done, but their understanding of the significance transcends their wish list.

My friend the city hall insider and new retiree says the only relevant (and frankly unromantic) question black people should be asking as we near the end of the Obama era is, how has he added value to us? Leaving aside the question of what she really meant by "value"—a marketplace word she applied directly to people who have spent much of their time in this country as property—I would say that he has. But value, like the price of gold, is a way of measuring. It isn't justice. And love is grand, but it's not justice either. It aligns the stars but nothing so pedestrian as racial disparity and black immobility. *They* still wait for a hero. I knew that going in. In following Obama, I really only wanted a chance to do what I'd never done—to swoon, to give in, to follow someone and something with my heart instead of the heartless statistics of race, to pull out of what I'd been slogging through for fifty years and re-cast it as an adventure with a fellow black American of my generation and temperament who, despite being president and being so far removed and mistaken much of the time, always seemed to be walking next to me. He still does. He may always.

Epilogue I ♥ Obama

It's March 2015, and Obama is back. The house around the corner from me, the one that for years had displayed the life-size figure of the president in its front window against the drawn shades before it was inexplicably taken down, has just as inexplicably been put back up. It's a little worse for wear; the color around the cardboard edges has faded evenly from the sun. But it's clear. It is him. And this time the image has a banner, a message printed across the bottom in white block letters on red: "Celebrate Black History."

I'm a little perplexed. Black History Month is done. Is this a late addition that will run a week or so, fly its flag for the record, and then disappear again, and for good? Days pass and the modified image, and its message, remain. Slowly, I begin to feel heartened, or re-heartened, restored to some earlier point. Once again, it feels as if Obama is watching over the street, the neighborhood, over our precarious fortunes as black people living barely out of the shadows in America's most fortunate big city. "Fortunate" is always relative for us, its meaning not fixed or secure. It never has been. Aggrieved Baltimore was recently burning; aggrieved Los Angeles may be next. Any place, anything could be next.

And yet this hologram, this mere suggestion of Obama and all that he has meant and will mean, anchors me. Every time I pass the house I meet his openly sly, resolute gaze, and the world of impending black trouble, our eternal struggle, falls briefly away. In these moments, we are only two children of fortune, with history well in sight but at our backs. I almost laugh in astonishment and a certain delight at being suddenly and completely released, and I shake my head—really, who would have *thought?* Obama is stepping into the breach, he and I, he and everybody else. It's all still so mad, impossible. As he passes from sight, I wish him luck, though not necessarily success in everything, a reflexive tempering of this strange love that persists, sometimes against my will and sometimes because of it, though in either case the truth, six years later, is undisturbed. I no longer fight it, though I'm still seeking the courage—the audacity—to say it aloud: I ♥ Obama.

Bibliography

Berlin, Ira. *The Making of African America*. New York: Viking, 2010.

Bolton, John. "The Coming Crash of American Diplomacy in the Middle East," *Los Angeles Times*, February 18, 2014, www.articles. latimes.com/2014/feb/18/opinion/la-oe-bolton-obama-mideast -failure-20140218.

Harris-Perry, Melissa. "Cornel West Vs. Barack Obama," *Nation*, May 17, 2011, www.thenation.com/article/cornel-west-v-barack-obama/.

Levine, Lawrence. *Black Culture and Black Consciousness*. New York: Oxford University Press, 1977.

McClelland, Edward. *Young Mr. Obama*. New York: Bloomsbury Press, 2010.

Marable, Manning, and Kristen Clarke. *Barack Obama and African-American Empowerment*. New York: Palgrave MacMillan, 2009.

Obama, Barack. *Dreams from My Father*. New York: Broadway Paperbacks, 2004.

Reed, Adolph Jr., "Nothing Left," *Harper's Magazine*, March 2014, www.harpers.org/archive/2014/03/nothing-left-2/.

Reed, Ishmael. *Barack Obama and the Jim Crow Media: The Return of the Nigger Breakers*. Montreal: Baraka Books, 2010.

Remnick, David. "Going the Distance," *New Yorker*, January 27, 2014, www.newyorker.com/magazine/2014/01/27/going-the-distance -david-remnick.

Rhoden, William C. "Joe Louis Moment." In *Best African American Essays*

2010, edited by Gerald Early and Randall Kennedy. New York: One World Books, 2010.

Sullivan, Andrew. "Andrew Sullivan on Barack Obama's Gay Marriage Solution," *Newsweek*, May 13, 2012, www.newsweek.com/andrew -sullivan-barack-obamas-gay-marriage-evolution-65067.

Walker, Rebecca, ed. *Black Cool: One Thousand Streams of Blackness*. Berkeley: Soft Skull Press, 2012.

Will, George. "Obama's Epiphanies on Governing," *New York Post*, December 12, 2012, www.nypost.com/2013/12/12/obamas-epiphanies -on-governing/.

FOR FURTHER READING

Coates, Ta-Nehisi. "The Champion Barack Obama," *Atlantic Monthly*, January 31, 2014, www.theatlantic.com/politics/archive/2014/01/the -champion-barack-obama/283458/.

Cruse, Harold. *The Crisis of the Negro Intellectual*. New York: New York Review of Books Classics, (1967) 2005.

Dix, Carl. "Obama's Trayvon Speech: Massa Trying to Keep the Slaves on the Plantation by Acknowledging Their Pain," *Black Agenda Report*, July 23, 2013, http://www.blackagendareport.com/content/obamas -trayvon-speech-massa-trying-keep-slaves-plantation-acknowledging -their-pain.

Karenga, Maulana. *Kawaida and Questions of Life and Struggles: African- American, Pan-African and Global Issues*. Los Angeles: University of Sankore Press, 2008.

Smith, Robert C. *We Have No Leaders*. New York: State University of New York, 1996.

CS-18